William T. Vollmann

*A Critical Study and
Seven Interviews*

Michael Hemmingson

McFarland & Company, Inc., Publishers
Jefferson, North Carolina, and London

LIBRARY OF CONGRESS CATALOGUING-IN-PUBLICATION DATA

Hemmingson, Michael A.
   William T. Vollmann : a critical study and seven interviews /
Michael Hemmingson.
      p.   cm.
   Includes bibliographical references and index.

   ISBN 978-0-7864-4025-2
   softcover : 50# alkaline paper ∞

   1. Vollmann, William T. — Criticism and interpretation.
2. Vollmann, William T. — Interviews.   I. Title.
PS3572.O395Z75   2009
813'.54 — dc22   2009017960

British Library cataloguing data are available

Cover image: *William T. Vollmann* by Derek Fenner, courtesy of the
artist; background ©2009 Shutterstock

Manufactured in the United States of America

*McFarland & Company, Inc., Publishers
   Box 611, Jefferson, North Carolina 28640
     www.mcfarlandpub.com*

To Liv Kellgren,
for both helping and hindering
this project over the past four years

Acknowledgments

I would like to acknowledge the journals *Fourth Genre, Modern Language Studies,* and *Review of Contemporary Fiction* for publishing the reviews and review-essays of mine that were the basis for some of these chapters.

A truncated, somewhat different version of Chapter Four appeared as "William T. Vollmann's Prostitute Trilogy" in *Critique: Studies in Contemporary Fiction.*

I would like to thank the interviewers for allowing me to reprint their conversations with Vollmann.

Finally, I would like to thank Dr. Matthew Bruccolli for his comments on early drafts of this study and Dr. Larry McCaffery for first suggesting that I immediately check out Vollmann's work back in 1991.

Contents

Preface

I wanted to write a critical study on Vollmann as far back as 1994, when I was living in a motel room in downtown San Diego and read *The Rifles*. For years I thought about it, tried to start it, then put it aside. I knew one day I would get back to the project. I also knew it would be some time before I could find the time and the desire. In the meantime, I wrote an academic essay for *Critique*; a handful of review-essays for *American Book Review* and elsewhere; capsules for the *Review of Contemporary Fiction*. Then I co-edited *Expelled from Eden: A William T. Vollmann Reader*, a necessary contribution to the canon of contemporary American literature. My co-editor was Dr. Larry McCaffery — he had suggested at a *Fiction International* party I read Vollmann (at the time I was a manuscript reader at the journal). He was telling everyone this; I may have been the only one there who took his advice. It is fitting that he worked with me on that reader, which, due to various delays in the publishing business and in life, took three years to select and compile, just as this book took me three years to get together. I am not usually that slow, but there were certain interferences. I made an independent film, *The Watermelon*. I wrote some novels and screenplays. I moved in and out of the academic world, switched from literary criticism to anthropological field work. However, I always came back to this overview.

During the time I worked on this study, Vollmann won the National Book Award for *Europe Central* and received the Strauss Living Award. He also published *Poor People* and *Riding Toward Everywhere*. *Imperial* is being released as this book is in its final stages. If you are reading this years after the 2009 publication date, there are most likely half a dozen Vollmann titles not addressed herein. I will leave that to future Vollmann scholars. This is the first book-length critical work on Vollmann; it is my intention that this study will be the starting point for all Vollmann studies.

This book is divided into two parts. Part I, "Freedom, Redemption, and Prostitution" consists of seven chapters that examine Vollmann's work by theme and series — books on prostitution and the lives of sex workers and their clients; books on travel; short story collections; the Seven Dreams series; and the seven-volume *Rising Up and Rising Down*. Part II, "Seven Conversations," collects interviews conducted over the years by both academics and fans, from print journals, e-zines, and forums, as well as two previously unpublished dialogues. The number seven is an intentional motif, reflecting Vollmann's use of it.

I have specifically chosen these interviews for their content, their chronology, and their relationship to my critical study. The reader can find certain aspects that I discuss drawn out in further detail in Vollmann's own words. The first interview, "Moth to the Flame," is the first major interview with Vollmann, conducted by Larry McCaffery in 1991. At 15,000 words, it has never been published in its entirety until now, although parts of it have appeared over the years in *Mondo 2000, Review of Contemporary Fiction,* the book *Some Other Frequency,* and the Japanese magazine *Positive.* The bulk of the interview deals with Vollmann's early works — his first novel, his first collection, the first volume of *Seven Dreams.* The second interview, "The Write Stuff," is the first interview to be posted on the Web, in 1994, on the ground-breaking Alt-X.com. This interview delves more into the darker side of Vollmann's work — prostitution, drugs, guns, and war. The third, "Vollmann Shares Vision," also originally appeared online. The fourth, "Pattern Recognitions," has never been published before and centers on *Argall* and the challenges of producing a large novel written in Elizabethan prose. "Drinks with Tony" is the fifth and is a transcript of an interview broadcast on Internet radio. It is more informal than the others — just two guys talking about literature. Kate Braverman's "The Subversive Dialogues" is the sixth and first appeared in a much truncated form in *The Bay Guardian;* it appears here in its full original version with a prose poem at the top. This interview reads like a performance piece, a short play, as the conversation is interrupted by a ringing telephone and the two characters popping pills. Finally, Teri Saul's interview, the seventh, is an essay about a trip to Vollmann's art studio in Sacramento and focuses on his paintings and book arts rather than his commercial books.

In each interview, the reader will find information that will help in understanding Vollmann's work as a whole. He is a complicated artist working on multiple levels of expression — whether in fiction, essay, journalism, poetry, ethnography, photography, or oil paints, there are many ways to approach the work and life of William T. Vollmann.

Now he would never write the things he had saved to write until he knew enough to write them well....
— Hemingway, "The Snows of Kilimanjaro"

PART I

FREEDOM, REDEMPTION, AND PROSTITUTION

Introduction

In order to understand this we need also to consider the following....
— Wittgenstein, I.181

Biography and Background

William Tanner Vollmann appeared on the contemporary American literary scene in 1987 with the novel *You Bright and Risen Angels*. He has since published fourteen additional books and won the PEN/Hemingway, the Whiting, the National Book, and the Strauss Living awards. His work has never been easy to pigeonhole: it is a combination of fiction, memoir, erotica, journalism, social critique, ethnography, history, and speculative fiction. In stealth mode, Vollmann moves from one category to another, whether it is a study of sex workers or immigrants or Noh Theater artists, mixing genres with the skill and grace of a well-trained Yakuza assassin. In a 2006 interview with *Poets & Writers Magazine*, he contends the "different genres are like different paint brushes you might pick up, which create different effects.... It doesn't really matter whether you are writing a detective story or a science fiction story."[1]

He was born in Santa Monica, California, on July 28, 1959, to Thomas and Tanis Vollmann. His father was at UCLA, completing a Ph.D. in business. The following year, the family moved to New Hampshire. Thomas had been hired as an assistant professor at Dartmouth College. Two more children were born that decade: Julie in 1962 and Ann in 1965.

Young Vollmann was shy and introverted, finding solace in the world of books, usually science fiction. He devoured every novel and short story he could find, especially by his favorite writers, Philip K. Dick and James Blish. Still in elementary school, he wrote a first novel: a space adventure about astronauts who are killed off one by one as they try to explore a new solar system. "I have wanted to write ... ever since I was six or seven," he explains in his "Biographical Statement."

> While the other children played games, I sat indoors reading stories; and in those days it often seemed to me that I was inside the book, riding with the Caliph upon his magic carpet, and all I had to do was tap him on the shoulder for him to see me and greet me and accept me as his Vizier [*Expelled from Eden*, 3].

In 1968, his six-year-old sister Julie drowned. He had been left to watch her. In a *Paris Review* interview with Madison Smart Bell, Vollmann confesses the pond "had a shallow bottom, which dropped off abruptly and ... she couldn't swim." He was haunted by his sister's death, troubled with nightmares of her up until he left home for college. He has examined this event and his feelings about it in several works. He deduces in the story "Under the Grass" (*The Atlas*) that his attempt to save a young prostitute in Thailand — also resulting in a photo essay for *Spin Magazine* — was a feeble act to atone for failure to rescue his sister. The curse of culpability and the need for penitence also haunts the protagonists of *The Rifles, Butterfly Stories,* and *The Royal Family*; the men in these books live with the aftermath of a death or suicide for which they feel responsible and guilty. Vollmann's sister becomes his influence, his muse, his curse.

He graduated high school in 1977 and was accepted at Deep Springs College, an all-male liberal arts institution in the high desert of southeast California. Deep Springs is located on a cattle ranch and alfalfa farm, established by electrical pioneer L.L. Nunn in 1917 "on the three pillars of academics, labor, and self-governance in order to help young men prepare themselves for lives of service to humanity."[2] There are only twenty-six students at any given time; they are required to perform manual labor for upkeep of the ranch, along with intensive academic studies. There Vollmann discovered Ludwig Wittgenstein; he identified with the philosopher. He started an autobiographical novel, *Introduction to the Memoirs*. The manuscript eventually morphed into *An Afghanistan Picture Show: Or, How I Saved the World* (1992). He picked up *A Tomb for Boris Davidovich* (1980) by Danilo Kiš, and his view of the possibilities of literature forever changed. The Yugoslavian short novel inspired a significant amount of his future work.[3] That same year, he took a trip to Alaska, the first in a lifetime of journeys away from home. He continued his undergraduate studies at Cornell (residing in Telluride House, founded and funded by Nunn for Deep Spring graduates) and submitted *Introduction to the Memoirs* to literary agents and publishing houses. Like many young writers on a first outing, he collected a stack of rejection letters praising his talent yet stating the book would not sell in the commercial marketplace.

He graduated *summa cum laude* in 1981 and accepted a fellowship from the graduate program in literature at the University of California, Berkeley. He moved to San Francisco and deferred his fellowship; he had his heart and mind set on joining the Mujahedeen rebel resistance in Afghanistan, fighting against the Soviet invasion. An idealist, he felt it was his duty to defy what he determined was a social and political injustice. He took a job as a secretary in a reinsurance company and saved money to fund this call to adventure.

He made his way to Pakistan, and then Afghanistan, in 1982, chronicling his travels in *An Afghanistan Picture Show.* He began work on an essay about violence, *Rising Up and Rising Down*; it became a twenty-three-year project consisting of seven volumes. In the same year he started work on *You Bright and Risen Angels* and his graduate studies. He dropped out of Berkeley, though. He submitted *Picture Show* to agents and publishers with little luck; he received the usual encouraging comments on his talent, but no representation or publishing offers.

At this time, he crossed paths with Ken Miller, an iconoclastic photographer whose images influenced the direction of Vollmann's career. In the preface to Miller's collection of photographs, *Open All Night* (1995), Vollmann offers this insight:

> What most people call beauty annoys him; what they call riches disgusts him, and the manners of his own class, the middle class, incite him to grinning personal taunts. This genuinely ugly side of his character frames his work, because it is what is called the *ugly* that attracts him.... These squashed lives are not just isolated bugs on the windshield, but *parallel worlds* of hermetic secrets, like the nine cities of Troy stacked one upon the next inside the earth [iv].

Miller was compiling a series of photographs documenting the seedier side of San Francisco life in the Tenderloin District — Neo-Nazi skinheads, drug addicts, alcoholics, the homeless, pimps, and prostitutes were his subjects. These members of America's sub-cultures were now Vollmann's new research interest. While *Angels* is a work of the fantastic, bordering on surrealism and science fiction, his second book, *The Rainbow Stories*, is an assemblage of "gonzo" journalism along the lines of reportage in the tradition of Hunter S. Thompson, Mark Twain, and Tom Wolfe.

In 1984, Vollmann took a job as a computer programmer in Silicon Valley. He knew very little about programming and obtained the position through a fellow Deep Springs alumnus. He took advantage of the situation and wrote the bulk of *You Bright and Risen Angels* on the job site. At the time, he did not own a computer or typewriter and was sleeping on the floor of a friend's apartment. He stayed after hours at the company, working on the manuscript long into the night, subsisting on candy bars from the vending machine. He slept under his desk, placing a wastebasket in front of him so the janitors would not notice his body as they came by to vacuum.

He did not have an easy time finding a home for *Angels*; the typescript made the usual rounds of publishers and did not receive a single response. It was nearly 300,000 words. Conscious of his budget and the expense of printing, copying, and mailing such an unwieldy typescript, he printed it out single-spaced, on both sides of the page. *Angels* eventually wound up on the desk of Esther Whitby, an editor at British publisher André Deutsch. She acquired *Angels*, publishing it in 1987 with U.S. rights going to Atheneum. The publishers "made one or two weary attempts at selling the first serial rights ... somebody at the *New Yorker* [said] that the violent language and subject matter ... would be 'absolutely unacceptable to Mr. Shawn,' who was then in charge" ("Morrow's Conjunctions: A View from Below," 143). Nevertheless, *Angels* did what every new writer hopes a first novel will do: earn critical attention. It did not earn an abundance of money, but it marked Vollmann's arrival as a published author.

Career

While waiting for his first novel to come out, Vollmann worked on *The Rainbow Stories* and *Whores for Gloria*. He was dismayed by the mixed reactions *Angels* received. "Some people seemed to be really bothered by the 'diffused' quality of the book," he says in Larry McCaffery's collection of interviews, *Some Other Frequency*, "while others have been increasingly disappointed with succeeding books" (318) "because they are not like *Angels*."[*] Sales were modest; Deutsch's first printing was 2,500 copies, and there was not a second.[4] The Whiting Foundation, however, acknowledged his talent with a $25,000 grant.

Deutsch did not accept *Whores for Gloria*. Filled with drug use, despair, and unsavory sex scenes, *Gloria* was rejected by a number of American publishers[5]; Pan Books U.K. released it as a paperback original. The late writer Kathy Acker read the short novel and recommended it to her American editor, Fred Jordan, a Grove Press veteran who was at Pantheon Books. Pantheon published *Gloria* in 1991; actor Dennis Hopper's production company optioned the book and hired Vollmann to adapt it into a screenplay. Never having written a screenplay, he bought a how-to book and followed the instructions. The screenplay, still owned by Hopper, has not yet been produced.

He switched American publishers for the 1990 publication of *The Ice*

---

[*]*See "Moth to the Flame" for the full interview.*

Shirt, Volume One of *Seven Dreams*. He was now with Viking Penguin, where he has maintained a long working relationship with then-editor now publisher Paul Slovak, whom he has credited as a great ally of the same magnitude as legendary editors Maxwell Perkins and Malcolm Cowley. He was hard at work on the second *Seven Dreams* installment, *Fathers and Crows*, writing sixteen hours a day. He developed carpal tunnel syndrome. Concerned about his condition, his parents bought him a computer with voice recognition software. This did not help.[6]

In 1991, he embarked on a hazardous excursion to the magnetic North Pole. This trip cost $12,000; *Esquire Magazine* paid part of it, in exchange for a feature article. Vollmann wanted to experience firsthand the weather conditions endured by the doomed John Franklin Expedition through the Arctic North in 1847. He was dropped off as close to the magnetic North Pole as he could get. He found shelter in a metal shed while a storm came in. In *The Rifles*, he reports that his alter-ego, Captain Subzero,

> wondered if he would live until morning.... It was still unnerving, to lie down shivering, on the near edge of a dark night, and to know that he'd only get colder and colder.... The first drop of ice-cold water ran down the mask and across his nose ... the sweat on back and buttocks and belly turned to ice ... [and] clung too ferociously to be scraped off with a fingernail or a knife [275].

He was eventually rescued, walking away from the icy ordeal with frostbite on his hands.

His second volume with Pantheon was *Thirteen Stories and Thirteen Epithets*, a collection of fiction, autobiographical narratives, and prose poems. In 1992, Viking and Deutsch published *Fathers and Crows*. Farrar, Straus and Giroux released *An Afghanistan Picture Show* the same year. *Fathers and Crows* was his longest book to date; both his publishers wanted the page count reduced. Vollmann passionately argued against any cuts to the text, a defense he would have to make more and more as his books grew in size.

Most of the 1990s, Vollmann traveled the world on assignment for *Esquire, Gear, The New Yorker, Time, Los Angeles Times* and *Spin*. His fiction regularly appeared in the literary journals *Conjunctions, Grand Street, Paris Review, Granta*, and *Fiction International*. Anthologies began reprinting his work. He was a frequent reviewer for the *Philadelphia Inquirer, Los Angeles Times Book Review*, and *New York Times Book Review*. *Butterfly Stories* was his next book, from Grove Press in 1993. *The Rifles* was published by Viking in 1994. The literary community certainly took notice of his prolific output: seven books from four publishers in four years. The reaction was not always positive. Critics questioned whether he was publishing too much and being repetitive in themes and topic, mostly his obsession with prostitution.

He gradually moved into the next stage of his career, as a foreign correspondent. He made the first of many visits to Sarajevo for the *Los Angeles Times Magazine* and BBC Radio 4. His broadcasts, "The Yugoslavian Notes," were nominated for a Sony Award in News and Current Affairs. He continued traveling to Thailand, Burma, and Malaysia, as well as Serbia, Croatia, and Bosnia.

May 1, 1994: On assignment for *Spin*, Vollmann was riding in the back seat of a jeep en route to Sarajevo. The jeep drove over a land mine. Will Brinton — his friend since high school, working as a freelance photographer — and interpreter Francis William Tomasic both died at the scene. Vollmann was the sole survivor, injured by shrapnel, his life spared because he was wearing a bulletproof vest. The incident was covered by several wire services and was the talk of the literary community for weeks.

Viking released *The Atlas* in 1996; it received the PEN/Hemingway Award, an honor usually given to works of fiction. It is a mixture of genres: journalism, essays, short stories, meditations, and prose poems, a compilation of his experiences traveling the world as a war correspondent and reporter of the exotic — an ideal subject for the Hemingway Award. That year, he married longtime companion Janice Kong-Ja Ryu.

The Royal Family was published in 2000. A 1400-plus-page manuscript, it was 780 pages when printed, with small type. Critical response was mixed. It is his most structured and conventional novel, essentially a private-eye yarn. In 2001 came the publication of the fourth (and one of the most challenging) of the *Seven Dreams* volumes, *Argall*. Written in imitation Elizabethan prose, it was ignored by the general public and challenging even for his most devout readers.[7]

Vollmann dubs *Rising Up and Rising Down* his life's work. At 3,296 pages and seven volumes, no publisher had the staff, resources, or wish to tackle the ungainly project. He decided publication was a pipe dream and a lost cause. Writer and publisher Dave Eggers wrote a letter pledging that he would publish all seven volumes simultaneously (Vollmann did not want them to be released serially) through his company, McSweeney's Books.[8] In late 2003, a year after the first announcement of publication (fact-checking and proofing causing the delay), McSweeney's released the seven volumes in an impressive slip-cased edition of 3,500 copies. It was a minor literary event. Despite a nomination for the National Book Critics Circle Award, there were no further printings; the complete set has now become a much sought-after collector's item fetching far more than the original $120 retail price. HarperCollins/ Ecco published a condensed, 733-page version in 2005.

In 2004, while riding his bicycle in Sacramento, he was hit by a car and broke his hip; he was hospitalized and, for a while, could not travel for work and research. Later in the year, he suffered from a stroke and then a series of smaller strokes; while these did not result in permanent damage (other than slight problems with equilibrium), it was a wake-up call that middle age had arrived.

The 2005 publication of *Europe Central* assured Vollmann his place in contemporary American literature, winning the National Book Award for Fiction. A collection of paired stories and novellas about Germany and Russia during World War II, the volume was close to succumbing to obscurity before being awarded the prize. It was in the bookstore remainder bins when nominated.[9]

A departure in subject and style, *Uncentering the Earth: Copernicus and the Revolution of the Heavenly Spheres* was published by Atlas Books/W.W. Norton in 2006. In 2007, Ecco published a book-length essay, *Poor People*. It is an inquiry into why some people in the world are poor and others not. In 2008, Ecco released *Riding Towards Everywhere*, an essay about hopping freight train cars, the American subculture of hobos, and the search for freedom.

In November 2007, the American Academy of Arts and Letters announced that, along with Madison Smartt Bell, Vollmann was the recipient of the $250,000 Harold and Maude Strauss Living Award, paid out in $50,000 installments over five years.[10]

Style and Technique

Readers may find some difficulties with Vollmann's approach and syntax. In general, he does not use quotation marks to denote dialogue. Most of the large magazines he wrote for added them into his features. In Volume Five of *Rising*, he notes:

> You will find minor stylistic differences in the case studies.... Some chapters ... deny themselves the convenience of quotation marks in direct speech. This so-called innovation ... was a source of some distress to my patient editor.... Other chapters show the influence of market pressure.... Should I have standardized these inconsistencies? I recall Lawrence of Arabia's comments to the proofreader who warned him that he had spelled the name of his favorite camel every which way in *Seven Pillars of Wisdom*. Lawrence replied simply, "She was a splendid beast" [9].

He employs kinetic, run-on sentences that can go on for pages in single paragraphs, reminiscent of Jack Kerouac, another influence from his youth. The best examples of this are found in *Gloria* and parts of *Thirteen Stories and Thirteen Epithets*. A syntax quirk in his early prose is the use of three spaces instead of commas or semicolons when writing dialogue. He drops this stylization after *Atlas*.

He does not keep to traditional narrative points-of-view and authorial voices. He mixes first and third person freely. For instance, *Angels* is generally in the third person; the story is "launched" via keyboard by a character named the Author. Later, Vollmann's alter-ego (and various real people in his life) enter the narrative and interact with fictional characters. In *The Rifles*, Vollmann (as "Captain Subzero") travels to the icy Northwest Passage and comes across the entrapped soul of Captain John Franklin. Franklin's soul possesses Subzero's body and Franklin is resurrected. In essence, as all the *Seven Dreams* volumes are told by "William the Blind," there are three narrators competing in *Rifles*, just as there are three in *Angels*. In *Europe Central*, the authorial voice jumps around from first to third to the collective "we."

Vollmann's novels do not "end" — at least, not according to what modern readers may believe constitutes an ending in the contemporary text. He offers no easy and clean wrap-up with problems solved and all questions answered. In *Gloria*, the protagonist, Jimmy, suddenly disappears for no apparent reason (he could be dead, as rumor has it, or he might have simply walked away), and no resolution is presented. In the table of contents of *Angels*, sections and chapters are listed that are not included in the novel; reading the sub-headings creates a secondary narrative that outlines what happens after the last page.

Vollmann's use of copious chronologies, glossaries, cited sources, and bibliographies often take up a good chunk of the back of the book. In the four published volumes *Seven Dreams*, the historical source material and footnotes create a running dialogue between author and data to present historical events, fact or myth, showing the reader that the events in these books are usually and literally true, yet remain mere interpretations of the available data. "I've always felt that the more we know about our own history the better off we are," is his philosophy,

> but today a lot of people get their histories mainly from movies, television or other media sources where things don't have to be accurate. People will see movies like *JFK* or *The Patriot* and end up thinking, Okay, now I see how it really was. But the truth is that it's really, really dangerous for people to be thinking that way. It's so easy to be manipulated by the media, whose main goal isn't to provide historical accuracy but entertaining versions that will sell. I don't want to put people in that position in my books.... I want to encourage readers to understand what my versions were based on.[11]

Vollmann's aim is for the reader to get to the end of the narrative and discover there are still more words. The reader is three-fourths finished, but discovers the story has actually come to a finish of some sort; the main text has "ended" yet there are more than one hundred appended pages, with further narrative and information. The approach avoids the novelist's device of closure, what Vollmann's calls "a dramatic convenience, a way of pandering to the reader's desire for resolutions." *Seven Dreams* works against this expectation: there are the source notes that comment on matters introduced in the novel; there is the main text, introduced by a long introductory note (e.g., "Ice-Text" and "Rifles-Text"); and then a series of what-happened-next commentaries, dubbed "further history."

Some readers, who are not used to such text in fiction, may find this extra material pretentious and annoying. It is possible to ignore these pages and still absorb the essence of the book. Vollmann's commentary, however, can be amusing; in the first source note in *Poor People*, he claims that Henry David Thoreau "was interviewed by ouija-board" [295] for consultation; when interacting with prostitutes, he will note how much each encounter cost him. The reader also sees the process (and methodology) of Vollmann's research with the inclusion of correspondence with scholars, librarians, and foreign government officials (such as the Russian consulate in *An Afghanistan Picture Show*) whom he asks to read and comment on manuscripts.[12] His comprehensive glossaries of names, terms, and places, as well as inclusive chronologies, help readers better understand and interpret the story. By allowing readers a gaze at his procedure, to view the nuts and bolts of what it takes to create a book-length work, he demystifies the writer's craft and the scholar's labor.

Themes

There are three major themes to Vollmann's work that I focus on in this study: freedom, redemption, and prostitution. I will show that the majority of Vollmann's fictional characters and non-fictional actors seek freedom in their lives — personal, political, spiritual, sexual. When restrictions are imposed, they rebel like the insects in *Angels* or the American Indians in *Seven Dreams*; when society disagrees with their lifestyle, they engage in that life even more, such as the prostitutes in *Gloria* and *The Royal Family*; when personal circumstances are a cause for being trapped into an unwanted life, Vollmann's actors will break free from their confines and escape, as in *Butterfly Stories* or even Copernicus and the religious doctrine that did not allow him to freely think.

The Vollmann narrator, or alter-ego, is always seeking redemption in his travels and actions, such as the Butterfly Boy living with the guilt of his dead sister; the private eye in *The Royal Family* who goes on a journey to run from the guilt of his lover's suicide; Captain Subzero's icy travels as he deals with the suicide of an Inuit lover; and Vollmann himself, in *Ride Toward Everywhere*, who discovers he understands his father better now, as he gets older, while he travels in box cars, goes to war zones, his father always questioning why he has to do this — can't he just sit behind his computer and write stories?

Then there is the theme of prostitution; there is no getting away from that in Vollmann's literature. He has been condemned by critics and encouraged by fans. It is indeed the oldest profession, the sale of counterfeit intimacy, but in prostitution (for Vollmann) also lies the ideals of freedom and redemption: the Madonna/whore image, and the act of paying another for love and sex, a slippery freedom in the postmodern world.

1

You Bright and Risen Angels (1987)

Somewhere in the world there exists an exceptional philosopher ...
— Truman Capote, *Answered Prayers*

You Bright and Risen Angels was released when cyberpunk literature was introduced as a sub-genre of science fiction, after the publication of William Gibson's *Neuromancer* (1984) and Bruce Sterling's *Schismatrix* (1985). *Angels* possesses similar themes, motifs, and imagery to those found in cyberpunk fiction. It was not, however, recognized by (or marketed to) science fiction readers. It is about revolutionary insects, set in the virtual universe of an apparent program operating inside a computer system. Subtitled "A Cartoon," the novel recounts the video game-like narrative of a data programmer who, referring to himself as "the Author," produces a colossal cast of characters from his fingertips and keyboard. He observes, and is fascinated by, their violent, apocalyptic interactions. *Angels* anthropomorphizes non-human creatures in the same vein as Orwell's *Animal Farm* (1945), Adams's *Watership Down* (1972), and Spiegelman's *Maus* (1988). These three books are political metaphors, and Vollmann follows suit; literary critic Larry McCaffery notes that "the motifs of bugs and electricity ... develop an allegory about the failure of revolutionary impulses to counter the evils of racism, fascism, and industrialism" (*Expelled,* xxii). Rave reviews were printed in the *New Statesman, USA Today,* and *The New York Times Book Review.* It is unlike typical first novels, which are obvious apprenticeship and outright autobiography. Some critics believe it remains his best novel. He has never returned to this whimsical form; subsequent work is grounded in realism and observational journalism.

It is the type of first novel that signifies a writer has left the starting gate of a major career, similar to Pynchon's *V.*, Fitzgerald's *This Side of Paradise*, and Mailer's *The Naked and the Dead*— all, respectfully, lengthy novels by writers under 30 years of age, employing pyrotechnic and acrobatic uses of language and formal innovations of structure.

The "Transcendental Contents" include sections and chapters not found in the volume; it is read as an outline to further content, what happens after "the end." So when the last page is reached, the reader can go back to the beginning to find more narrative. There is an epigraph from Adolf Hitler: "Surely I have the right to remove millions of an inferior race that breeds like vermin" (3). Quoting Hitler is a risk for any novelist, sure to achieve negative attention and disapproval. *Angels* is about war, tyranny, and oppression; using Hitler's words is an effective choice. In the prologue, "Shape-shifting," the Author asserts: "I may disguise myself as any other animate or inanimate object as follows" (4) as he seems to have the power to take on various personae. So begins "The History of Electricity," an introduction to the lonely Author who wishes to create life because "there is no one left in the world" (9). At his computer terminal, he presses the "resurrection button," summoning forth his "bright and risen angels" (9) from their graves: a cast of characters brought to being by the electrical current. There is the hero, Bug; powerful villain Mr. White; and the treacherous Big George, who is able to take control — indeed, hack — the narrative and change the course of events and history. Big George is described as a mysterious entity and "math nerd" (417), who is "pure electrical consciousness itself, insinuating itself everywhere, drifting in and out of all stories and machines" (111). The chapter structure is similar to Vollmann's future books: unnumbered, titled, each with an epigraph from sources such as Lautrémont, Marx, Hobbes, and Edison. "I will remain especially faithful to those first few pages," the Author states before Big George can take over, "since in the beginning of the story I cannot but be reminded that every key-stroke I make upon my typewriter may be transmitted through the wall outlet just behind my head (for I do not pretend to understand electricity) and left naked to the public" (12).

Knowing the circumstances behind how and when this novel was written, one can imagine Vollmann huddled in the corporate office, at his desk, late at night, in the dim light of his cubicle, conjuring up the lives of various insects and human beings while on a sugar high from the candy bars he has had for dinner. "The keys of my typewriter depress themselves and clack madly," the Author explains (15). There is no sense of linear time and space; events simultaneously occur in the past, present, and future. The Author observes Big George's military adventures in the jungles of an unknown foreign country and Bug's education and problems growing up an awkward, bookish insect. The Author recalls his own biography, when he once lived in San Francisco with a woman named Clara Bee. She calls him Beetle and grows weary of the relationship, resulting in the Author's attempted suicide. The biographical information for Bug and the Author overlap and mirror one another. Bug is a loner who never seems to fit into any social order; he does not know his direction in life until he joins and becomes the leader of a terrorist cell that is battling against the Blue Globes. In *Some Other Frequency*, Vollmann explains the inspiration for the Blue Globes:

> The first commercial transmission of alternating current took place in Telluride, Colorado, around the turn of the century. They originally used wooden power poles, which weren't creosote or anything, the way they are now (they didn't have these PCB resistors or anything like that). As a result, often times the power poles would short and even catch on fire, and there would be these huge blue globes of ball lightening on top of the globes [326].

The Blue Globes are anthropomorphized evil entities of electrical current; they are operatives for a tyrant known as Mr. White and do his bidding. He is a power-hungry man with world conquest as an agenda. Since *Angels* is "a cartoon," Mr. White fits the role of the typical cartoon villain with delusions of grandeur, such as Marvin the Martian, who desires to rule Mars and Earth. Mr. White wishes to do the same, his sights set on both worlds.

The real enemy lies within the Society of Daniel (for Daniel Boone), founded in the early twentieth century by the racist megalomaniac Mr. White. The Society of Daniel discovers electricity, or perhaps they are mere pawns for the greater agenda of the Blue Globes and their shared desire for world domination. Either way, one hand washes the other. Students at the Society "memorized statistics on pig-iron production and prepared to be engineers in the erection of that transnational superstructure known variously as the White Man's Burden, the Good Neighbor Policy, the Open Door, and Our Oriental Heritage (Vietnamization)" (33). Technological knowledge becomes a means for imperialism, exploitation, and the hierarchy of the elite ruling over the common folk (and insects). On the eve of the industrial revolution, Big George claims "we were all separate but equal then, you see.... It was only later, in the mysterious days when electricity had grown up all around us, there were the little folks and the big folks towering like weeds" (38). Mr. White embraces expansion and rule; he is a fan of Manifest Destiny; he is a blue-eyed Aryan idealist and shameless sexist who also sexually abuses his wife and daughter. He wants the nation to be safe and clean for white people, electricity, and the good old-fashioned American Way. He instructs his followers: "Kill anyone that tells you different and fight to keep what you have and obey the guy that pays you because what's good for him is good for you; and that, gentlemen, is freedom" (103).[1]

A collective resistance hatches out of the oppression within the metaphorical form of "The Great Beetle," a hodgepodge of idealistic humans and insects. There are allusions to Marxism and Russia's history; Bug is compared to a young Trotsky (248). The revolution against electricity is compared to "those happy, unambiguous days of 1917" (273), the insect army resembling the Bolsheviks. But Vollmann points out that those who gain power eventually become despots themselves. Bug begins with pure and moral motives; his intentions are for the good of all, the planet, and the environment. Bug's moral fiber is gradually degraded and eliminated as he evolves from the bookish geek to weaponized, bloodthirsty terrorist. Bug and his cohorts smash up computer terminals, murder software programmers, and capture two Blue Globes, torturing them during a cruel and brutal interrogation. The Author is helpless to stop this carnage; and so is Big George, who escapes the conflict between reactionaries and revolutionaries while the machines and the insects escalate into ever-increasing butchery and tyranny.

In the aftermath of this animated war, Vollmann jumps to present-day San Francisco. A real-life person, a prostitute named Brandi, is introduced (she also appears in *The Rainbow Stories, Thirteen Stories and Thirteen Epithets,* and *Fathers and Crows*):

> Sure enough, there she was, nodding her head back and forth, standing there on the corner of Cole and Haight.... Her beautiful junky's face went up and down as if she were listening to secret music through a headphone cassette player, but there wasn't any music and her head hit the wall [607].

She interacts with fictional characters, and real people are absorbed into the fiction. Frank, a "double agent" employed by the Blue Globes, is looking for Brandi, to have a good time and perhaps extract information about who the Author really is and how much control he has over the reality within the book. When Frank finds Brandi, the two smoke crystal meth from a glass pipe that feels "bitter and icy" (618). This reads as an odd, sudden insertion into this imaginative text, something the reader will not expect after digesting so many pages of battles between insects and electricity.

The text shifts from cartoon to reality and to allegory. The final chapter, "World in a Jar," is Big George's recount of an experiment where fruit flies are put in a glass jar with yeast; they eat and procreate and eat, and then their dead bodies cover the food as they continue to feast on the dead and procreate more, "encrusted with fecal dots," until the jar is so black with excrement and corpses that one can no longer gaze into it. Big George notes that the "larvae took over and grew wings and buzzed about the steadily more polluted vial like traffic helicopters in New York as cars snorted and farted in the blue-grey air" (624). This is a warning for the human race, devouring and using the planet, trapped in the Greenhouse Effect as "they went on buzzing and swarming until the vial dried up completely and then they were still" (624); it is commentary on humanity's disregard for the resources of the planet and for each other: an endless cycle of war, death, consumption, and the obsession, to be forever repeated. Big George understands that humans, like the fruit flies, never learn, building mounds of excrement upon more mounds of excrement. "Bugs are a good metaphor," Vollmann says,

> bugs are amoral. You can't blame them for being that way. Bugs aren't coura-geous. They're always scuttling in and out of crevices, always trying to better themselves; they're always prepared to hide, and always ready to attack. With the possible exception of social insects, they don't have concept of friendship or kindness, or mercy. In other words, bugs have developed the same kind of prac-tical survival mechanisms that all the people in *Angels* have. Survival by this amoral expediency of hiding, scuttling, grabbing what's available, attacking when you have to [*Some Other Frequency,* 327].

In the epilogue, Big George and the Author struggle for control of the final pages. The Author writes, "We bright and risen angels are all in our graves, as I, the Author, can assure you; for Big George has locked me into the Soci-ety of Daniel for the sake of productivity, and when I close my eyes I can remember only the framed colored plots of silicon micro-wafers" (632). The reader is directed to the Transcendental Contents to read the chapter titles for the seven missing sections, and conclude what would have happened next: more oppression, more wars, a Bug Senate, and finally the death of all the players (yet again). The insects wanted revenge for "unequal development" but in the end, the bugs lose and humans continue to exploit and pollute until, like the fruit flies in the jar, everything is used up and everybody simply dies. The characters wait in their digitized graves until the next time the Author presses the resurrection button and the morality play is reenacted again.

Angels was an auspicious debut; the first novel earned Vollmann a Whit-ing Award, the attention of influential people in the publishing community, and the regard of literary critics. The book is taught in many courses on post-modern literature and science fiction, but it is not the type of fiction Voll-mann continued to write. It stands alone in his oeuvre; on the other hand, being a cautionary tale on war, violence, and tyranny, it fits precisely with the thematic content of most of his other books.[2]

Freedom is the core of *Angels*— the quest for freedom from tyranny; political and even religious freedom is the ideal. The novel shows us, how-ever, that the fight for freedom can become addictive — once you win the struggle and the war, what is left to do? One may seek enemies of freedom where they do not exist, simply to keep the war machine and the killing continuous. History — as Vollmann will discuss in *Rising Up and Rising Down*— proves this to be true.

2

The Rainbow Stories (1989); *Thirteen Stories and Thirteen Epithets* (1991); *Europe Central* (2005)

In our first listening, under the pressure of "accepting a call," the telephone will in fact emerge as a synecdoche of technology.
— Avital Ronell, *The Telephone Book*

These three volumes are set in America, Europe, and southeast Asia; placed in the past and the present; and written in the context of history, fable, fantasy, autobiography, and ethnography. They are made of fiction and fact and something in between; sections range from one page in length to the novella.[1] Vollmann's collections are not compilations of random short stories written over a certain period of time, as many collections tend to be. Each is compounded on a high concept, a grand metaphor; the volumes are cycles of related texts with recurring topics and motifs.

Europe Central almost functions as a novel, coupling related stories together, one set in Germany and the other in Russia; they share similar premises and moral inquires about war, patriotism, love, and art. *Thirteen Stories and Thirteen Epithets* also pairs off texts — a prose poem (or flash fiction) mirrors a longer story; also, the same characters (like the prostitute Brandi from *Angels*) reappear throughout the book. *Rainbow*, however, mixes fiction with journalism and memoir with interviews. Vollmann employs the same mixed-genre method ten years later in *The Atlas*.

Vollmann's second title appeared two years after the publication of *Angels*, and if readers expected another exercise in postmodern quirkiness, they got just the opposite. The style of narrative journalism in *The Rainbow Stories* reflects the overall presentation of Vollmann's future work. Here he explores the reality of streetwalkers, skinheads, murderers, strippers, junkies, unrequited love, romance, spirituality, and cruelty in postmodern performance art. Asked in an interview at website Alt-X.com about the genesis of the book, Vollmann replied:

> I guess it was because I was able to meet this guy, Ken Miller, the street photographer. At that time, he was in his heyday on Haight Street. He knew everybody. Everybody knew him. He'd just go out, and all the alcoholics would call out "Hey Ken!" He'd just shaved his head, become a skinhead, and he lived with the skinheads. So they kind of liked him. He took all their pictures.

The collection revolves around the colors of the rainbow; spectrum; each story is dedicated to a specific color: white, red, orange, yellow, green, blue, indigo and violet — with two stories each given to red, yellow, and blue — and range from five to 110 pages. "I won't pretend that once I had the color scheme pretty well fixed in my mind," Vollmann admits.

> I started cold-bloodedly trying to go out and make every experience I had try to fit this scheme. I knew more or less what I wanted this collection to be about, and the color scheme simply seemed to supply a kind of overlay or connection between the things I wanted to talk about. I thought of the book almost like a novel because it has a structure that allows specific patterns of themes and symbols to develop and clarify themselves [*Some Other Frequency*, 330–31].

As he did in *Angels*, Vollmann inserts himself as an omnipresent force: "Because I, William T. Vollmann, am the Holy Ghost, I am able to understand all tongues" (530). While he may not speak the white-power tongue of Neo-Nazis, Vollmann is allowed to accompany them and observe their way of life in "The White Knights." The publication of this disjointed story — a compilation of scenes and vignettes — in both the journal *Conjunctions* and this collection caught the attention of critics and readers. Here was a writer who was willing to go to extreme and very fascinating lengths to get his story, similar to Hunter S. Thompson in *Hell's Angels*. Vollmann hangs out with a group of social outcasts who call themselves the SF Skinz: young men and women with names like Dagger, Bootwoman Marisa, Dan-L, Spike, Dickie, and Yama. They are angry at the world; they hate anyone whose skin is not white and whose ancestry is not pure Aryan (as with Mr. White in *Angels*, Vollmann seems to be fascinated with issues of white supremacy); they love to get drunk, do drugs, have casual sex; they enjoy participating in violent acts. They open up to Vollmann in a way they would not with a more casual. Vollmann jots down his observations like an anthropologist taking field notes.

He reports that a Skinz female, attached to a Skinz male, is called a "boot-woman." Dagger's bootwoman is named Spike and she's pregnant. Boot-woman Dan-L waits hand and foot on the men, getting beers; she tells Vollmann she dearly loves her mother even if her mother does not understand her. Dee is "a thin bootwoman with big teeth" (51). Sixteen-year-old Boot-woman Marisa has a missing front tooth and a conviction for assault with a deadly weapon on her record. Her shaved head is "clean and marbled like the freckled stone stairs fronting San Francisco houses" (45). She loathes Brandi — that ever-present prostitute from *Angel, Thirteen* and *Fathers and Crows*— who makes a brief appearance: It is no surprise that "the skinheads hated Brandi because she was black" (44). Their opinions are blunt: "She's a walking stinkbag,' said Bootwoman Marisa" (44).

When Vollmann, playing the vulnerable observer, buys Marisa a white rose, she is surprised and delighted; it is probably the first time any man has ever given her a flower. A black woman sees the rose and Marisa says, "Yes, it's a *white* rose" (49). Marisa's hatred of black women stems from her miss-ing tooth; she was in juvenile detention and always getting into fights, and one day a bunch of black girls held her down, got a pair of pliers from a guard, and pulled out her tooth. When Vollmann asks, "So the girls held you down?" she replies: "No, the guards did" (50). Is she making this up? Is this true? If true, what does this say about the juvenile corrections system and the safety of minors in the United States? It paints an ugly, biased world, and there appears to be little that is beautiful or tender in the world of the skinsheads — the white rose being the one exception.[2]

While a white rose signifies racial purity for Marisa, the story "Yellow Rose" is a heartfelt love story between the narrator (Vollmann?) and a Korean woman, Jenny. It begins: "When I put Jenny's picture up against my glasses her face fogs into a pale yellow moon mistily aswim in the darkness of her hair and high school uniform" (205). The story has a youthful, innocent frenzy; the narrator can't wait to tell his love about his feelings even though "she came from a very traditional family. If her mother ever suspected her of being involved with a Caucasian, Jenny would be cast off" (209). She is "*soon-jin*" ("innocent" in Korean) (210). She is a virgin but curious about sex. She taunts him about getting engaged to another man, or meeting men and leav-ing with them; she always says she is "kidding" (211) and enjoys his despon-dent reactions, his jealousy repressed. He is afraid of doing or saying the wrong thing and losing her.

"Ladies and Red Lights" is Vollmann's first extended study of prostitu-tion, the seed of what would later become *Gloria, Butterfly Stories*, parts of *Thirteen,* and most of *The Royal Family.* The story opens in a peep booth and ends with Brandi asking for change on the street. Like Jimmy in *Gloria* and the private eye in *Royal*, the narrator interviews various San Francisco street-walkers, dancers, and call girls, getting the stories that illustrate how they got into the business. Vollmann provides footnotes on how much each conversation and encounter set him back: "This paragraph cost me seven dollars" (80); "This ended up costing two dollars, for naked girls must have their tips" (81); "This revelation cost me twenty dollars" (110); and, finally, at the end, "I gave Brandi twenty-five cents" (141).

In "The Blue Wallet," his awkward relationship with Jenny continues as "she had never told her family about me" (312). Jenny loses her wallet at a party she throws and is convinced his skinhead friends stole it from her. Jenny is paranoid, deadbolting her door, fearing the skinheads will return and steal more from her. Vollmann comments, "If this had been a Chekhovian story ... the blue wallet would have turned up eventually, proving by its determined refusal to be elsewhere that all suspicions had been reified to the point of logical and moral death" (323). Similar to other stories in this volume (and the novels), there is no conclusion. There are only snapshots, interwoven so that *Rainbow* is almost, but not quite, a novel — the same way the stories in *Thirteen* and *Europe Central* are laid out.

Rainbow is also connected to his first novel. At the end of *Angels* is a four-page paragraph, a prose poem really, about a woman named Catherine "who would never love me or love anyone" (633) although "we talked about how we each wanted to have children" (633). The paragraph ends with the narrator "sad because by the time I close my eyes each night I suspect that as usual I have been fooling myself, that she, too, is in her grave" (635). She is dead at the end of *Angels*, and this the read runs to the second to last entry in *Rainbow*, "Violet Hair," subtitled "A Heideggerian Tragedy." It is about Catherine, aka Saint Catherine of San Diego "or rather, to be more concrete, Solana Beach"[3] (487), who "had violet hair" (483). She is the same Catherine from *Angels* and it seems she is still dead; she is a ghost, and the narrator is none other than the Holy Ghost himself (aka Vollmann), who writes that "most of her life, Catherine had been reading, sometimes taking her book to visit me in Heaven where it is cold and foggy and she must lie on the couch wrapped in a thick Canadian-Indian sweater and a reindeer skin" (485). The Holy Ghost visits her; the two watch TV and talk back to what they hear and observe on the TV. She does not actually see the Holy Ghost, she feels his presence, "a peculiar feeling that something in the air is trying to talk to me" (487). She has a "badboy" friend named Beelzebub; he is studying the works of Heidegger and often quotes the philosopher: "Anyone can dream in the sunlight which is so ready-to-hand" (496). Catherine too quotes Heidegger in an attempt to interpret what is happening to her: "The world is a *structure* ... and when you look at how it's structured there are these sequences of *steps*" (515).

"Violet Hair" can be read, on one level, as a tale of the fantastic, that Catherine is a lost soul on the earth who is not aware that she is actually dead and needs to rise up to Heaven with her pal the Holy Ghost. On the other hand, it could all be a metaphor about a woman who is simply lost in her life path and does not know which direction to go, essentially a ghost in society: in Heideggerian terms, her *Daisen* (self-aware person) has no career, no goals, no foreseeable future. The story is a clever allegory about unrequited love (while "Yellow Rose" is realism concerning the same), the sorrow a person can feel when loving another who does not return the feelings and the loss of what could have been. Someone on the TV says at the end: "Things could be different" (531), which can sum up any failed relationship.

Vollmann puts the journalist's hat back on in "The Indigo Engineers" and profiles the San Francisco–based performance art troupe Survival Research Laboratories, led by Mark Pauline. SRL's iconoclastic performances of machines and dead animal flesh in the 1980s–90s are legendary in the underground cyberpunk and art scene of Northern California. One has to attend an SRL installation/show to fully understand what it is about; it is visual social commentary that has to be gazed on and experienced; words alone cannot describe what happens, although Vollmann attempts to, in prose befitting *Angels*:

> Winged like maple-seeds and insects, their thoughts fell to earth in a thousand ways — always verified by the smell of machine grease. First there were the martyrized pigeons, then the posters, then the rockets and the crawling robots viscously battling for possession of decayed freeway underpasses or rubble-covered parking lots, while spectators cheered, fulfilling their own function of ghouls reveling in devastation [443].

Vollmann's mission as a reporter is to find out the reason behind this art and the fascination people have with observing the destruction of both dead flesh and machines. SRL's performances are the simulacra of violence, a *spectacle* that, according to Guy Debord in *Society of the Spectacle* (1970), "is not a collection of images, but a social relation among people, mediated by images" (4). The audience immerses itself in dead animals torn to pieces and robots battling each other for supremacy. (This sounds a lot like the battles of insects and electricity in *Angels*, something Vollmann must have been aware of when watching SRL performances.) The performance reflects the duality of mankind's relationship with technology: technology is *needed*, and also *feared*. Jean Baudrillard discusses this concept in *Simulations* (1988):

> Of the same order as the impossibility of rediscovering an absolute level of the real, is the impossibility of staging an illusion. Illusion is no longer possible, because the real is no longer possible.... Transgression and violence are less serious, for they only contest the *distribution* of the real [38].

"The spectacle does not realize philosophy," contends Debord, "it philosophizes reality" (18). Mark Pauline is thinking along the same lines when he explains to Vollmann that "cruelty ... doesn't make any sense any more." For instance, why is it "cruel" to make machines fight each other? They have no feelings. We are projecting our emotions onto inanimate objects. "In the old days," Pauline says,

> when philosophers talked about identity, it was never an issue for inanimate things. Inanimate things could not recognize in each other any kind of identity. You had to be alive; you had to have an intelligence in order to have an identity.... In these shows, what we're trying to do is bring inanimate objects to a level where they can act, and people can relate to them as identities [457–58].

Humans, he means, feel a need to anthropomorphize what has no life. Vollmann feels an affinity with Pauline and his theories; he sees his own interests manifested in the performance. Vollmann comes to believe that all things are ultimately connected, whether they be fiction or fact, justifying *Rainbow's* mixing "the documentary stories with the imaginative stories to make the point that it doesn't matter in these worlds whether these things literally happened or not. They're both true in different ways" [*Some Other Frequency*, 323].

The twenty-six prose texts in *Thirteen Stories and Thirteen Epithets* have their own identity; they are paired up and unified: for each short story, there is an accompanying one to three-page prose poem, such as "Epitaph for Ken and Yummy," "Epitaph for Peggy's Pimp" and "Epitaph for President John F. Kennedy." They act as both supplement and sidebars to the longer works. A novella, "The Ghost of Magnetism," tells of the narrator's last days in San Francisco, before he leaves for New York, and a doomed love affair (yet another one) with Elaine Suicide. The style is frenzied, feverish, and nervous, with single paragraphs going on for up to twelve pages; there is a plethora of run-on sentences without standard punctuation or conventional grammar. The influence here is Kerouac; *The Subterraneans*, a short novel that employs long rambling paragraphs and is also set in San Francisco, is about a doomed love affair. Elaine Suicide and Kerouac's Mardo Fox are curiously similar:

> She had to tell me everything — no doubt just the other day she'd already told her whole story to Adam and he'd listened tweaking his beard with a dream in his far-off eye to look attentive and loverman in the bleak eternity, nodding.... Her own little stories about flipping and her minor fugues, cutting across boundaries of the city, smoking too much marijuana, which held so much terror for her [*Subterraneans*, 26–27].

> Getting to know Elaine was like listening from start to finish to the Suzanne Vega compact disk that she brought in order to record one particular song onto the soundtrack of her film with maximum fidelity and then Elaine was finished with the compact disk forever because she did not have a compact disk player

and never would since she had given up being an Assistant Media Buyer in the advertising office on Market Street [*Thirteen*, 53].

Thirteen contains more examinations of prostitutes ("The Bad Girl," "The Happy Girl," and "Flowers in Your Hair"); Elaine Suicide appears again ("The Handcuff Manual" and "Kindness"); and Vollmann reveals his deepest, darkest self in the three-page "Epitaph for a Coward's Heart," where, sitting on the steps of the New York Public Library one day, he spots a young girl in a Catholic school uniform who is accosted by a man walking by, telling her, "You shouldn't be showing your legs like that" (208), embarrassing the girl. People around the library pretend to ignore this; no one, not even Vollmann, does anything to stop the man. In retrospect, Vollmann is haunted by "that girl whose integrity I did not repair, those burned ghosts whose memory I did nothing for" (209). It seems to be the death of his sister all over again, that dreadful feeling of helplessness. He has to live with his guilt and believe that the next time he witnesses something similar, he will act, he will be a hero and good citizen, worthy of a medal or an award for his valiant deeds.

The 2005 National Book Award[4] in fiction was given to *Europe Central,* an ambitiously big book of interlinked texts set during World War II. Each of thirty-six fictions is paired off, one set in Russia, one in Germany, about real and imagined people caught up in actual historical events. "For my own narrative purposes I have invented much of the interrelations," Vollmann notes in a postscript (807). The actors include artists, musicians, and poets such as Kurt Gerstein, Käthe Kollwitz, Anna Akhmatova, Elena Komstantinovskaya, Dmitri Shostakovich, and documentary filmmaker Roman Karme, who is caught up in a fictionalized love triangle between Komstantinovskaya and Shostakovich — that is, fiction to the extent that there is no basis in historical fact other than some archived letters Vollmann discovered in his research. In the appendix, he writes:

> It is unlikely that Shostakovich never got over Elena, as has been imagined in this book. There is equally no reason to suppose that Elena's marriage to Karmen failed because she was still in love with Shostakovich. Moreover, Elena was not blonde, but darkhaired, and I have no grounds whatsoever for believing her to have been a bisexual cigarette smoker.... She remains an enigma to me.... I had various reasons for making my version of her as capable of love for both men and women.... As I have written in this book, "above all Eurpoa is Eleana" [808].

Then there are the men of war. *Europe Central* includes representations of real generals who served on both sides of the eastern front. Field Marshal Friedrich Paulus listens to "Beethoven on the gramophone" (328) before going into battle with his counterpart, Lieutenant-General A.A. Vaslov, "one of those heroically immaculate men of Soviet marble" (260). Vollmann writes with such authority and familiarity of historical time and place that readers unfamiliar with his work might mistake him for a European author. Unlike his previous historical books, "Vollmann" does not appear in the pages as meta-character, alter-ego, or himself—although one may wonder who the intermittent drifting "I" is who pops up now and then. There is also a "we" who occasionally asserts attention — it is a culture speaking, the collective conscious:

> We journeyed for thousands of kilometers, sometimes in windowless train cars, the rest of the time on foot. Most of us remembered how it had been the first time, with Ivans and Natashas struggling ahead of our Panzers.... They carried us east in boxcars; we rode railroad tracks as narrow in guage as the strange note-strung segments which begin in measure ninety-six of Shostakovich's Eighth Symphony [533–34].

Within the wide array of characters, Soviet and Nazi, Shostakovich is the protagonist; he and the people involved with him weave in and out and are the narrative glue that makes this collection a quasi-novel. Shostakovich's symphonies operate as a soundtrack; the music is referred to throughout the book as the characters listen to and have emotional reactions to it. The section "Opus 40" is a meditation on the melodic movement:

> Each of Shostakovich's symphonies I consider to be a multiply broken bridge, an archipelago of steel trailing off into the river. Opus 40, however, is a house of four rooms. In front, it is true, there is an ornate golden staircase ascending out into a snowy plain, the ending unconsummated in the air ... the first movement, composed to firelight and kisses, remains the most romantic thing that [he] ever wrote [85, 87].

Europe Central is dedicated "to the memory of Danilo Kiš, whose masterpiece *A Tomb for Boris Davidovich* kept me company for many years while I was preparing to write this book" (iii). In his afterword to the 2001 Dalkey Archive Press reprint of Kiš's novel, Vollmann tells how he came across the book as a teenager, and how it influenced him:

> The books in the "Writers from the Other Europe" series were thrilling and shocking incitements not only to my political development but also to my creative purpose.... Why has this book in particular been always on my desk or at my shelf for twenty years? ... Growing up in a society whose historical memory and political perceptiveness are attenuated in direct proportion to its commercialism ... I vaguely understood that something was amiss in my surroundings [*Expelled*, 335].

Europe Central opens with a telephone ringing, "a squat black telephone ... an octopus, the god of our Signal Corps, owns a recess in Berlin.... Somewhere between steel reefs, a wire wrapped in gutta-percha vibrates: *I hereby ... zzZZZZZ ... the critical situation ... a crushing blow"* (3). The ringing telephone continually appears throughout the text, either as a benign object of technology or "scream[ing] like an eagle" (534). It is a wake-up call to a world gone mad with warfare: "He told the telephone: Get somebody over here with the order of battle" (76). The ringing "black octopus" at the opening of *Europe Central* is also an invitation to war, its tentacles of doom initiating battles that will result in the deaths of millions.

Despite its dense, meditative, elegant prose, *Europe Central* may confuse and aggravate some readers, unless the reader is familiar with not only the political landscape of Germany and Russia during World War II, but Eastern European literature, opera, art, and cinema too. There are many obscure references that require the reader to refer to the 59 pages of cited sources. However, *Europe Central* is a deeply researched work of historical fiction, worthy of the attention that the National Book Award Foundation gave it, a declaration that the once promising author had transformed, like the larvae from a cocoon, into a major voice in American letters.

*   *   *

Again, the theme of freedom is at work in these three collections. The Russians fight for freedom from the tyranny not only of Germany, but of the old ways that have enslaved the common man before the start of the war. We know that the Russians did not find the freedom they craved while in battle, but they could not foresee the downside to a communist government at the time. *Europe Central*'s cry for freedom is for art, music, and love; at the heart of the book, we see men and women whose lives are shadowed by world events they can neither escape nor control. The same can be said for *Rainbow*; the collected lives strive for freedom against poverty, bigotry, and the pressures to conform to society's expectations — the Skinz want the freedom to be Nazis; Survival Research Laboratories performances reveal man's inner wish for freedom from machinery, while the group enacts freedom of speech within performance; Brandi portrays a freedom from conformity by smoking crack and selling her body; the strippers and sex workers Vollmann studies exhibit the freedom of the female body.

Vollmann's next major theme, redemption, starts to show in *Thirteen*. The narrative "I" seeks redemption for his desire for Elaine Suicide and the fact that he was unable to help her find happiness, and there is the need for redemption for not defending the honor of a young girl verbally accosted in public. Perhaps by writing about it, Vollmann redeems his failures and guilt.

3

Seven Dreams: A Book of North American Landscapes (1990–2001)

Destiny is written concurrently with the event, not prior to it.
    — Jacques Monod, *Chance and Necessity*

History

Vollmann envisioned *Seven Dreams* while writing *Rainbow*. He noticed there were many parking lots in the San Francisco Tenderloin where prostitutes congregated and conducted business. He wondered what was the land was like before all the parking lots were paved, before the continent was colonized.

Seven Dreams is a work of post-colonial literature and magnifies the narrow, dogmatic points of view of European superiority. At issue is foreign interaction with, and oppression of, Native American Indian populations: how the introduction of European weapons, philosophy, and religion affected cultural and ethnic identity. The genre is the historical novel, using the formal innovations of metafiction and the qualitative methods of ethnographic research to form the "dreams"— an interpretation of history and treatise on how the past has influenced the present. Vollmann also considers contemporary representations of the past in historical scholarship, biographies, propaganda, revisionism, and the media (e.g., Disney's versions of the life of Pocahontas).

There is no such thing as a truly accurate historical account, according to Norman K. Denzin in *Interpretative Biography*:

> Ethnographies, biographies, and autobiographies rest on *stories* which are fictional, narrative accounts of how something happened. Stories are fiction. A *fiction* is something made up or fashioned out of real and imagined events. History, in this sense, is fiction [41].

Real people interact with imagined characters in the *Seven Dreams* volumes; this is accepted poetic license in historical fiction. Vollmann is *free* to interpret and represent the past as he chooses; these are *his* dreams, after all, of what once was, of what history is interpreted as. Nevertheless, his exhaustive method of research is to be as accurate as possible. He states the books operate ethnographically,

> in addition to being a symbolic history of America ... a classroom-type ethnography work that could be read for real information. I wasn't really thinking of this as something that would actually be used in a classroom, but I did want readers to feel confident that if they picked up, say, *Fathers and Crows*, they could be pretty sure that every detail about the Micmac Indians was correct and that what happened between the Micmacs and the Algonquin Indians had been rendered as correctly as I could make it.[1]

In *The Paradox of History*, Nicola Chiaromonte argues that the "history of historians" is "unreal or mythical" when compared to "reality itself, history as it is actually experienced by the individual and the community" (19). The past, for Chiaromonte, is moot without a personal connection — the way a person approaches the concept is far more import than what is found in scholarly texts. Vollmann follows this theory by mixing historical events with autobiographical narrative as each book jumps back and forth through time.

The Volumes

The dreams have not been published in chronological order. *The Ice-Shirt* and *Fathers and Crows* are the First and Second, while *The Rifles,* published third in line, is actually the Sixth (and has a more contemporaneous setting than the others). The Third, *Argall,* was published seven years after *Rifles.* Unpublished, and in various stages of completion,[2] are the Fourth (*The Poison Shirt,* concerning the Puritans vs. King Phillip of Rhode Island), the Fifth (*The Dying Grass,* about the destruction of the Plains Indian tribes), and the Seventh (*The Cloud-Shirt,* regarding the Hopi vs. Navajo in the 20th century land rights issues[3]). Each volume is the fevered reverie of William the Blind, a narrator who cannot be trusted to tell the truth because he is biased and cannot see well. He is a remake of Homer and an omnipresent storyteller, the symbolic representation of Vollmann. The name reflects Vollmann's actual bad eyesight.

Method

For *Ice Shirt* and *Rifles*, Vollmann conducted research by traveling to the coldest regions of Canada and the magnetic North Pole. He had no prior experience with such harsh environmental conditions, as he did not on his first journey to Afghanistan; he put himself at physical risk for the sake of writing authentically. On the other hand, for *Argall*, he studied hundreds of texts written during the Elizabethan era, immersing himself in the rhetoric and thought-patterns of another time and place, so that *Argall* would have an authentic narrative voice.

The overall model Vollmann had in mind was Ovid's *Metamorphosis*:

> I wasn't thinking in terms of doing a whole series of books but just a single, seven-part volume that would be this symbolic history of North America over the past thousand years. It would rely heavily on European and Native American myth, and I would retell these stories with my own slant as a way of providing some idea of the way that things changed. I stuck fairly closely to that conception. I retold lots of Norse myths and two or three Inuit myths as well, using those as a kind of a basic paradigm for other things that happen. I found that all the materials I wanted to deal with simply could not be compressed into a single volume.[4]

In *Ice Shirt,* the Norse engage a process of assimilation by introducing *ice* into "Vinland." The classical Norse sagas claim there was no ice during the winter when they came to North America — for a culture that co-existed with ice year-round, Vinland must have been Shangri-la for the Norse explorers. The ice they bring, of course, is clear metaphor: the chill in their hearts and the love of violence. Just as the Europeans had an apparent destructive influence on the Native American Indians, so did the Norse hundreds of years earlier. Vinland offered new opportunities for Norse warfare and conquest. With their characteristic amalgamation of raw courage and carnal brutality, they were determined to take over this newfound real estate. In their eyes, the natives were outlaws, subject to the judgment of the iron axe. With stone axes, the native Indians could not prevail in battle. They do not lose in the long run, however, because their numbers are great and the Norse technological superiority is not as powerful as first perceived. In a battle scene from *Ice Shirt*, one of the Norse axes has killed a native; another native picks it up and kills a Norseman with it; understanding how sharp and strong it is, and what the new axe can do, he throws it away. "This really happens in one of the Norse sagas," Vollmann says,

> and when I came across it, I thought it was a really odd and extraordinary moment. Here was the first confrontation between a native, established way of life and this new power which the natives had never seen before. That ice was the beginning of this new power which was going to transform the landscape

and pretty much ruin them — and pretty much ruin us, as well. Rejecting that power was an act which you can call the opening of American history [*Some Other Frequency* 317].

The Norsemen represent pure, raw freedom — they conquer, pillage, and plunder at will, never caring for the consequences, their main desire victory. At least, this is the popular conception of the virile Viking male, supported by historical fact. The Norsemen are similar to the Skinz — they believe in their people's right (and destiny) to rule over those they deem inferior; the way Neo-Nazis view Jews or blacks is the same way the Norse gazed on the natives of Vinland. The natives fight for their freedom from the invaders the way the insects battle the Blue Globes, the Russians resist the Germans, and the prostitutes defy the law. The struggles encompass a freedom of land, a freedom of creed, and a freedom of the body's placement and use in the world

The Stream of Time

Seven Dreams examines how different societies — worlds, really — attempt to mesh together and become one, intentionally or by force. *Fathers and Crows* concerns the failed integration of cultures, the pitfalls of oppression, and the hubris of religious colonization. Vollmann's literary device is a concept he calls the Stream of Time; it flows forward, never back. It is a time/space continuum encompassing all of history, sinuous in its movement out of the past and into the future. He conceived this concept while visiting a friend in upstate New York, "on whose creeked, waterfalled, and wooded property I first conceived the idea of the Stream of Time as employed in my novel *Fathers and Crows*."[5] Vollmann's concept recalls the "chronotope" as theorized by M.M. Bakhtin:

> The chronotope is a formally constitutive category of literature ... [within which] spatial and temporal indicators are fused into one carefully thought out, concrete whole. Time, as it were, thickens, takes on flesh, becomes artistically visible; likewise, space becomes charged and responsive to the movements of time, plot and history.[6]

For Vollmann, the past is a force of its own, coercing itself onto the present, so that "history devours what happens, without any reason" (*Fathers & Crows,* 215).

Myths and Legends

Ice Shirt goes back to the beginning of time, to the creation allegory according to the Inuit. In the section "The Hermophrodite," a fable that possibly dates back prior to 30,000 B.C., long before the time of Odin, the Inuit tell the story of mankind's beginning. It starts with Elder Brother and Younger Brother, who "lived on the ice without knowing where they had come from" (85). They are just there, with no apparent origins; they live together, hunt together, learn together. Younger Brother has some identity issues; he is

> less sure who *he* was. Sometimes he thought he was a seal, and lay on his stomach barking.... At other times Younger Brother was convinced that he must be a polar bear.... One day he was sure that he must be a gull [86].

One day, after a horrible storm, they are visited by a mysterious Spirit Woman: "I am the blue snow-shadows all around you. You can always hear me; you can sometimes see me; you can never kiss me," she says (90). She strikes the ice and makes an island, and the two brothers, injured, "feebly crawl to shore" (91). She bends over Younger Brother and "did something to him, but he did not know what it was." She tells the brothers: "I have fitted you for each other" (91). The encounter has exhausted them and

> for a long time the two brothers slept.... When he awoke, Younger Brother felt a warm wetness between his legs that had never been there before. His fresh boy-strength became as feathers whirling in the air.... The nipples flowered on his chest, and bore fruit. Then his brother looked at him as men look at women [91].

Elder Brother forces himself onto Younger Brother. After the rape, babies come and the human race begins.

Fathers and Crows interprets the life story of Dekanwida. The Iroquois (as spelled in the book) myth of the great Christ-like peacemaking leader Dekanwida ("Two River Currents Flowing Together") is an apparent combination of Iroquois oral story and the influence of the Jesuits who attempted to convert "the savages" to Christianity. It tells the narrative of a young girl in an Iroquois village who becomes pregnant; she is a virgin and does not know how this happened to her. She considers killing herself out of shame, but the soul of her son whispers from the womb: *I will be born soon* (320). When the unnamed girl's mother asks her how it is possible she is carrying a child, the girl replies, "I'll tell you the truth ... the truth is I don't know" (320). In a dream, the spirit of the child tries to soothe her fears: "*Be comforted, my mother ... I'm going to be a great man ... I am going to go to the Flint People, to the Many Hill People; I'm going to raise up the Great Tree of Peace*" (321). When the child is born, she tries to kill the boy, as predicted by the girl's mother: "Well, Dekanwida ... You have no father, so Your mother is going to drown You" (323). The girl does drown the boy child, several times, happy to be rid of the burden. Each time she does, he returns: "Later that night, they found Dekanwida at His mother's breast." The girl's mother tries to kill the baby, too, but Dekanwida again returns to his mother's bosom. The family starts to believe Dekanwida has a destiny to be a great man. Indeed, he does become that great man, but it is not an easy path to accolades, fame, and legend. When he grows up, Dekanwida goes off to unite the Iroquois with the warrior-tribe the Flint People, part of the Mohawk nation. He has to dazzle the Flint People with miracles channeled from the Great Creator (327) before they will listen to him and accept his claim that he has been sent on a divine mission. He eventually goes to many other tribes and communities, bringing them all together in peace rather than war:

> Now it is to be told that after the United People healed the wounds that they had inflicted upon each other, they came into the fullness of their strength and began to look about them.... The United People had a law that all Nations must accept the Great Peace [336].

Despite the Great Peace, however, it is only a matter of time before the United People disband and start to slaughter one another other again. Dekanwida's life mission seems to be a failure.

Rifles tells of the legend of Sir John Franklin, who, for several years, tried to complete the journey of the North Pole's Northwest Passage on four missions, three of which he commanded. He did not return from the last voyage of 1847. He died an icy death, and he is resurrected, Christ-like, in the body of Captain Subzero. It is the legend of one of history's greatest explorers of the unknown; his desire for conquest and need to succeed become his downfall. Vollmann attempts to separate popular myth about Franklin from the truth, hinting that he may have not been as brave and courageous as often represented; he is unhappy, running away from the reality of his life in England, perhaps inviting death to take him rather than returning home less than the legend he once enjoyed being.

Resurrected, Franklin finds that he is a stranger in a strange land, but he quickly integrates himself into the life of Subzero, participating in a sexual relationship with his Innuit translator and guide, Reepah, a native, a single mother, and an alcoholic with no apparent career or future other than raising a child, drinking, and living day-to-day, hand-to-mouth. In desperation to keep Subzero/Franklin from going back to the United States and his wife, Reepah claims she is pregnant.[7] That turns out to be a lie. She is a burden and a liability for Subzero/Franklin. This is evident when takes her to a party; she wants to go although she does not like crowds when the people are not her kind. She wants to drink and Subzero/Franklin forbids her to, because she loses control of her social graces when alcohol runs through her blood. She receives attention at the party and "everyone loved Reepah because she was a native American and that meant she was ecological" (189). A party is a good place for people to be fascinated with the Other, putting the Other on display. Subzero/Franklin asks people not to give her anything to drink, yet she winds up drinking and knocking things over and becoming obnoxious. "He did not yet acknowledge that the nightmare time was coming" (189) is an understatement. It is a struggle to remove her from the party and get her home, while she screams and yells at people. She is unhappy and feels trapped in her life, hoping for something better to come but knowing it never will.

> On the subway car she tried lunging out of her seat to try to hug someone ... and he had to keep slamming her down.... Everyone looked away. She was ranting about Jesus in broken English and Inuktitut.... She snatched a half-empty bottle of Seven-Up from the trash can and drank it. She picked up a dirty beer can from the sidewalk and licked it ... then she kissed Subzero on the lips.... When he finally got her home she was screeching at him because he wouldn't marry her and he had to give her four blue pills and lie on top of her all night to keep her still [190–91].

He is her rifle. When that weapon was introduced several hundred years before, it was like an intoxicant, and the Inuit got drunk on bullets and violence, following that legacy, Reepah, depressed and alone, commits suicide with a gun.

At the core of *Argall* is the myth and legend surrounding Pocahontas, the young Powhatan princess who has been the subject of many novels, movies, and cartoons. Contrary to Hollywood's narrative, she did not marry John Smith, and she may not have saved him from execution; there is evidence that Smith made this up in his published journals as added spice for his readers, also creating legend around himself as Franklin did. Indeed, the two characters were not lovers, nor had they any desire to be (she would have been eleven or twelve at the time). Pocahontas was kidnapped by Argall, Deputy Governor of Virginia, to blackmail her father, Chief Wahunsunacock, and make him bend to Argall's will. She later married an English businessman, John Rolfe, moved to London, and was integrated into European culture with a new name, as Lady Rebecca Rolfe. The Londonization of Pochahantas is symbolic of Great Britain's conquest of the colonies and subduing the native savages. By possessing and changing the body of the Indian heathen into a woman of British society, the dream of one culture is engulfed by the desires of another; the old world lost in the Stream of Time. She gave birth to a son, Thomas, mixing the genetics of the two races.

In March 1617, Lord and Lady Rolfe were on a ship heading to Virginia. They only made it to Gravesend on the River Thames when the former Pocahontas was struck ill and succumbed. She reportedly said, before passing away, "All must die, but 'tis enough that her child liveth" (Rolfe, 71). She was buried 21 March 1617, in the parish of Saint George's at Gravesend. There, she is memorialized with a life-sized statute.

Argall is problematic for any reader, difficult to comprehend and digest. Vollmann is true to style and syntax of the time, using long, rambling sentences, Elizabethan rhetoric and use of capitalization and punctuation. Reviews were not favorable; the *Los Angeles Times* assigned William the Blind, a hundred years in the future, to write a self-review. Making best use of this genre of self-mockery, Vollmann writes:

> *Argall,* whose story emblematizes a personified and of course feminine Virginia, is no better or worse than any of the other *Seven Dreams.* That is why nobody reads *Argall.* No one looks for *Argall.* No one can find *Argall.* Good riddance, say I.... This book's first sin ... consists in its so-called Elizabethan language, whose archaicisms, variant spellings, and preposterous figures of speech substantially impede the reader in any attempt to envision the ball in any uniform fashion [*Expelled,* 368].

He acknowledges that *Argall,* as a commercial product, is a failure, and possibly not the best idea if he wants the rest of the *Seven Dreams* volumes published.

4

Whores for Gloria (1991); *Butterfly Stories* (1993); *The Royal Family* (2000)

It's enough to make an honest soul vomit ...
— Gustave Flaubert, *Letters*

Prostitution

"I have worshipped them and drunk from their mouths," Vollmann confesses in "The Shame of It All: Some Thoughts on Prostitution in America" (*Expelled from Eden,* 167). He claims to have "studied at their feet" and that "many have saved me; one or two I have raised up" and "they've cost me money and made me money" (*Expelled,* 167). He has written many words about prostitutes and the world they inhabit, perhaps too many. In the November, 2005, installment of the book review and literary website Bookslut.com, he explains:

> I have a lot of love and respect for prostitutes. Of course they're out to get what they can, and take advantages of the johns occasionally. They rob them, they give them disease; well, that's life, that's how people are. And at the same time, they make their customers very happy, they keep marriages together, they console lonely people. I think they're very, very spiritual in what they do.

"No story is anything more than a list," he writes in Volume Five of *Rising,*

> so we might as well begin with one. At the top of the list are the prostitutes who really love you, the ones who marry you for life or even just for a night but always with sincerity; the ones who sing after making love. Next come those

> who love the money, the vacations and the new clothes. They are honest about what they do, at least sometimes. Well-paid, professional though they are, they may become fond of you. If not, they will pretend that they are and have a good laugh later [187].

The three novels discussed in this chapter are devoted to the oldest profession in the world, inspired by his personal experiences in San Francisco's Tenderloin District and travels to Thailand. At the core of each is a love story. While not published as romantic works, they are interconnected in theme, style, and autobiography and form a *de facto* trilogy. The protagonists — all anti-heroes — are on a quest for human connection, a search for what they consider is love in the guise of a prostitute. In *Whores for Gloria*, a Vietnam vet seeks the whereabouts of a streetwalker whom he believes he has known since childhood. In *Butterfly Stories*, a journalist, unhappy with his marriage, falls in love with a young prostitute in Thailand and takes her as a second wife, but leaves her there. Discontented in the United States, he returns to Thailand to find her after she disappears. In *The Royal Family*, a private detective is hired to find the Queen of the Whores. When he locates her, she provides him with everything he requires to soothe the pain and guilt inside his heart. When she leaves him, he sets out on an Arthurian quest to get her back; she is his Holy Grail (or his Cold Mountain; see Chapter Eight). He is lost without her; with her, he is whole and complete.

The men in these novels are misplaced and delusional. They believe their salvation is found in the embrace of the hookers they are enamored with, even if they know such adoration is fleeting, absurd, and futile. What these men seek and need is to live in the moment of that perceived love. Whether the feelings are true or purchased does not matter. These are not romance novels in the traditional sense of the genre or love stories one would expect from mainstream, commercial fiction. These are sordid tales of affection for the apparent outcasts of society, a triptych that constitutes an ironic version of "romance fiction," vindicating the many varieties of love (even if unsavory) that life presents. "Beauty is in the eye of the beholder" is the old saying; the men in these novels find that beauty where others see only the horrendous.

Freedom

"I have had more trouble publishing this book since my writing career began," Vollmann states in his "Note to Publishers," included with the manuscript when submitting it to editors. "*Whores for Gloria* is, in my belief, of the same quality of *Let Us Now Praise Famous Men* and *The Grapes of Wrath*" (*Expelled* 317). It is his shortest book, 138 pages in contrast to his others that, on average, range over 600–800 pages. More novella than novel, it tells the story of Jimmy, a sad and lonely Vietnam veteran who wanders San Francisco's Tenderloin district, desperately searching for a prostitute named Gloria. He believes he has known Gloria since childhood and has a unique spiritual connection with her. It is questionable, however, whether Gloria even exists; she never makes an appearance other than in his head. He talks to her in his imagination. In the second chapter, an undercover police decoy (pretending to be a streetwalker), Loredo, spots Jimmy having an animated conversation on a pay phone: "Gloria? Gloria, what did the doctor say? Are you crying, Gloria? If I can buy you a plane ticket tonight, will you come tonight?"(6). When Jimmy gets off the phone, Loredo realizes this man is most likely crazy because "the pay phone had been broken for weeks"(7).

In a review, John Rechy suggests *Gloria* "might be described as a love story set in a hell" and that Jimmy is "Don Quixote in the Tenderloin [who] journeys through the squalor of his territory in search of his own Dulcinea." Jimmy is an alcoholic, living in an $85-a-week flophouse and spending most of his SSI check on prostitutes. He is not a likeable character. He is pathetic, vulgar, probably insane — readers will have difficultly having empathy for Jimmy. He does not possess the humor of the down-and-out drunks in Charles Bukowski's work. Understanding why Vollmann has chosen to spend time with a pungent central character is like approaching Dostoevsky's *Notes from the Underground*: a dreadful examination of how far human beings, full of hubris, fall as they make their way through mainstream society, rejecting what is deemed normal and acceptable. Rechy compares this book to

> the growing school of literary cruelty that includes Brett Easton Ellis's *American Psycho*, Dennis Cooper's *Frisk*, and Paul Russell's *Boys of Life*. It abounds with scenes of assault and violent sexuality. But Vollmann's novel quickly separates from the cool, fascinated voyeuristic slumming of those other writers because of its compassion for the denizens of the hell he explores, the world of whores, pimps, and derelicts.

Jimmy has sex with a streetwalker named Nicole, whose legs are "speckled with boils and lesions"(15) and covered in abscesses and needle tracks from heroin use. His encounter with her is eloquent and pornographic, but hardly erotic. He wears a condom with Nicole but later visits a free clinic to see if she gave him a sexually transmitted disease. The doctor tells him: "Anyone who'd go to a prostitute ought to have his head examined" (17). This does not seem to matter to Jimmy, although after Nicole he does not have sex with the other prostitutes he meets (as much as he desires to), claiming he is faithful to his true love, Gloria. Instead, he pays them to tell stories from their lives — about a recent john, a painful or sweet memory, a tender regret. He asks this of Melissa:

> Tell me how much you have to spend and Jimmy said I have forty and
> Melissa was happy with that which made Jimmy happy and Melissa said what
> do you want me to do with you and Jimmy said I want you to tell me happy
> stories about when you were a little girl and I'll just kind of sit down and *watch*
> you and *listen* to you and Melissa said OK honey... [24].

Melissa shares some happy memories from an innocent childhood: her first
train ride, a nice Christmas with family, getting a puppy dog. Jimmy enjoys
hearing this. She reminds him of Gloria, although "they're her memories and
not Gloria's"(29), but it does not matter since he "paid for them" (29). Jimmy
crosses paths with colorful Tenderloin characters. There are Dinah and Phyllis: Phyllis is a transsexual who also seems to be searching for love. Jimmy
also meets "a lovely black whore who stood smiling at him and fixing her hair"
(40) that he dubs the Queen of the Tenderloin, who becomes a major character in *The Royal Family* as the Queen of the Whores; thus the novels connect and solidify the trilogy. When he gives her this noble title, "the whore
said big deal that means I'm the Queen of Nothing" (41).

Eli Gottlieb writes in the *Village Voice Literary Supplement*:

> Not much happens in the book, and yet the lack of narrative movement
> never palls. Somebody buys someone else a drink. Somebody, for no particular
> reason, bursts into tears.

Jimmy wakes up each day and his days are the same: he wanders the streets,
gets drunk at the bar, spends his money on prostitutes first for their stories,
later for a lock of their pubic hair so he has something tangible to remind
him these women are real. For Jimmy, "that's all there's left to get: sad stories" (128).

Jimmy disappears from the text and there is no resolution, no real ending to the text. There is rumor that Gloria, or her pimp, murdered him. He
becomes the subject of street folklore:

> Lit him right up, man, right in front of my eyes! And she knew her shit! She
> had some kinda training or somethin' like that. She knew how to kill. She had a
> .38. She didn't miss 'im [138].

He died for love. The protagonist in *Butterfly Stories* is not as tragically heroic,
but disastrously ignorant, and also dies because of his love for a prostitute.

Redemption

Butterfly Stories is about prophylactics and the results of not using them,
"so that is the real moral of this story, and those who don't want anything but
morals need read no further" (43). The story: A lonely but adventuresome
journalist engages in sexual tourism throughout southeast Asia without using

condoms, falls in love with a prostitute named Oy, and gets AIDS. Is the moral really that he should have used a condom? Maybe. And yet, *Butterfly* is about love, or loving the wrong person, and not receiving that love in return, just as *Gloria* is. From the very beginning, as a boy, the protagonist who never has a real name, constantly falls in love/lust, only to be disappointed, hurt, and confused: a pattern that will follow him all through his life and eventually to the grave. He is "a shy child known as 'the butterfly boy' who was not popular in the second grade because he knew how to spell 'bacteria' in the spelling bee, and so the other boys beat him up" (10). He likes girls, so that makes him a playground outcast because "boys are supposed to hate girls in the second grade, but he never did, so the other boys despised him" (10). Simultaneously with this introduction, Vollmann writes about a turbulent, violent Southeast Asia where some slaves escape from their captors and go into Thailand, some meeting death by land mines or snakes. He contends it "did not matter whether the land mines were Russian or Chinese because they rended people with the same sudden clap of smoke-pleated flame" (9). That death foreshadows the Butterfly Boy's future, when he grows up to be the journalist, but for now he is suffering the humiliation of being bullied and beaten on the playground. Since none of the boys like him, his only friends are girls. He has an allure to, and weakness for, the opposite sex: "sometimes he kissed them, and sometimes they kissed him" (12). The Butterfly Boy eventually falls in love with a "big" girl; she hits the bully who is picking on him. The Butterfly Boy loves the big girl and the big girl feels the same, but both are too shy to admit it, until they are forced together by the bullies of the playground, seeking revenge for having been humiliated by the girl. In a moment of what seems like the romantic ending of doomed lovers, it all comes out:

> He kissed her the only way he knew how, as he would have kissed his mother's cheek or his aunt's cheek or the cheek of the nice ladies who came to visit.... He felt something happening to her but he did not understand what it was [22].

This is possibly the only incident where the protagonist will experienced true idealistic romance; the rest of his experiences with women, even his wife, are sordid and gritty, yet he still holds out hope for some kind of traditional love, even with a prostitute.

From the cruel playground to foreign countries, the Butterfly Boy emerges from the cocoon of adolescence as a hopeful journalist, falling in love with various women — "the gentle girl" and "the girl who wanted to be a linguist" and finally a Thai whore who will, inadvertently, kill him. It is an intrepid sensation of a man caught in a downward spiral of repetition: constantly connecting with the wrong people when deep down he knows they are the wrong people to try to connect with. Yet he does it anyway, because of his aspiration for love.

He goes to Thailand and meets a "taxi girl" with a character based on Ken Miller, called "the photographer," who has been to Thailand before. Their motivations are neither political nor journalistic, but self-serving: "Once upon a time a journalist and a photographer set out to whore their way across Asia. They got a New York magazine to pay for it" (43). There is nothing romantic about the encounter with the Thai taxi girl — it is the sordid connection of a man with money and a young girl who has nothing in her impecunious life but to sell her body. She is a virgin, though; she has just entered the sex trade. He is deeply affected that he has paid to ruin an untouched girl, so much that he tells himself: "I certainly deserve to get AIDS" (51). He becomes obsessed with her, though, and is only happy when finally connecting with (and paying her) again. He marries her, then she disconnects from him, not wanting his love, only wishing to be a taxi girl, to return to that life — so she disappears. The journalist goes back to the States, distraught. He discovers he has AIDS, returns to Thailand to find this other wife — who must have AIDS as well — so he can die with her. The thought that "soon he'd be sleeping beside her forever"(277) gives him comfort.

This is a morality play, but Vollmann is not standing on a platform promoting safe sex by telling this story of one man's deadly fate; it is a story (cautionary or not) about cause and effect. *Butterfly* serves as commentary on the changing nature of human sexuality for men such as the journalist and the photographer who wish to wanderlust: it is not the same as it used to be, and the condom speaks a different language, delivers a different message, than it once did. It also about the extremes a lovelorn man will go to find a cure for loneliness; like Jimmy, he dies in his quest. In that regard, Vollmann is working within classic traditions of tragic love stories.

The Royal Family is also a simple story for its 780 pages; like Jimmy and the journalist, the characters are searching for something missing in their lives. This time a private eye is on the case. The book's structure, conforms to the conventions of a traditional genre novel, unlike Vollmann's other volumes. It is broken down into 37 "books" and 593 chapters.[1] The central character is Henry Tyler, a down-and-out San Francisco gumshoe in the tradition of Phillip Marlowe, yet closer to the seedy private eyes found in Carter Brown's trashy 1970s soft porn mysteries (e.g., Rick Holman in *The Pornbroker*). Like many a broken shamus, Tyler is haunted: his sister-in-law, Irene, has committed suicide. He was in love with her; she was pregnant, most likely with his child. Tyler now walks the city with the symbolic Mark of Cain on him, having betrayed his more successful brother, John, a young lawyer. But Tyler is "unlike Cain ... jealousy never drove him to the commission of actual evil"

(23). The relationship between Henry and John "promoted aloofness rather than feuds" (23). John has been neglecting his wife; she is in love with Henry, and now pregnant, her depression is so deep that she kills herself. A wealthy client of John's firm, Mr. Jonas Brady, has heard about an elusive Queen of Whores in the Tenderloin District. He wants to find her and employee her in a new casino/brothel he has opened in Las Vegas, for a stage show called the Feminine Circus. Henry is hired to track her down, a job he welcomes to keep his mind off Irene's suicide.

The idea of the Queen of Whores goes back to when Vollmann was researching *Gloria*. He had written a play and hired streetwalkers to act out what they thought the Queen of Whores might be like. At the website Beatrice.com, Vollmann says in an interview:

> It was really interesting because almost invariably, I really brought them alive. I thought they would just think it was stupid, but they found it really exciting to imagine themselves in charge and I started realizing that there were several different kinds of imaginary Queens. There were some that just wanted it to mean that they were extremely sexy, erotic prostitutes, then there were some who would have liked to use their imaginary power to help the others, such as the good queen in my story. And there were others who just would have loved to be able to dominate others with that power.

The project came out of a profile the BBC was producing about William T. Vollmann, maverick American writer. In another online interview with the Commonwealth Club of California (that awarded *Royal* the Silver Medal for its California Book Awards), he recalls:

> The BBC guy was hiding in the closet with the microphone. He didn't feel like being out there. He would just hand out his twenties and we'd go out and bring out enforcers and prospective queens and listen to what they all had to say. The prostitutes were all very much taken with the idea. I was sort of surprised. I was originally just thinking of something to fill in time....

Royal opens with Henry and Brady in a room with Domino, who charges "the same for spectators as for participants" (3), and denies knowing who the Queen is although she is actually one of her loyal royal subjects. The novel ends with John standing before the Queen on a stage. Domino tells him: "You have been summoned" (773). In between is an epic adventure where Tyler travels through the Tenderloin, Las Vegas and the Imperial Valley, crossing paths with a variety characters: prostitutes Beatrice, Strawberry and Sunflower (loyal subjects of the Queen); Dan Smooth (a pedophile rapist); and the mysterious residents of a desert hideaway called Slab City (which partially inspired *Riding Toward Everywhere*, see Chapter Eight).

The Queen of Whores is also known as "Maj," the munificent ruler of a gang of prostitutes. She protects them, offering them crash pads, drugs, and her alluring, heroin-injected speeches. Some of her subjects adore her, some resent her, but they all have respect. When Tyler finally finds her, she sees his pain and provides him with rituals of degradation intended to purge his grief for Irene; when this doesn't quite work to cure him, she becomes his lover and even offers to give him a replacement for Irene, "the false Irene." A world where a queen rules over all the whores of San Francisco reads like an alternate universe, similar to the hyper-real world in the movie *Sin City*, where such a queen and her loyal subjects live in their own section of town. While *Royal* is a conventionally structured novel, there are sidebars, such as "An Essay on Bail" and "Geary Street," nods to the form of *Moby-Dick* and the works of Jonathan Swift which make use of similar textual asides. Vollmann asserts himself (as his actual self, not one of his alter-egos) with various editorial comments throughout the book, a device he compares to John Dos Passos's camera eye (*Expelled*, 323). "An Essay on Bail," for instance, reads as straightforward journalism as Vollmann interviews bail bondsmen about how their business works. He examines the judicial system of San Francisco, finding that "the more charges stuck, the more weighed down becomes the defendant by crushing bail" (232) and the more money a bond agent will make on the 10 percent. As he goes about his investigation, he muses on how his findings may affect his fictional characters: "Unlike birth, bail may occur at practically any phase of gestation within the lion's barred womb — or, as Strawberry knows, it may never happen at all" (234).

"Geary Street" is a meditative prose poem, noting "of all the multitudinous arteries of San Francisco, Geary Street is perhaps the most important of the overlooked" (569). Vollmann has described *Royal* as his "love letter to San Francisco." His descriptive passages are finely, affectionately detailed:

> After Little Russia comes Little Korea with its Hangul newspapers, its excitable, clannish grocerywomen, and above all its temples of grilled meat where for a price one can offer up to heaven the greasy incense of barbeque-smoke, faithfully attended by many small round dishes of pickles. Do I write too much about food? Geary Street knows that everybody has to eat, just as sooner or later everybody needs an undertaker's services, and, as I recall, there's a funeral parlor right here [571].

Vollmann had wanted to write more about other San Francisco streets. In the Commonwealth Club of California interview, he says, "Originally I wanted to make the book much longer and have a prose poem about every district ... the book would have become really unmanageable.... I didn't want to wear out my readers."

Henry's detective work and experiences are wrought with religious overtones supplied by epithets and references to Gnostic scripture and Canaanite mythology. God set the Mark of Cain upon the brow of Abel's murderer so he would be avoided by all decent and righteous people. Henry comes to view prostitutes — and eventually himself— as members of Cain's tribe: the outcast, the untouchables, haunted by the pain of their past. Similar to the prostitutes in *Gloria*, each subject has her own hard-luck story about how and why she got into the business. Henry hears these narratives the same way Jimmy gets autobiographies.

> The tale of Beatrice, of sweetnatured Beatrice who very rapidly chewed gum with her black black teeth as she swayed herself down the curbside of life, illustrates above all else that whenever Queen Destiny marches in her lethally imperial purple, free will must fall down naked and trembling in every groveling ritual of hopelessly humiliating abasement suffered not merely by the bitter-comprehending brain alone, not only by the heart which would be proud, but even by the entrails, for free will, stripped bare, must squat down exposing its haunches, to be kissed, whipped or raped as sparkling Queen Destiny may please [175–76].

Henry takes in one horrible story after another, but none is as bad as those from Dan Smooth, a Sacramento low-life, police informer and child-molester. The descriptions he relays, about sexually assaulting his niece, are graphic and unsettling. Steven Moore, reviewing in *Rain Taxi*, critiques:

> I was reminded of Samuel R. Delany's transgressive novel *The Mad Man* and even of Sade's monstrous works.... Whoring is only one of the activities depicted here that will discomfort the reader.... A lively character named Dan Smooth, an enthusiastic pedophile, regales Henry (and the reader) with a number of stories. At one point Henry interrupts Smooth to say, "Your filth gets pretty boring after a while" ... and I almost gave up at that point in hearty agreement.[2]

Henry needs Smooth, who initially helps him find the Queen, and goes with him to find her again when she disappears. For his love, Henry gives up his profession and becomes a hobo, riding the train routes in boxcars and heading down to California's Imperial Valley.[3] He simply disappears, the way Jimmy vanishes and the Butterfly Boy dies, all because of an involvement with, and love for, a prostitute.

Vollmann concludes in "The Shame of It All":

> ...I said that the conventional understanding of a prostitute's client envisages a man who rents a woman's body as if it were a machine. Never mind the many men I've met who weep when the street-whores they love go to jail. Never mind the case of the man who would run to buy a hamburger and fries for his favorite bar-girl whenever he saw her drunk; he'd help her eat; he'd spoon-feed her black coffee right there at the bar; he'd drive her to her mother's house.... Never mind all that, because it's perfectly true that some men do rent prostitutes as if they were machines [*Expelled* 183–84].

They are "machines" that certain men come to love. The core of this *de facto* trilogy, this triptych, is the pursuit, and need, for that love: Jimmy haunts the Tenderloin, the journalist travels half way around the world, and Henry Tyler wanders across Southern California. "I'm wondering whether if someday I ought to prove my love," Vollmann continues, knowing "De Sade proved his in prison" but "for now, the answer is to keep writing what happens" (*Expelled*, 308). Vollmann does keep on writing about prostitutes and lovesick people; these are obsessive themes that he comes back to and re-explores in subsequent work. While this may seem repetitive, Vollmann — like a private eye for eros — always finds new aspects of love and loneliness to investigate.

5

Rising Up and Rising Down (2003)

But why have I told of all these scenes of pain and distress, and perhaps
aroused painful emotions in my readers?
— Henry Dunant, *A Memory of Solferino*

Publication and Reception

What started out as a monograph grew exponentially during the two and half decades Vollmann traveled the world independently and as a foreign correspondent. With his continued experiences and observations, he added more pages to the essay, creating a work of philosophy, history, and memoir. It also works as ethnography in its observations of foreign cultures; it is investigative journalism for its reportage of gangs, crime, war, and human rights violations. The volumes are divided by two themes: first is theory, with examples of "moral actors" and their place in the history of violence, from Alexander the Great to John Brown, Buddha, Jesus Christ and Gandhi, to Adolf Hitler and Ho Chi Minh, David Koresh, Louis XIV, and Pancho Villa; the second is empirical, comprising Vollmann's meditations on his lived experiences, labeled "Studies in Consequences." He states *Rising Up* is "a just act of violence" where "both means and ends are legitimate" whereas *rising down* is "an unjust act of violence" and a "means, ends or both [that] fail to meet legitimacy's standard" (48–49).[1]

The publication of this massive work proved to be a difficult, but admirable, task for the small publishing operation McSweeney's Books. On their website, Timothy McSweeney's Internet Tendency, is a page called "An Oral History of *Rising Up and Rising Down*" that contains testaments and reflections by the people who worked on the book, from Vollmann's literary agent to the interns and production staff. Publisher Dave Eggers writes:

> I saw an excerpt ... and I tried to find out when it would be published as a whole. I wrote to Vollmann, offering to publish any other excerpts from it, and that led eventually to his giving us "The Old Man," which we published in our seventh issue.... A while later, I saw him read one night at Black Oak Books in Berkeley, and during the Q&A he mentioned that *RURD's*, publisher had backed out, and the book was orphaned. So I went home, did some rudimentary math, and wrote him a letter to the effect that McSweeney's might be able to figure out a way to get the book out.

Critical reaction ranged from admiration to outrage; reviewers questioned why a writer would devote the time, and so many precious pages, to such an unwieldy undertaking. In the *Boston Globe*, John Freeman writes, "No other American writer alive today is as crazy and as productive and as willing to risk his life. " Steven Moore, in the *Washington Post Book World*, claims the work is

> a monumental achievement on several levels: as a hair-rising survey of mankind's propensity for violence, as a one-man attempt to construct a system of ethics, as a successful exercise in objective analysis (almost non-existent in today's partisan, ideological, politicized, spin-doctored, theory-muddled public discourse), and a demonstration of the importance of empathy ... beyond the realm of mere mortals.

Scott McLemee, in the *New York Times*, chastises Vollmann for "passages ... swept away by the flood of logorrhea. He is fond of the overwrought and the overwritten. Truisms bloviate into the purplest of profundities ... with so much polish that they form little globules of self-parody." Likewise, a reviewer on Amazon.com, Jane Graham-Roberts, accuses Vollmann of having "forgotten that the primary purpose of writing a book is communication.... I submit that Mr. Vollmann wrote this book, not to inform his readers, but to vanquish his own demons."

The Volumes

Vollmann's inquiry is: "When is violence justified?" He then searches for the answer. The first volume is called "MC" for Moral Calculus and is the shortest of all: 282 pages, containing seventeen pages of annotated table of contents for all seven volumes, twenty photographs (combined, all volumes have more than 300 pictures of people and places), an index of "moral actors" that he offers up for study in Volumes II, II and IV, annexes lettered A-H, a 43-page bibliography of primary and secondary sources, four pages of acknowledgments, and 212 endnotes. Vollmann considers it "a resource ... to be referred to whenever useful" (iii). At the center of the volume is "The Moral Calculus" (33–133), a philosophical treatise where Vollmann argues, ponders, and contextualizes acts of violence past, present, and hypothetical — attempting to find the proper answers to when violence is wrong or right, necessary or evil, justified or criminal. He is influenced by Benjamin Franklin's *Moral or Prudential Algebra*, where "Franklin used to divide a sheet of paper into two columns, one in favor of a decision, the other against" (41).[2]

"Should you find fault with this calculus as you ought to," Vollmann advises,

> I respectfully ask you do not leave a vacuum, but to construct your own. The translator of two old collections of Zen koans has noted that there is no 'correct' answer to a koan, and, indeed, one student's right answer may be wrong if uttered by another [41].

The fallibility of "The Moral Calculus" is that it will not ring true with every reader, depending on the reader's personal experience and philosophy. Religion and society are major points of criteria, too — for instance, while Western culture may find suicide bombings an atrocity, the non–Western suicide bomber believes he is on a mission of the highest order: blessed, doing a holy act that his faith and culture will view as heroic. Likewise, a religious zealot who bombs an abortion clinic and kills doctors may be prosecuted and incarcerated for the crime, but this person's moral compass makes the crime justified. "The Moral Calculus" considers opposing views of rightful violence, but does not side with one or the other. Vollmann does offer insight into his personal ethics; he states that suicide "to be justified ... must be an act of assertion" (237) and "offers the only way to freedom" (241). *Freedom!* Vollmann advises, "Follow your own inner logic in order to postulate laws of conduct which seem good to you" and "choose the right regardless of local authority or custom, and then act accordingly" (44). He brings up the Golden Rule — "do as you would be done by"— with the caveat: "The Golden Rule is justified only when applied to acts which all parties affected agree will contribute to their conception of goodness, or when the dissenting party is a bona fide dependent of the moral actor" (45). Setting up his scale of the just and unjust, he categorizes acts of violence committed in the name of defense, policy, choice and fate, with the subcategories of honor, class, race, culture, creed, war aims, homeland, earth, animals, and even sadism.

Vollmann walks through the catacombs below Paris, where the

> walls of earth and stone encompassed walls of mortality a femur's-length thick: long yellow and brown bones all stacked in parallels, their sockets pointing outward like melted bricks whose ends dragged down, like downturned bony smiles, like stale yellow snails of macaroni — joints of bones, heads of bones, promiscuously touching, darkness in the center of each, between those

twin knucklespurs which had once helped another bone to pivot, thereby guiding and supporting flesh in its passionate and sometimes intelligent motion toward the death it inevitably found — femurs in rows, then, and humerii, bones upon bones, and every few rows there'd be a shelf of bone to shore death up, a line of humerii and femurs laid down laterally to achieve an almost pleasing masonry effect, indeed, done by masonry's maxims, as interpreted by Napoleon's engineers and brickmen of death, who at the nouveau-royal command had elaborated and organized death's jetsam according to a sanitary aesthetic [9].

Next, he is in Northern California, interviewing Dr. Boyd Stephens, then Chief Medical Examiner of the city of San Francisco. It is 1995 and eight thousand people died in San Francisco County that year, many by natural means, some by homicide and manslaughter; the others are suspicious and questionable. Vollmann sits in and observes a number of autopsies. "Determining the cause of death is the prerequisite for some kind of justice, although justice, like other sonorous concepts, can produce anything from healing to acceptance to compensation to revenge to hypocritical clichés" (14). As he watches one cold, clinical autopsy after another, he engages Dr. Stephens in the thesis of *Rising*. "I would say that about twenty-five percent of the suicides we have here are justified by real physical illness," the doctor states. Vollmann recalls a woman he once loved who died of cancer and the first time bullets were shot at him: "I pledged to be happier, to be grateful for my life" (23). He expounds on a constant need to justify why he has written this work. Perhaps the Amazon.com reviewer is right: he is not out to educate or inform, he is exorcising his inner torment and exploring the tarnished landscape of his broken soul.

At the beginning of Volume II, Vollmann suggests, "Please imagine yourself in the judge's seat" (7). His aim is for the reader to make his/her own final assessment whether certain life performances of the moral actors are right or wrong. The first justification is *honor*; examples given are Joan of Arc and Sun-tzu, who composed *The Art of War*. Vollmann posits that "honor in our context will therefore be defined as the extent to which the self approaches its own particular standard of replying to or initiating violence" (15). He states there are four types of honor: outer, inner, individual, and collective. In the case of Joan of Arc, her call to violence is for the honor of France's throne. Sun–tzu executes a concubine for embarrassing him, thus defending his personal honor, both outer and inner (taking into account the cultural expectations of the society he lived in). Next is *class*; examples are Lenin justifying violence against landlords and rich peasants, and Stalin against all peasants. For the defense of *authority*, he offers up Abraham Lincoln, Thomas Jefferson, and even Adolf Hitler, ordering acts of violence because they have the power, the authority, to do so. For defense of *race and culture*, there are John

Brown, Martin Luther King, Jr., and Booker T. Washington. "Slavery is a state of war," Vollmann observes and quotes Brown's philosophy that "the slave has a right to anything he needs for freedom" (436). For defense of *creed*, he brings up Montezuma, Cortes, and Jesus Christ (Christ allowing violence to happen against his body as a symbol for a religious movement).

The reader will find more profound chapters in Volumes Five and Six, the "Studies in Consequence," collecting his observations and experiences as a foreign correspondent. His findings are more empirical than theoretical. These last two volumes read like extensions of *The Atlas*. The sections are broken down by continent — Southeast Asia, Europe, Africa, North and South America — and culture, such as "the Muslim World," that groups several nations into the category. He goes anywhere he can, wherever the magazines and newspapers are willing to send him; as long as these publications foot the bill and pay him a fee, he is ready to pack up and go. He journeys to Yemen, Iraq, Canada, Columbia, Thailand, Burma, Japan, Madagascar, the Congo, Somalia, Malaysia, Cambodia, ex–Yugoslavia, Jamaica, the United States, and finally, his necessary return to Afghanistan, coming full circle.

Each case study is "accompanied by introductions only, not conclusions" (13). In the introduction of southeast Asia, Vollmann writes, "Prostitutes clasp their hands and bow to Buddha when they get a nice customer.... People tend to submit to their destiny" (17) because the culture and religion requires such compliance. "The Skulls on the Shelves" is a 93-page account of two trips taken to Cambodia, in 1991 and 1996; he interviews members of the Khmer Rouge, including Pol Pot's brother. Such places in the world are not safe for members of the press:

> The Japanese journalists ... threw their money around and generally managed to cross the minefields by one secret way or another until they got to Battambang. The Khmer Rouge finished a number of them off there. The police general had told me one story of a Japanese with a video camera worth one million bhat. The Khmer Rouge shot him in the face and sold the camera for a hundred thousand, which means that the only one who got any kind of story out of it was me [135].

Regarding the Khmer Rouge's rule of Cambodia, the Western world views Pol Pot as a genocidal tyrant; to his followers, he is a righteous savior.

The next two chapters, "The Last Generation" and "Kickin' It," examine Cambodian immigrants who have migrated to America. In Long Beach, California, the young Cambodians form gangs and wage small wars with the Crips and various Latino groups in Los Angeles County. Just as the skinheads had turned against him when he was writing "The White Knights," Vollmann is aware that with these gang members, the wrong look, the wrong attitude, and the wrong color of clothes could easily get him killed. Most of them admit they just "hang out" or are "kickin' it" (161), yet have more fear of the police than other gangs. When he asks a fellow known as "Cruel" about justified violence, Cruel tells him violence is expected "when we see a Mexican, 'cause no other choice.... They just beat us down. Any Mexican, we beat them down" (163). He hears about older gang members coercing schoolboys into committing crimes by threat — "I will kill your family and eat 'em" (166). Vollmann wonders:

> Should I have watched a gangbanger kill somebody's family and eat them? I didn't feel like it.... Sometimes the feature editors who pay my way tell me I ought to "push the envelope." If I had hung around the right people I could have seen some kid's dead body [166].

In the chapter "I'm Especially Interested in *Young* Girls" from 1993, Vollmann and Ken Miller pay for an underage prostitute, Sakanja, in Thailand, and reportedly set her free. *Spin* published a photo essay about this particular excursion that was met with controversy and condemnation for the magazine, questioning the ethics of the editors and publisher, as well as the writer and photographer. Some critics have wondered if it was all made up — after all, Vollmann *is* an author of fiction. If true, was their deed borderline illegal and immoral, or were they gallant heroes out to save the helpless? Or was it all just to have a fascinating story to publish and be paid for, something that will add (and has) to both men's already established notoriety?

Who was this female they allegedly rescued from the horror of child prostitution and sexual slavery? Vollmann describes Sakanja as a girl who

> sat on the chair in dirty pajamas and answered that she was fifteen. During the weeks that we knew her we had her age variously as sixteen, fifteen and fourteen. After a while we gave up asking. She looked twelve. She looked so scared that I wondered how she would ever trust us. The answer, of course, was that she never would [216].

Given his previous written accounts of prostitutes, the cautious reader might question his moral compass about doing this, and where it fits in The Moral Calculus. He and Miller pay her handler (pimp) to spend time with her, then smuggle her away to a social organization in Burma, called the Women's Education Center, whose mission is to assist young girls out of the sex trade and educate them, so they can find better ways to make a living.

Sakanja's father sold her to the pimp. Vollmann goes to see this father with the local authorities in tow.

> The father was skinny and middle-aged.... He twitched his mouth a little, squatting on a mat, answering questions in a rapid and surprisingly deep voice. I had expected him to be meeker in the presence of police and soldiers, who

now demanded his identification to see if he might be receiving support from Taiwan, in which case the sale of Sukanja would look worse [231].

Why did he sell her? Because she did not make enough money, for him, at the restaurant she used to work at; he states his son-in-law got her into prostitution, it was not his doing. He believes he is innocent of any crime. The father is not angry with the son-in-law for doing this because "prostitution no problem" and "any job that get money is no problem" (232). This story reveals the differences of morality and sex in other cultures, which is Vollmann's aim — not that he agrees with it, but he understands that in a culture where sons are a man's pride and daughters a burden and to be used, this father sincerely believes that Sukanja's familial duty is to be a source of revenue, no matter what she does — washing dishes or performing sex — as long as money comes in. Vollmann decides that any violence against the father would be justified for having put his child into the hands of a pimp who would quickly murder her if she refused sex, contracted AIDS, or tried to run away. In this case, the rescue also puts her in danger.

Next, Vollmann jumps to 1998, and he's in Japan, interviewing members of the Yakuza — another tricky, dangerous assignment that requires a lot of fast-talking and the spreading around of cold hard cash (his interpreter also happens to have translated Thomas Pynchon's novels into Japanese). The Yakuza is another Asian gang, but with much more history and strength in numbers than the youth gangs in Long Beach and Stockton — and certainly more stylish in suits. Each Yakuza member has a "Confucianist loyalty" to their bosses (313). The bosses are known as "parents" and the underlings "children" or sons (313). Like old school Mafia mobsters, the Yakuza offers "protection" to local businesses in exchange for weekly payments, but does not traditionally deal in counterfeit money, drugs, and prostitution. Interviewing a 56-year-old fellow who has been in the Yakuza for decades and killed several men, Vollmann asks him if he had his life to live over, would he still be Yakuza? The man replies, "No ... I'd be a schoolteacher" (322).

The Yakuza's justification for violence is defense of honor, class, and creed. "Although feared by society and hated by the police," Mr. Suzuki says, "we have our pride" (323). The would-be teacher will never leave the organization because "it's more easy for me to be here" (322). Vollmann understands that these men, in order to survive, have no other choice but to be Yakuza; after the choice is made and the life lived, there is no way out, just as it appears there is no way out for the members of various ethnic groups (Muslim, gypsy, Albanian, Serb, Croatian) in the former Yugoslavia.

"Yugoslavia was never a country," he writes in the introduction to the case study of Europe, "as much as one of many experiments in confederation"

(327). This section covers his travels from 1992 through 1998, across Bosnia-Herzegovina, Croatia, Kosovo, Sarajevo, and Montenegro. The defenses for violence are homeland, race, and culture. He meets one desperate, trapped person after the other, whether civilian or solider, freedom fighter or terrorist. A Serbian woman offers to let him see her naked for 15,000 *dinars* (372). In a cellar, hiding from bombs, Serbian soldiers take Vollmann's bulletproof vest and test out the Kevlar, trying to shoot holes in it.

He tells the narrative of Vineta, "fiercely frightening, beautiful, racist, loyal, proud, honest and filled with hate, [she] is my friend" (403). She belongs to the Serbian Radical Party (SRS), a somewhat extreme political group. Vollmann hints at a sexual relationship: she tells him to stay in his hotel and not go out one night because it is too dangerous, but if he insists on going outside, she wants him to give her money (405). She seems to be another "guide" like Reepah in *Rifles*. Understanding Vollmann's work, the reader must consider his bold, if not foolish honesty — that he pays money to his female guides *for more* than advice, guidance, and translation. This fact probably draws more readers to his work — and where is his moral compass there? Perhaps it is just how things work in certain parts of the world — just as it is common for ethnographers to go from observer to participant, becoming sexually intimate with study subjects, journalists become involved with, and in Vollmann's case often pay, their informants and assistants for extra interaction. Neophyte journalists quickly become aware that in war zones, with death and adrenaline in the air, the need for connection, and sex, is heightened. War sparks off hormones and a basic human drive to procreate; in war zones (and disasters) people who would not necessarily be attracted to one another in civilized society will reach out for mutual comfort and intimacy — at any given moment they could be killed; they have no idea what events will occur tomorrow, so they seek the moment, possibly the last time they will be close to a fellow human being.

Vollmann does not play by safe rules when in the field; this is what makes him an exciting journalist to read. He notes that his editors ask him to go to extremes, because they know subscribers will not be interested in prudent and mundane articles. There is, however, the risk of tragedy with this side of the literary life — in his quest for adventure, truth, and the next feature, people sometimes get hurt and die. It is in this section that he goes into detail about the deaths of his friends Francis Tomasic and Will Brinton, as he did briefly in *Atlas* as well and "Three Meditations on Death." He writes in heartbreaking detail about not playing it safe — they were advised not to drive off the main roads because there are land mines scattered about, but they did so anyway, and they drove over a land mine. The jeep is turned over, the driver is dead and his friend is nearly dead. Vollmann watches his friend die — a true journalist to the end, he takes a photograph of this scene, which is included in the volume. His leg is injured; shrapnel is embedded in his flesh. He knows that had he been sitting elsewhere in the jeep, and had he not been wearing his flak jacket, he too would be dead. He is trapped there for hours; he is hiding behind the jeep because soldiers in the hills are taking shots at him. He is trapped with the dead bodies of his companions, watching the flies swarm around, smelling the scent of decay. Spanish soldiers in the U.N. peacekeeping forces happen by; they are amazed that he is alive, flabbergasted that he takes photos of his dead friends. They transport him to the medical unit. The Associated Press and Reuters run the story of the maverick American author who escaped death. Sales of his books increase for a short while. His colleagues and family worry about him — will he suffer survivor's guilt, post-traumatic stress disorder? Will he never take another assignment again? (In *Riding Toward Everywhere*, his father pleads with him to stop taking such risks, to just stay home and "cool it" [5].) No; when he heals and is able to, Vollmann is back on the job....

"It's said that the human race was born in Africa," he writes in the next case study. "The complexity of Balkan tribalism stretches back beyond 1389; but the kingdoms, customs and tribes which have come and gone in Africa extend beyond comprehension" (503). He discovers two different Congos: the eastern part that has been ravished by the civil war in Rwanda, spreading to other nations, and the western section, "the other Congo ... [where] people may be less hungry, but they remain no less ready to plead or threaten" (504). On the island of Madagascar, he hears of a woman "who stabbed a pregnant lady in the belly so that she could sell the victim's clothing" (505). In the prisons, inmates will starve to death if their relatives do not bring food. In Madagascar, he explains,

> a beggar will approach you and calmly express his expectation of receiving, not everything, just something, an amount varying between reasonable and unreasonable; if you give it to him, he will be satisfied; if you refuse, he will become, as they constantly say there, "jealous," and he will stab you if he can [505].

Vollmann first learns of this cultural jealousy in a disco, when a bar girl he calls O. asks him to buy her a drink. He then has to buy drinks for all the females there, or else they will become jealous and violent with one another, and maybe towards him too. "Of course jealousy and dishonesty are essentials for the human apparatus," he concludes, "but the Malagasy seem to be more matter-of-fact about them than we are" (523). He learns about various tribes outside the major cities, like the Bara clan, where a "man of the Bara race is not a man until he steals a zebu."[3] If he does not perform such a socially expected crime, "no woman will marry him" (527). A zebu thief will not fight if he is pursued after the theft, and is expected to kill the zebu owner "only if the owner ... discovers them in the act of theft" (527). Vollmann's companion O., now sharing his bed at the Hotel Glacier, gives him further examples of the zebu's importance in Malagasy culture:

> If you marry me, must pay my Papa one zebu. If you fuck another girl, me no understand, no problem. If me understand you fuck another girl, then you must buy me one zebu, then no problem. You no buy me zebu, me never stay with you. Zebu is for eat. Zebu is for money. Zebu is for dead [529].

In the sixth and final volume, Vollmann wants to know why certain sects of Muslim culture want every Western man and woman either converted to Islam or killed. "I feel as strongly about what happened on September eleventh as do most of my fellow citizens," he admits, and "that the acts of murder committed on September eleven were unjustifiable, evil, wrong" whereas "the great majority of people I met in Yemen a year later considered them justifiable" (8). This is the first indication of Vollmann expressing a clear political, dogmatic, and patriotic point of view. He witnesses, in Mogadishu, Somali men pay small children to throw rocks at the U.S. Marines because they know the soldiers will not shoot children. And if the children get hurt?— the end justifies the means, in defense of the land. In Malaysia, Vollmann interviews Hadji Amin Tohmeena, aka "the Old Man," leader of the Pattani Unification Liberation Organization (PULO) which had committed "terrorist" attacks, but any deaths resulting were justified in the defense of creed. When a bomb is set off in the town of Hat Yai and seven innocent bystanders die, Hadji Amin claims his group is not out to murder anyone but "placed the bomb to make the police afraid, just to make trouble in general" (67). His goal is to create an idealistic and pure Islamic state in Malaysia, free from outside influence.

Vollmann goes to Iraq for Hussein's birthday and finds statues of the dictator on every street, in public squares, and portraits of his smiling face on the walls of most business establishments. In Baghdad, Hussein "had been idealized onto a concrete slab, and an Iraqi flag flew over his head" (82)— and of course, five years later, in a televised display for the world, an American soldier would replace that flag with Old Glory; Iraqi citizens would tear down the statue and smash it to pieces. "By the end of my first day in Iraq," he reports, "the portraits of Saddam had already made my eyes begin to glaze" (83). He finds Iraqis who truly admire Hussein and do not live in fear of his rule; they are not obliged and coerced into worshipping him and celebrating his birthday. "I had expected a Serbian welcome in Iraq," he reports,

> but from the very first they greeted me warmly when they learned that I was from America. Oh, I haven't completely forgotten the solider who playfully

pressed his machine gun to my heart and pulled the trigger, the tea-shop proprietor who, after I photographed his little child with his permission, suddenly began shouting that I was a Jew spying for the Israeli intelligence service Mossad, the butcher who shook his bloody knife at me when I asked to take his portrait [95].

The concluding bulk of Volume Six brings Vollmann to North and South America with his case studies of guns, gun culture, and gun cults. He interviews the Guardian Angels, muses on their methods and philosophy, as well as rock star Ted Nugent's radical views of weapons and hunting. He heads down south to Colombia, where "a gun is primarily a tool of terror, deterrence, retribution, revenge" (213). These final segments of Volume Six are stylistically different from the other sections, similar to *An Afghanistan Picture Show*, with shorter sub-chapters and "statements" by various interview subjects." North Americans are the quintessential lonely atoms," he claims (213), and what lonelier atoms could there be than the two teenage boys who went on a shooting spree in Denver, Colorado, at Columbine High School, a mass murder that traumatized the nation, created a cultural crisis and media frenzy ("the vultures" is his term [338]), and resulted in a handful of copycat campus shootings? "There are some stories that should be written only for money," Vollmann contends, admitting "this is one of them" (337). On that day of April 20, 1999, a newspaper editor calls him to fly out and cover the incident. Too many special interests, he finds on arrival, are using this tragedy to promote agendas, philosophies, religion. He is overwhelmed by the great amount of sadness, grief, and anger. He can find no justification in the violence that happened in Denver; it has no place in The Moral Calculus. He comes to understand that human beings, at the core of their nature, are violent animals that will always kill one another. Nothing will change that — certainly not his words. Vollmann cannot save the world like he had once hoped when he went to Afghanistan in the 1980s.

Abridged Edition

There is more to *Rising*, so much more; an entire monograph could be written about these seven volumes. Since only 3,500 copies were printed, most readers will have to visit a library, where *Rising* is usually kept in the reference section of social sciences. An abridged trade edition was issued by Ecco in 2004; at 733 pages, much of the original has been left out, especially appendices, end notes, bibliographies, and the bulk of the photographs. "The abridgement ... has only one justification," he writes in the preface: "I did it for the money.... I can't pretend that a one-volume reduction is any improvement (over) the full.... It's not necessarily worse.... The possibility now exists that someone might read it" (xi). The most important segments are intact: "Three Meditations on Death," "The Definition of Lonely Atoms," "The Moral Calculus," and all the theories of justifications for violence. The sections discussed in this chapter are found in this edition, although it is advisable that the serious Vollmann reader try to seek out the McSweeney's version.

Copernicus

Nicolaus Copernicus died around the same time that his treatise, *Revolutions*, was published in 1543; his death probably saved him from suffering the Inquisition and the fate of Galileo, who, decades later, was forced to renounce his theories or face execution for the crime of heresy.

How did Vollmann come to write this small volume about Copernican theories? The Atlas Books series, Great Discoveries, pairs today's high-profile literary authors with biographies of historical figures and their grand discoveries in science, mathematics, and biology. David Foster Wallace wrote about the concept of Infinity; Madison Smartt Bell about Lavoisier and new scientific theories before the French Revolution; and David Leavitt about Alan Turning and the evolution of the computer and artificial intelligence. It is fitting that Vollmann would be chosen for the planet earth proven as nothing more than a mere lonely spec of dust in the vast spinning universe, rather than the center of everything. Copernicus is an example of a man true to his convictions, who strove for truth based on reality and logic and fought for the freedom of his thoughts.

Uncentering the Earth is Vollmann's attempt to make Copernicus's life and work accessible to the general reader. Copernicus, taking into account astronomical theories posited by Aristotle and Ptolemy, watched the heavens and deduced that the sun and the stars — and the other plants, heavenly bodies all — did not revolve around the planet earth, and earth was not the center of the Universe. Vollmann does not have much to work with because little biographical information on Copernicus is available for scholars. "What moves me most about [Copernicus]," Vollmann states, "is the struggle [he] represents to free the human mind from a false system"(61). This book represents Vollmann's continued interest in history, personal growth, and the repercussions — the justifications — of engaging in dangerous viewpoints that bring about milestones of change.

Uncentering is also Vollmann's weakest book; it reads as hastily written; the style is awkward and occasionally incoherent. Its brevity is a stark contrast to *Rising*'s abundance. The book was generally ignored; reviews were few and not favorable, noting it as little more than an oddity in Vollmann's oeuvre. What the study does show is Vollmann's continued interest in the idea of *freedom*— Copernicus, like Galileo, sought the freedom to explore his scientific ideas that went against the doctrine of the Church. The freedom of thought and research is at the core of Vollmann's quick look into the life of the man who changed the way we gazed at the heavens.

6

An Afghanistan Picture Show (1993); *The Atlas* (1996)

> *One of the ways I can mark my own corner is by going off to someplace where a lot of other writers wouldn't dare to go.*
> — Vollmann[1]

These two books can be categorized as travelogues and memoir, although *The Atlas* contains a few pieces of fiction and prose poems. *An Afghanistan Picture Show* is an account of Vollmann starting out as world explorer, on a quest to understand the Other and, from its telling subtitle, "save the world." *Atlas,* like *Rising,* is the product of foreign correspondence; following in Hemingway's footsteps, Vollmann is paid to go to other countries and report on war and civil conflict. In the process, he also obtains material for books. "Some years ago, I sold my soul to the magazines," he writes in Volume Five of *Rising*:

> The price I got was excellent: money enough to buy whatever I wanted ... adventure in exotic countries, and more liberty of expression and behavior than my friends get accorded. In exchange I laid down my illusions about painting The Big Picture, not to mention "making a difference" [551].

Picture Show is a portrait of the author as "The Young Man"—literally; this is the name Vollmann gives himself. It is written partially in the third person, a method of examining the naiveté of an estranged and younger self. It is a coming-of-age narrative, a memoir of folly. The Young Man is straight out of college, idealistic, dreaming of the Quest, seeking extreme experiences he believes all hopeful scribes must endure to produce great literature (the Hemingway effect). He realizes the shortcomings of his academic existence and wants to rectify this. He gets a firsthand glimpse of war when he joins the Mujahadeen in their effort to end the Russian occupation of Afghanistan. He comes to understand the true nature of foreign policy and how things are not what they always seem to be. He goes from naïve to jaded in the months he is there, yet remains hopeful that one man can indeed change the world. He goes back home thirty pounds lighter and with a slightly broken heart. Needless to say, his escapade is not the adventure he dreamed of when he was that child who read many books and fantasized about astonishing and wondrous lands:

> I wanted to go to Antarctica. In New England there was the snow and the woods, but it was gloomy among the trees and when I went sledding with Julie we would always crash into old stone walls. Antarctica sounded much better; my father told me that hardly anyone lived there. I imagined a sunny space of snow, a smoothness of ice that sparkled blue and green. There were penguins, of course. Icebergs moved through the ocean like ships, and far away could be seen jumping porpoises, and I could build snow castles and have my own ice-cream mine [20].

When he does get to travel and arrives in Afghanistan, he finds he is not physically ready for the harsh terrain and hot desert weather. Foreign countries also mean foreign germs and bacteria — The Young Man falls ill for most of his journey. "I did not understand the nightmare that I was seeing," he confesses.

> Partly it was because I was sick that I was sometimes little more than a data collector; partly it was because I was so young that the exoticism of the experience made the greatest impression on me; partly it was because, thanks to my background, I was little understanding of physical suffering [150].

An Afghani general admonishes him to take better care of his health and that "you have the brains — but you are not physically fit and you have no money" (247).

Picture Show exhibits all the unsophisticated trappings of a first autobiographical novel (although published in 1993, it was started in 1983, a rewrite of his first autobiographical manuscript, *Welcome to the Memoirs*): the uneven shifts in point-of-view, employing a disorderly textual technique with different font sizes and faces, intermingling short passages of interviews, letters, statements, scanned documents, illustrations, flashbacks, flash-forwards, quotations from Wittgenstein and the Qur-ān; footnotes, a postscript, and an appendix. The effect Vollmann is attempting is a mixed-media presentation, a slideshow of textual images; hence the title. His heartfelt innocence is exhibited in the postscript; he reprints a letter, dated 6 November 1987, sent to the Consulate General of the Soviet Union in San Francisco, along with a copy of the typescript of *Picture Show*. Does he still hope to change the world by showing a Soviet government lackey his unpublished tome? "I frankly believe the Soviet presence in Afghanistan is wrong," he states in the letter, offering the government "five or ten pages" (252) to present their foreign policy position in the book: "I will not edit or alter your remarks in any way without your permission" (252). He ends the letter by writing that if he does not receive a response, "your silence will speak for itself" (252). Since no reply is printed, it would seem the Consulate General either did not read The Young Man's words of wisdom or did not take his words seriously.[2]

The structure of *Atlas* is inspired by Yasunari Kawagata's "palm-of-the-hand stories," fitting a novel's worth of information into several pages.[3] "A piecemeal atlas of the world I think in" is how Vollmann considers the 52 prose texts. "The book is difficult to categorize," writes Steven Moore in a review,

> ... it resembles a short-story collection ... made up of four or five brief vignettes — the prose equivalents of postcards or vacation slides — linked by a particular image or memory. It is like a gazetteer in that you can focus on particular places to read about, if you wish, for the stories are all self-contained. It is also a mathematically structured fiction like Georges Perec's *Life: A User's Manual* or John Barth's *LETTERS*.[4]

In the same spirit as his other collections, *Atlas* is not a mishmash of short works; it operates thematically so that each selection relies on the others to create a whole. In the "Compiler's Note," Vollmann states that "this collection is arranged palindromically: the motif of the first story is taken up again in the last; the second story finds its echo in the second to last, and so on" (xvi). At the center is a novella called "The Atlas," interlacing episodes from other parts of the book. *Atlas* resembles a novel the same way *Butterfly Stories* and *Europe Central* do, but is more personal: exploring the spiritual side of the narrator — a disenchanted man — who is becoming aware of the world within by experiencing the troubled world without, alternately in the first and third person, with an extraordinary list of locations, from Afghanistan to Zagreb, New York's Grand Central Station to the Alaskan Yukon, as well as Australia, Burma, Egypt, India, Italy, Japan, Madagascar, Mexico, Vatican City, and the Ocean Beach community in San Diego. His body has been everywhere; so has his soul, with entries set in the metaphysical space of Limbo as well as "The Sphere of Stars" (reminiscent of The Holy Ghost, traveling from Heaven to Earth in *Rainbow*). In the physical world, Vollmann explains in sordid and frank detail "The Best Way to Drink Beer," "The Best Way to Shoot H," "The Best Way to Chew Khat," "The Best Way to Smoke Crack."

Nudge that rock down into the end that's burned blacker.... Don't push it in too hard, or you'll break the mesh.... Just tamp it lovingly in with the black-burned hairpin. Lovingly, I said, because crack is the only happiness [171].

He is not afraid to admit that he has used drugs in his travels, either as research, to fit in with his subjects, or for recreation. "The Best Way to Smoke Crack" is often requested at readings, an audience favorite. Vollmann has publicly pointed out the irony of reciting the story in Italy, for a reading sponsored by the U.S. State Department, as an example of U.S. culture in literature. During Q&A sessions, readers and fans often ask him if he really smoked crack with prostitutes, or if he was making it all up. For better or worse, like Hunter S. Thompson, Vollmann's autobiographical portrayals of life's seedy side has been a significant factor in his cult status and how the literary community perceives him. A writer risks alienating and losing devout readers by moving away from the subject matter that has made him/her popular, but this is not Vollmann's concern. "I write to please myself," he notes in *Poor People*, and "the idea of *capturing a market* repels me" (287).

Atlas deals with the two major deaths that torment him: his sister and two friends in Bosnia. "Under the Grass" opens with the narrator reliving the day in 1968 when his sister drowned, as explained in Chapter One. Buried under New England ground, she is both spirit guide and haunting ghost: "Outside the night skull, you looked for me to hold your hand" (104) he addresses her, because now she is his "white witch" (104) when standing he is at her grave. The narrative is not completely grounded in realism. Jumping across time, Vollmann is at an airport in Mauritius twenty-five years later; he is so exhausted and disoriented from his world travels that he asks the authorities how to find his sister, a request that results in a comic misunderstanding and ends with a taxi driver assuming he wants a prostitute. Later, he is Thailand, at a prostitute bar; he is feeling proud and heroic for having recently rescued the child-prostitute Sakanja from the brothel she was enslaved in, as detailed in *Rising*. He dreams of his sister's coffin. He realizes that the rescue of Sakanja was nothing more than a failed attempt to appease the lingering spirit of the sister he failed to save when he was a child. The text ends in the catacombs of Rome; he visualizes a macabre revivification of his dead sister and knows he will never be free of her and his guilt; he will continue to wander the world, loveless and lost, atoning for the sin of her untimely death. Perhaps she, more than anyone or anything else, has been the greatest influence on his writing. Tom LeClair's review in the 6 May 1996 issue of *The Nation* is titled "His Sister's Ghost in Bosnia" and discusses this unifying motif, contending that Vollmann could be seeking atonement by placing his body into dangerous regions of the world, wanting to die so he can join his sister in the land of ghosts. As previously described, instead of achieving that transformation, while in Bosnia, the jeep he is riding in drives over a land mine and he survives, but two companions do not. Again, he is the survivor. In "That's Nice," he recounts dealing with the destroyed jeep and looking at photos of it with the rental car agent, who

> selected a good one that showed how the driver's side had been smashed and twisted and riddled.
> That's nice, I said. That's very artistic. Here. I'll show you a couple of nice pictures, too.
> I got up and went to the other bed and took the envelope of contact prints.
> This is Mr. B after I pulled him out of the car, I said. Isn't that nice? He was my friend for nineteen years. And this one here is Mr. A. Here they both are in the front just before I pulled them out.
> Mr. A. was driving? the rental man asked.
> That's right. See how the first burst got him right in the head? I'll be happy to make a copy for your collection [126].

Together, these two volumes create a fourteen-year arc in Vollmann's life: innocent in the first; experienced, cynical, and traveled in the second. In *Atlas*, he does not see the world so new any more; all his lofty, admirable ideals have waned.

> For a moment he felt melancholy as he always did the day before some journey to unknown climes, but then he found himself remembering one of those December nights when he'd come home from a trip, brought the duffel bag upstairs and was asleep within minutes; but he'd awakened early, his innards still flooded with another country's time where high over the cobalt sea there was nothing, then suddenly four low brownish-green islands ringed brilliant white — Taipei? No, blue space again [255].

He is poignant and somnolent, for he did not find a way to end his loneliness and pain. He knows he will travel again, and search again. In *Picture Show*, the last sentence is: "Two years after his return, he began learning to shoot a gun" (246). The Young Man understands the power of weapons and the need for self-defense, having witnessed war up close. *Picture Show* works as a blueprint for Vollmann's future interests and writing, moving away from the cartoon wars of insects and embracing real wars in Bosnia and Somalia. As a memoir, it reveals his roots and early influences.

7

Poor People (2007); *Riding Toward Everywhere* (2008); *Imperial* (2009)

All good writing is swimming under water and holding your breath.
— F. Scott Fitzgerald

Vollmann has been labeled a postmodernist, metafictionist, contemporary and historical novelist, pornographer, journalist, cultural/social critic, travel writer, and memoirist.[1] With these next three volumes, he explores interdisciplinary research and wears the hat of social scientist and anthropologist, employing methods of qualitative inquiry and autoethnography to present his findings and reflections. The rapid accretion of the varied genre forms and techniques that interest him shows no signs of slowing down or becoming staid.[2]

In Volume Five of *Rising*, Vollmann asks a Communist general of the Cambodian Khmer Rouge: "What's the best way to help poor people?" He is told

> first, the man must be a solider, and must help the citizen, must know how the citizen feeling, happy or unhappy. And he must looking for the safety for the citizens. Protect the country for all Cambodian people, to make them think that you are man of the country. And everyone must respect him [137].

This is not the answer Vollmann seeks; it does not satisfy his curiosity and concern. He asks the question over and over during his travels, compiling information that is the basis for the book-length essay, *Poor People*, which reads, stylistically, as Volume Eight of *Rising*. It is inspired by his lifelong fascination with *Let Us Now Praise Famous Men* (1941) by James Agee and Walter Evans, a project that came out of a *Life Magazine* assignment in 1936 to report on the conditions among white sharecropper families in the south. It was the era of Franklin Roosevelt's New Deal, a governmental effort to help the nation out of the recent Depression and assist those mired in the most desperate poverty across the United States. Agee and Evans spent eight weeks with three sharecropping families. The result was Evans's portfolio of bleak and desolate photographs — heartbreaking images of families with hungry, hopeless, withered faces; adults and children thronging together in inhospitable shacks in dusty, barren lands of a Depression-ravished landscape of the Deep South. Similar to Evans's photographs, *Poor People* contains 128 black and white images of the interviewees. The photos, taken by Vollmann, are in the front and back, bookending the text in the same format as *Atlas—* and *Famous Men*.

From Afghanistan, Pakistan, Japan, Burma, Australia, Ireland, the Philippines, Kenya, Mexico, Kazakhstan, and the United States, Vollmann asks numerous individuals of apparent little means: "Why are you poor?" It is a loaded question, an innocent interrogative, and an insulting inquiry. Reactions and answers vary from culture to culture, with philosophy, acceptance, and anger in context: it is the fault of the government, of the rich, or a punishment from God. Many of the subjects are trapped in the geography of their lives, without the means or opportunity to change their economic situation. Vollmann wanders the world once again in search of the truth. There is a cohesion in the text with the reoccurring Sunee, a weary, middle-aged woman in Thailand with too many children and husbands behind her. She works every day for twelve or more hours; looks forward to when she can come home, get drunk, and sleep, only to rise early and go back to work for meager wages. She believes she is poor because she was bad in a past life and is now paying a karmic debt. As Vollmann discusses his interactions with the insolvent on every continent, he comes back to Sunee, comparing her to the others; she is the unifying nexus of the narrative. There are the gypsies in Russia, the untouchables in Japan, the migrant, undocumented Mexican workers in southern California's Imperial Valley — no matter where he goes, and as much as he wishes otherwise, he is no longer The Young Man of *Picture Show* and it is futile to believe that he can still save the world. He has accepted the fact that he cannot change things for the better; he can only observe and report, like the indifferent anthropologist writing ethnographic field notes.

Fourteen years after his first trip to Afghanistan, we find Vollmann a much wiser, world-weary journalist in *Poor People*. He has survived death several times, seen good friends pass away; when he exists in a post–9/11 world far more violent than the days he joined the Mujahadeen. Everywhere he travels, he finds people who are desperate and starving, who lost all they once had or who never had a chance from square one. The Vollmann in *Poor People* is now a father with a young daughter; he is a prominent writer of contemporary literature, with major awards to his credit; his health is not what it used to be and he is more humble, less adventuresome than that Young Man from *Picture Show*, whose health was not all that great from the outset anyway. Instead of saving the world, all he can do is try to understand it, learning truths about his own self in the process. He is disenchanted and distrustful, admitting

> I am sometimes afraid of poor people.... I am a petty-bourgeois property owner. My building is an old restaurant on a corner parking lot just under the railroad bridge from the homeless shelter. People sleep in my parking lot. Some of them stay for months; others I see only once [263].

The book employs a non-linear structure. Chapters weave in and out of time and place; on one page, we find Vollmann in Russia and the suddenly Japan or Mexico. The work is a meditation rather than a dissertation. The tone is not as immediate as previous work; it possesses all the qualities of a mature writer in the process of evolution, and while it comprises a dozen years of research, everything contained in its pages rings true for today, and will for tomorrow. Vollmann creates portraits of subcultures and second-class individuals in non–Western countries who receive little, if any, consideration and press time outside specific studies in cultural anthropology. It serves as an educational work in that sense, such as Vollmann's reporting on the changing social and economic atmosphere of Japan, where "we used to say: water, air, and safety are free. Now safety is no longer free" (201). In the last decade, a new organized crime syndicate has arrived from China, different from the Yakuza, called "snakeheads."

> Why were they called snakeheads? I never found out.... The Yakuza had their proud and brilliant full-body tattoos of dragons and demons, but snakeheads, I was told, owned at most a small black dragon hidden in the armpit.... For all the risks I took and all the expense money I spent, I never to my certain knowledge met a single snakehead in the flesh. This essay on snakeheads and their relationship to poor people can thus proceed only by indirection, sketching the shadows which snakeheads cast as they flickered through other Chinese and Japanese lives.... They had no permanent organization, meeting only to finance specific ventures in alien smuggling — they wriggled through the bowels of Japanese society, sheltered by that society's xenophobia [199–200].

The snakesheads' business is human trafficking in the sex trade, bringing destitute young women from China, Thailand, Vietnam, and Cambodia into Japan to work inside brothels or be sold into slavery to the highest bidder. Also:

the marriage tricks.... A homeless man ... a stinking drunk, told me with his own lips how six months ago a snakehead whose name was something like Big Fish Dragon had come and paid him eight thousand yen [**approx. $685–M.H.**] to enter a taxi which conveyed him to a windowless apartment ... where he was instructed to shower, then loan[ed] an approximately fitting suit and necktie which he wore to another apartment filled with shy downcast Chinese women one of whom was also dolled up; a snakehead took a formal portrait of the happy couple — how sweet to see two poor people benefiting each other! — and then they got married. They would never see each other again. The homeless man guessed that his wife paid Big Fish Dragon half a million yen [**approx. $2,825–M.H.**] to arrange her nuptials.... She was beautiful, he said, a real princess. Perhaps she's gotten a good "dating club" job after that ... [204–05].

Some of homeless in Japan are referred to the untouchables (discussed in detail in Volume Six of *Rising*), yet it seems they are touchable for a night to be used as legal husbands and secure citizenship, never to consummate the marriage or gaze upon their brief wives again. The untouchables are a sub-culture of deformed or mentally disabled individuals (or perceived as such, with an apparently different lineage from "true blood" Japanese citizens) who cannot function in a working society; the homeless are also those who have lost their jobs either from corporate downsizing or age restrictions. And then there are those who simply dropped out of the rat race and decided to live on the streets.

What Vollmann discovers is that poverty is not necessarily an economic factor. He meets apparent poor people who do not consider themselves poor, who do not need a lot of money and material possessions, who are content with their lot in life and find riches in children, religion, and freedom from the stress that comes with monetary gain; as long as they have a place to sleep and enough to eat, and friends or family to rely on for comfort and love, they are happy. That old saying "money can't buy you happiness" comes to mind. "Do you think you are poor?" he asks a Yemeni fisherman who earns about $13 a day (104). The answer is no. Angelica, a Mexican prostitute "stinking of urine and sweat" does not consider herself destitute because "I can work" (43). Big Mountain, a homeless Japanese man, does not consider himself poor if "we have a place to live, we go there ... if we have a job to do, we do it" (94). While Vollmann may be in a better economic position than some of his subjects, he is not as content and accepting of the idea of poverty. He does not understand Angelica's view "that there are no rich and there are no poor" (43) because some people "know how to take care of their money ... and some of us, we don't know" (43). One of the Japanese untouchables tells him "money just goes where it goes.... There may be some reason, but anyway money just goes to where it goes, and to us it doesn't come" (293). This is a revelation to Vollmann: "If only someone had explained this to me before! Then I never would have needed to annoy myself with the subject of poverty" (293). Javier, a "young man in Mexico," believes the rich stay rich because they

> have enough money to get a good education whereas poor people like me, we don't get ahead.... I couldn't go to junior high or high school, because I didn't have the money for the books. In elementary school I didn't even haves shoes [158].

Vollmann has to accept that the world is simply divided by the haves and have-nots; it always has been this way. Class differences are a fact of life and there is nothing he can do or write to change that. "Recently I happened to be walking the train tracks of Salinas, California," he explains:

> Within sight of the passenger station began a zone of drugs and prostitution whose separate deals ... were secluded in part by trees and in part by the urgent wavings-away of the participants. My two companions, both of whom were successful businessmen, remarked on how useful it was for them to be reminded of the existence of this mode of life, which I found somewhat sad and they found much sadder.... What rendered the gap-toothed crack whore and meth peddlers mostly invisible to them was the convenient social subdelineation variously called Jewish ghettos, the red light district, Niggertown, the combat zone, the *zona de tolerenica*, the bad side of town, or (here's one that fits) the wrong side of the tracks [113].

The image of the hobo, riding trains and boxcars across America, conjures another time and place, the Depression era of *Let Us Now Praise Famous Men* and after, where the homeless and unemployed hitch free rides and search the nation for work and a place to call home. *Riding Toward Everywhere* is Vollmann's portrait of the contemporary hobo, a subculture of men and women who have dropped out of mainstream life and travel the nation by freight cars. Not all the trainhoppers are necessarily poor or homeless; some do it for the thrill and some, like Vollmann, do it for lived experience and research. Vollmann explains that the man

> who camped by his dog's grave had said: There's two types of people on this railroad. One type is the type with nothing. Then there's the second type. They're here because they wanna be [180–181].

The man wishes he were the second type, like the thrill seekers from Portland who get money from an ATM machine before "their long freight train ride from Oakland to Kansas City" (181). What is the attraction of trainhopping? Is it the excitement of getting away with it, of "slumming," of capturing what it must have been like in America's past? Vollmann's guide — a somewhat lackluster Virgil to his Dante — is a man named Steve, who has a home and wife and has been traveling the rails since he was a young man, collecting magnificent experiences and gazing on the beauty of the national landscape from the boxcar, *gratis*. He tells Vollmann that, in general, the conductors and other employees (such as railroad bulls) did not hassle him or his friends when they trainhopped, because they understood the call for the voyage.

Vollmann's interest in riding the rails came out of his research of California's Salton Sea and the Imperial Valley for *The Royal Family* (Henry Tyler becomes a crack-addicted hobo, leaving behind his life and job, as he searches for the Queen of Whores) and *Imperial*. Interviewing people who lived in the desert, either in small towns or Slab City, consisting of motor homes and tents, he discovered that the trainhopping American hobo still existed — this was, after all, a convenient way to travel if one was transient and poor. There is a smooth transition from *Poor People* to *Riding Toward Everywhere*; they could have been published under the same cover. *Poor People*, however, is global in its perspective, while *Riding* is local and focused on one county. Vollmann is not seeking answers to a framed question this time; he is simply traveling, observing, and *being*, much like Kerouac in his later years with *Vanity of Duluoz* that, as noted by Matt Theado in *Understanding Jack Kerouac*, made a "brave attempt to reinvigorate his prose and to summon a sense of grace in the relaxed, conversational language of a story that has as its main purpose the deflation of the narrator's earlier seriousness" (180). Indeed, *Riding* has a calm feel, an assuredness, more than any other Vollmann volume. Gone are the frenetic run-on sentences, the long poetic paragraphs, and the grand philosophizing on politics and morality. He finds a Zen-like joy in the simplicity of the "pouring rain, then birds and frogs, fresh yellow-green wetness of fields" (29). "I ... have seen it all" (29) he notes, yet for all his wanderlust across the globe, home is a new discovery. After sleeping outside and in boxcars, he appreciates the comfort of a warm bed more than he ever has before. "Whenever I injure or tire myself on the rails," he admits, "I can rest, whether at home or in a flophouse" (23). He has a choice to walk away from the hardships of hobo life, whereas others do not.

> As for me, where was I going, and where was *here*? That was as mysterious to me as the shine of spittle on the track of an old bridge. As Kerouac's guru Dean Moriarty says: *We give and take and go in the incredible complicated sweetness zigzagging every side* [185].

Comparison to *On the Road* is inevitable. He cites *The Dharma Bums* more; like Kerouac, he is traveling for the sake of experience, to see America and explore its soul (and his own, too). He also cites Jack London, Thomas Wolfe, Mark Twain, and John Steinbeck — their literature of wandering and escapade — so much that *Riding* resembles a work of quasi-literary criticism, especially when he muses about Hemingway's Nick Adams stories. "Indians haunt Hemingway's work most beautifully in 'Fathers and Sons,'" he claims, "where Nick remembers making love to his Indian sweetheart Trudy, who still in another story is called Prudy.... Beautiful, promiscuous, unself-conscious (and) excellent at making love, she breaks Nick's heart and enriches his soul" (116). Vollman fondly remembers "that sweetheart I first went trainhopping with" (116) now estranged to him, leaving a hole in his heart.[3] The pain that comes with love and loss, Vollmann implies, is what creates a man's character — notably the Hemingway hero, such as Henry in *A Farewell to Arms*, who is "happy, safe, in love and in nature until the very end when Catherine dies" (194). Chapter Four is entitled "I Think We're in Switzerland, Cat" referring to the train that will take the lovers in *Farewell* to a neutral country, far from the war, where they can raise their child in peace. That never happens, of course (he does not, however, mention the train in Hemingway's widely anthologized and classroom favorite "Hills Like White Elephants" and where that train is going to). Vollmann contends that Hemingway's "great novels ... all evolve around journeys" and "each journey is a quest for death" (123).

> *A Farewell to Arms* details desertion to, flight with and death of the beloved; *For Whom the Bell Tolls* asserts the impossibility of escape.... In both *To Have and Have Not* and *Islands in the Stream*, unlucky sailors and Cuban waters flee domestic loneliness to win death from the bullets of bad men. Finally, *The Old Man and the Sea*, whose protagonist completes and arduous circle from poverty and failure to the same ... spells out the paradigm: It was the journey itself, with its hardships, triumphs, puzzles and unexpected joys, that made these books alive in the first place [123–24].[4]

Is this a book about riding the rails or is it a quirky discourse on 20th-century American fiction similar to D.H. Lawrence's *Studies in Classic American Literature*? References to Hemingway — London, Tawin, et al. — are fitting; Vollmann goes from state to state in his boxcar journeys; what he sees reminds him of the literature associated with different places in America. He is a writer, after all, acknowledging the masters who came before him, like "many of Hemingway's protagonists ... [who] can look at a landscape they have never seen before and suspect that it will be good shooting country" (194). What is missing (and disappointing when it comes to Vollmann's usual abundant data) is the wealth of description of the Other America that is in Kerouac's work. Vollmann glosses over the landscape he sees and focuses more on his reflections of the literature that has influenced him; this creates an inner journey over the outer journey. Vollmann could be watching a "beauty pic" documentary film, covering the same states and sights, and have the same distanced experience. At times, the reader may think to herself: "Get off the train car, Vollmann, and live a little like you did with the crack whores and Afghanistan freedom fighters in your other books."

Where are all these trainhoppers going? What is the end goal? Vollmann hears references to a place called Big Rock Candy Mountain, which he determines is a giant crack cocaine metaphor or the label for a personal paradise, a Shangri-la, an ideal and truly democratic America that embraces all freedom and equality. Throughout the text, Vollmann calls this vague autonomous zone "Cold Mountain"—not the Cold Mountain of Alaska, California, or Idaho, but the idea of peace as interpreted in Charles Frazier's popular historical novel, *Cold Mountain*, where Inman sets out on an idealistic quest to return to the bliss he once knew, to experience love again; his journey wrought with experiences good and bad that force a spiritual growth. The epigraph to Fraizer's novel reads: "Men ask the way to Cold Mountain / Cold Mountain: there's no through trail" (iii). Cold Mountain is the *satori* Kerouac strove for in all his travels; Cold Mountain is Switzerland where Catherine Barkley and the baby are alive, well, and happy; Cold Mountain is where Nick Adams can hunt and fish all he wants in peace, "because the essence of Cold Mountain is *aloneness,* and as it says in 'Fathers and Sons,' looking back to the time of 'The Last Good Country' before all the timber was gone: *But there was still much forest left then, virgin forest*" (116). Vollmann, however, admits he is alien to the concept:

> I never could have gotten to Cold Mountain because I lack Cold Mountain's mind. I love cities as much as solitude, prostitutes as much as trees.... Neither the ecstatic openness of Kerouac's road voyages, nor the dogged cat-and-mouse triumphs of London's freight-jumpers, and certainly not the canny navigations of Twain's riverboat youth define me. I go my own bumbling way ... knowing not precisely where to go until I am there [73].

Even if he does arrive at Cold Mountain, he thinks: "Isn't it for the best if I can never be sure I've found it?" (186). If he does find it, what is left to live for? People want heaven, but they will not know what to do with it when they get it. "Sometimes when I ride toward Everywhere," Vollmann ruminates at the end, "I believe in Cold Mountain" (187). He wonders what happens when and if he reaches Everywhere. Nevertheless: "The longer I live, the closer I get" (188). Again, however, the reader is left somewhat at a distance through the lacuna of actual experience, place, and literary rumination. Perhaps this is Vollmann as he gets older, post-stroke: more inner workings than outer experience. No longer The Young Man eager for first-hand experience in *An Afghanistan Picture Show,* Vollmann has settled into the role of the reflective observer.

*   *   *

Poor People is the object and *Riding* is the subject. While *Poor People* deals with the problems of others, *Riding* is deeply reflexive and is perhaps

Vollmann's most personal, mystical book. What it is really about is aging, death, and fathers and sons. It opens with Vollmann and his elderly father standing in line at a bakery during the Christmas season. An employee barks at his father to stop blocking the line. "My father turned to me," Vollmann writes, "and remarked conversationally: Give some people a little power and they turn into Nazis" (1), not caring who hears him, causing a scene or embarrassment for his son. Vollmann ruminates how his father

> grew up in an era when to be American ... was to be yourself. In some respects his generation was more ignorant, complacent, self-centered and parochial than mine.... My grandfather's time must have been even more individualistic. With his by–Gods and goddamns, my grandfather laid down opinions without great reverence for the judgment of others" [1–2].

The writer Harlan Ellison often publicly states: "You are *not* entitled to your opinion, you are entitled to your *informed* opinion."[6] Does freedom of thought include keeping your unbound thoughts to yourself or the agency of putting them out into the world, whether or not the thought is in the "right" or "wrong"? Vollmann's father was, in fact, blocking the busy line for other customers; in this case, he was being inconsiderate, yet when he perceives an employee as being power-hungry when pointing out his defect, that person is automatically a Nazi for speaking up. Vollmann does not let his readers know if he is embarrassed or if he accepts it as a character trait of his father's upbringing and personality. "I still go back to the bakery my father hates," he writes, and the woman who yelled at his father "nods at me" (3) as if they share a secret connection.

"I am my father's son," he muses, "which is to say I am not exactly like father" (3). He lists their many differences regarding politics and material possessions; he also finds similarities. Vollmann continuously comes back to the topic of his father throughout *Riding*, realizing that as grows older, he becomes more like his father, just like his father has become his grandfather now. "Would I really have preferred my grandfather's time," he wonders,

> when Pinkertons were cracking Wobblies over the head, or my father's, when Joe McCarthy cold ruin anyone by calling him Red? All I know is that I live a freer life than many people. I want to be freer still; I'm sometimes positively dazzled with longing for a better way of being [5–6].

He recalls a couple sleeping in the dirt by a wall in San Diego, as he slept outside too, waiting for the morning train to depart. "They may have been trainhoppers," he writes, concluding that "they live a free life, perhaps" (180). Freedom, then, is the core theme of *Riding*— the freedom for Vollmann's father to publicly call someone a Nazi; the freedom for Vollmann to study and write about who and what he chooses; the freedom for members of the FTRA ("Free Train Riders of America") to live their life as they choose, and so what if mainstream society looks down on them as hobos, drugs addicts, criminals, and homeless. Kerouac knew the open roads of America represented freedom just as Hemingway asserted the freedom to take his own life in his own manner of choosing.

As this book was going into production, the bound galleys of *Imperial*—all 1300 pages — became available (published by Viking Penguin August, 2009). I have a few moments to discuss this massive tome but not at length; there is simply not enough time to deeply examine all that *Imperial* offers; however, this monograph would find itself incomplete without some mention. As stated in the preface, I will leave the task of weighty critique to future Vollmann scholars.

Imperial is the result of ten years of obsessive research; when Vollmann becomes interested in a subject, he does so in a voluminous, comprehensive manner, apparent with American history in the *Seven Dreams* series and his-torical/global violence in *RURD*. In 1997, literary critic Larry McCaffery intro-duced Vollmann to the Anza-Borrego dessert in California (where McCaffery lives and writes) and the neighboring county of Imperial that encompasses thousands of acres of desolate desert, the contaminated Salton Sea, a curious mixture of Mexican, Chinese, and Indian culture, as well as the volatile and controversial issues of the U.S./Mexican border and the "illegal migrant worker" conditions and human rights. Vollmann set the last scenes of *The Royal Family* in Imperial County's Slab City, Salvation Mountain, and bor-der regions, populated by train-hoppers, drug addicts and the homeless. Sim-ilar to the prostitute trilogy, Vollmann has created a triptych with the books discussed in this chapter: the Mexican migrants of *Poor People* show up, as do those who travel by train cars. Similar to Vollmann's career, *Imperial* cannot be framed into any compact genre: part journalism, part ethnography, part memoir, part cultural study, part political manifesto, part prose poem.

Imperial acknowledges its debt to Steinbeck's *The Grapes of Wrath* (1939): like the dust bowl that was America during the Great Depression, Imperial County mostly consists of uninhabited desert, destitute small towns, "out-sider" communities, and havens for human smuggled from Mexico to the U.S., seeking a better life. The characters in *Grapes* resemble the people Voll-mann crosses paths with: desperate, poor folk searching for work, meaning, and better days. Some are hopeful, some have accepted their lot; and some are on the brink of self-destruction and suicide, involved in crime, drug abuse, and prostitution.

The book opens with Vollmann, the reporter, accompanying Border Patrol Agent Dan Murray to prevent non–U.S. citizens, led by "coyotes" (men who lead groups of people across the border for money from men and sexual favors, and money, from women), from crossing into "The Gardens of Paradise," so dubbed the first chapter (3). This scene occurs before 9/11 and the institution of Homeland Security; Vollmann inserts an aside: "As I reread this chapter almost a decade later, in these days of 'extraordinary rendition' and the Patriot Act [...] Our Department of Homeland Security seems disinclined to let me watch anymore hunts and chases" (9). That is, prior to the War on Terror, Border Patrol and Customs were hospitable to journalists; however, as a division of ICE (Immigration and Customs Enforcement), Homeland Security, and the FPS (Federal Protection Service), "national security" dictates that the free press witnessing tactics and methods of the Border Patrol could be used as intelligence for those of Arabic lineage, disguised as Mexicans, to elude capture.

Vollmann searches for what *may or may not exist* during his decade long jaunts into a region whose name (much like another county, Inland Empire, not far north of Imperial) ironically conjures up images of majestic colonialism. For migrant workers in Latin America, Imperial represents the American Dream, a path out of poverty, a promised land of blue skies and green hills; when they cross over, having paid $1500–2000 to a coyote, they find a harsh land with little work, and sometimes return home or are caught by *la migra* and forced back to Mexico.

Imperial County was once a land of promised milk and honey during the first half of the Twentieth Century. The failed development of Salton City as the new Palm Springs is evidence of this. A best-selling romance novel, *The Winning of Barbara Worth* (1911), came out of the development dreams of the time, when

> the Imperial Valley gave birth to one million, one hundred and twenty thousand pounds of cabbage and an almost equal quantity of grapeweight, Mr. Harold Bell Wright [...] sat down it Holtville in an arrow-weed house he'd built with his own hands (how Imperial of him!), write out eight manuscript drafts whose internal organs he reshuffled through a system of hanging pockets, and reified Imperial into somebody he could adore: Too look at Barbara Worth was a pleasure; to hear her was a delight [161].

Vollmann, as any reader might, finds the novel absurd on many levels: first, it is badly written commercial fiction on the level of a Harlequin romance, yet at the time found millions of fans and made the author wealthy; second, while Bell's novels sold better than many writers in the 1920s (such as Hemingway, Fitzgerald, and Sherwood Anderson), Bell's name is basically unknown in the canon of American fiction, the books long out of print and hard to find; third, Barbara Worth is about a land developer who names a new Imperial county town after his daughter, yet meets with economic troubles, rebelling workers, and the breaking of a dam that sends a tidal wave from the Colorado River into the valley, destroying the town and washing away all the lofty dreams of paradise. The purple prose novel reflects what Vollmann finds in his travels: ideals of a land that may exist in the minds of men and women, but do not exist in reality.

Vollmann also searches for the Chinese tunnels under the two border towns Calexico (U.S. side) and Mexicali. The Chinese communities on the border and the outskirts of the Salton Sea are descendants of the Chinese railroad workers of Nineteenth Century expansion. No one talks about the tunnels, many treat them as urban legends, yet Vollmann uncovers evidence that the Chinese folk on the border did indeed use tunnels to smuggle in good, drugs, people, and engage in illegal gambling (and possibly still do). Casting himself as a "private investigator," Vollmann outfits himself with a spy camera in the shape of a shirt button (paid for by *Playboy* magazine) and infiltrates a "sweat shop" to uncover the true conditions of those seeking the American Dream: Mexican women forced into backbreaking labor for little pay. Vollmann also searches for himself: inevitably, over a decade, the events in Vollmann's life, and his experiences while in Imperial, change his outlook. One event is the stroke he suffered in 2004, which hampered him physically from moving about the desert as he did before. He finds the invisible county, state, and country lines of the region "delineations and subdelineations" of the lives of the people he meets, and his own life, so that

> this book forms itself as it goes. Fields, cemetaries, newspapers and death certificates beguile and delay me; I don't care that I'll never finish anything. Imperial will scour them away with its dry winds and the brooms of its five-dollars-an-hour laborers.... Imperial is what I want it to be.... The desert is real ... but there is no such place as Imperial; and I, who (doesn't) belong there, was never anything but a word-haunted ghost [181].

Claiming that "books are whatever we want them to be" (181), and that this book has multiple labels and layers, Vollmann imagines an Imperial in his mind, an ideal place, in contrast to the physical Imperial County. It is much like Big Rock Candy Mountain: a state one achieves than actual real estate. It is a place where Vollmann gets away from his domestic life in Sacramento, his image as a major American writer, his role as the danger-seeking journalist, a place where "I know that I'll sleep happily and well" (1118). "Imperial is the father and son who sit high and gently swinging in one car of the otherwise unoccupied ferris wheel which reigns over a sandy night carnival" (1120) he muses. Imperial is also a space where he finds and loses love — when "until a week ago, this place had been hers and mine, *our place,* she said, and so it had been for years" (99) to a painful delineation: "And so what if we had made love one more time after she said it was over? [...] I take back what I said at the beginning" (100). Imperial is no longer "theirs" but his and his alone, long after "she'd been begging me to let her go, but I'd been too blind and too selfish" (100) wanting to share Imperial, the idea of Imperial, when in fact it is a solo state of being. It takes him a long time free himself from the pain of this failed relationship; when he does, his view of *Imperial*, the book project, and Imperial the real estate, and his reasons for the research, change from idealism to fatalism: the land goes from "green, green fields, haystacks, and wide mountains" (49) to "the poorest county in California and its water [...] robbed away by state threat and federal intimidation" (159). The county's predicament becomes a reflection of Vollmann's experiences and scarred soul.

Imperial does not have to be read from page one onward. Vollmann has structured the text so that each of the 208 chapters operates as a stand-alone entity, jumping back and forth through time (akin to The Stream of Time) in a stream-of-consciousness non-linear phenomenon. It is possible to begin the book in the middle at Chapter 82, "The Long Death of Albert Henry Larson" (511) and then jump backwards or forwards, going to Salton Sea's New River, or experiences in Mexicali brothels with the midget whore, Elvira. We find Chapter 10 titled "Preface" where Vollmann is still thinking about writing the book, a meta-reflection on the birth of a text that is yet to exist: "All these delineations and subdelineations had persuaded me that if I were going to write *Imperial*, the book should probably investigate what used to be called 'the American dream,' with some broader strips of its Mexican counterpart" (158). Vollmann muses on how "this book forms itself as it goes" (181) and is not confined to an outline or chronological layer. As with other Vollmann books, mainly the *Seven Dreams* volumes, *Imperial* does not arrive at a completion that adheres to normative expectations of narrative; in the end, Vollmann finds "America itself, empire of ingenuity, progress, equality, enrichment and self-sufficiency and now a wavering half-symbol of imperiled decrepitude" (1121) and the text smoothly merges into 167 pages of back matter: chronology, source notes, bibliography, and acknowledgments (reading the long list of those who aided the writer over a decade is a narrative curiosity in itself). Just as Vollmann advocates creating an Imperial that can be anything in the mind of the beholder, he wants the reader to enter this book on any page and make it whatever the reader wishes it: history, ethnography, debauchery, journalism, fiction, or love story.

Within the pages of *Imperial* are the three themes I have been focusing on throughout this work. First, we find prostitution aplenty, on either side of the border: streetwalkers and brothels a significant part of the economy in Mexicali. Freedom, of course, is the goal for the illegal aliens who dream of a better life in America: the freedom to cross the delineated lines of nations, the freedom to work, the freedom to be. Vollman seeks a freedom to create

Imperial into whatever he wants it to be, as well as redemption from the life and role he plays outside Imperial.

* * *

Outside the text, I feel a need to comment on the physicality of *Imperial*, and other Vollmann books. At 1300 pages, this is Vollmann's heftiest volume, albeit *RURD*, essentially one book, divided into seven manageable volumes. When *The Royal Family*, at 780 pages, was published, I found I could not carry it around — comfortably anyway; nor could I lie down on a couch or in bed and attempt a blissful vetting. The book required placement on a flat surface to manage. This is also the case with *Imperial*; this is not an object one can take to the beach, read on the train or bus, or feasibly carry around in a purse or backpack. The softcover galleys alone weight five pounds; the hardcover weighs more. *Imperial* becomes a challenge to digest on the material, practical level; that is, it cannot be read at times and in places where one might read an average book. Critics have applauded and condemned the girth of Vollmann's volumes (competing in size with David Foster Wallace's *Infinite Jest*, Don DeLillo's *Underworld*, or Thomas Pynchon's *Mason & Dixon*), yet have not discussed their place in the history of The Big Book. Consider the illuminated manuscripts of antiquity, placed on podiums or shelves where they remained and could only be read while standing up. The bulk, and hulk, of a book such as *Imperial* becomes as pertinent as the text within: the actual land of Imperial County is just as taxing to navigate and explore as the act of reading about it.

* * *

One last aspect of freedom, to conclude this monograph: Vollmann's work expounds on various forms of, and need for, it. *You Bright and Risen Angels* finds Bug with a desire to free the insect world from the tyranny of electricity; in *The Rainbow Stories*, people express their freedom of politics (the SF Skinz), freedom of lifestyle choice (the prostitutes and exotic dancers), and freedom of cultural critique through performance art (Survival Research Labs). The freedom from colonial influence, religious and cultural integration, is at the center of the *Seven Dreams* series; *Whores for Gloria, Butterfly Stories*, and *The Royal Family* are about the freedom to love; nations fight for freedom or assert the right to go to war in *Europe Central*; mankind's desire to be free from, or engage in, violence unifies the volumes of *Rising Up and Rising Down*; Copernicus maintains his theories of the universe's structure, free from the dogmatic pressures of the Church; Afghanistan struggles to be free from Russia and Russia free from Nazi rule ... and Vollmann freely travels the world in order to understand why people do what they do. The freedom of happiness in poverty, without the pressure of wealth, the freedom to travel, the freedom from invisible lines of nations and ownership, the freedom of imagination — these aspects weigh heavily in the three books covered in this chapter. This is, perhaps, the direction Vollmann's career shall focus on the most in the future, and what scholars and researchers will zero in on when gazing back on the body of Vollmann's many words and pages. As an American writer concerned with issues of autonomy, and given that the United States is *based* on the *concept* of *liberty*, it would be safe to deduce that *all of American literature* is, essentially, about the varieties of freedom that are available to the human experience. As a practitioner of contemporary American literature, William T. Vollmann is simply doing his job representing the hypothesis.

Part II

Seven Conversations

Moth to the Flame (1991)

Larry McCaffery

Larry McCaffery: The writing of several of your books has required you to put yourself into a situation of personal danger or physical challenge, adventure: entering into Afghanistan with Islamic commandos for your first book, hanging out with skinheads, pimps, drug dealers, prostitutes and other street people in *The Rainbow Stories*, traveling to the Arctic wilderness in *The Ice Shirt*, and so on. What's your explanation for this — do you find these situations interesting from an aesthetic standpoint (because you think they'll produce good writing) or mainly because you find these situations personally interesting or fun or challenging?

William T. Vollmann: Every dog likes his own little corner that he can mark with his own piss. One of the ways I can mark my own corner is by going off to someplace where a lot of other writers wouldn't dare to go. That way I don't have to worry about the competition writing better things than I could. I guess I also feel attracted to the extreme because I feel like frequently the extreme case will illustrate the general case — and that it can sometimes do this more forcefully and memorably than just dealing with the general or the ordinary. But the other thing is, sure, I'm still fascinated by exotic things. I suppose I always will be. And very often, if you want some kind of direct contact with exotic things, you find yourself in a dangerous situation, almost by definition. If there isn't some barrier between you and the exotic, then usually it's not exotic. What creates this barrier has to be either danger or difficulty. When I have time and I'm feeling like a coward I take the difficult things; when I need to get things done quicker, I do the dangerous things. On the other hand, nothing I do is *that* dangerous. Others have built a mystique around my activities.

LM: In one of your biographical statements, you emphasized your absorption as a kid in books — this sense of riding on the magic carpet with the Caliph, and so on. Did inhabiting these exotic places so long and so deeply in your imagination have anything to do with wanting to actually visit them now that you're grown up?

WTV: Sure, there's something of that. The truth is, I get kind of bored with a lot of ordinary people. It's not that I think that I'm better than they are. If anything I think they're probably better than I am. It's easier for them to be happy and just live their lives, whereas for some reason I don't seem to be happy just living my life. It always feels like I'm looking for something new, something that's not ordinary. Given that predisposition, I'm always trying to find people who don't seem familiar, and oftentimes that puts me into that dream world I experienced as a kid, because the more extreme and exotic the experience and the more difficult the people, the more I learn, and the less remains that's not ordinary. Then even the process of searching for the exotic becomes a habit. Like a dream.

LM: How does your new book, *The Ice Shirt*, fit into the sequence of seven dream novels that you plan to publish over the next few years.

WTV: *The Ice Shirt* is the first book in a septology of what I'm calling "dream-novels." My idea for this sequence came about in a complicated way. When I went to Afghanistan in 1982, I was lured there by the thought of this unknown exotic experience — or by a whole bunch of exotic experiences. I guess what I wanted was to confront this foreign "other." Later on, I began to realized that's it pretty hard to know yourself and harder still to know the other. And hardest of all to know something which is really foreign. So my book on Afghanistan ended up being basically about the unknowability of their experience. That made me want to focus my interest more and more on things closer to home and that was one of the connecting threads underlying the different sorts of things you find in *The Rainbow Stories*. The simplest way to put it is that in *The Rainbow Stories* I wanted to understand what America's like. There was still this element of my fascination with the exotic experience — I wanted to look at lost souls and marginal people, with the hope that maybe by understanding them I could help them somehow, as I had done with the Afghans. The experience of writing *The Rainbow Stories* lead me to realize that I *still* didn't really understand anything about America and that I probably never would. But it occurred to me that one way of starting to understand would be to see where we as Americans have come from and how we've changed. So it seemed like a nice idea to go back to the Indians — in fact, go back as far I could, which is to the first recorded contact with Indians — and describe everything which has happened since then in a series of books that winds up covering roughly a thousand-year period. The first people that we know of to come to this continent after the Indians were the Norse, who came here around 1000 A.D.

The Ice Shirt, which is the first in the series, describes how the Norse came and how they tried to stay but weren't able to. I've always been very interested Ovid's *Metamorphoses*, and from Ovid I got the idea that there had been a series of different ages on our continent, with each age being a little bit inferior to the age that preceded it. So, for poetic or didactic purposes I decided that there would seven dreams and therefore seven ages. In the first dream of *The Ice Shirt* the Norse begin this process of degradation by introducing ice into "Vinland" (which is what they called North America). In the Norse sagas they talk about how there was no ice during the winter when they came. Of course, maybe they were exaggerating (because they came from Greenland, what they thought of as "ice" or an "icy" landscape might be different from what we do), but it was nice to suppose that there really *wasn't* ice here when they landed. In which case, one can imagine that perhaps they brought the ice with them — in their hearts somehow. Maybe winter was the first curse that came to Vinland. The other dreams will carry on different aspects of this motif until we end up at the present when everything was sort of concreted over.

LM: Your earlier work displays a similar fascination with change and metamorphosis — it was obvious, for example, in *You Bright and Risen Angels*, where you depict the same kinds of literalized interaction between people, plants, animals, and nature. What lies behind your decision to depict these kinds of interactions that seem so fantastic from a realistic standpoint?

WTV: Metamorphosis is one of the main activities of human beings. We're always trying to transform ourselves into things that we are not yet — and may not ever become. We do this either because we're bored or unhappy with what we are, or because we're satiated, or because we want to improve ourselves. But whatever underlying motivations there are behind this, it's a central activity. A lot of creation myths (probably *all* creation myths) deal with this. In a way, history is basically a description of metamorphosis. As we go from myth to history, people lose a lot of their powers. Suddenly they're not able any more to change themselves into birds, or to gain superhuman powers (or they can do these things only very rarely) but they're still able to change themselves from one kind of person to another. *The Ice Shirt* is partly about that particular barrier between myth and history. In the old days people could change into bears (at least men could), and then suddenly that doesn't become possible any more. We actually get into the ken of memory and history. People can imagine that there was such a thing, but whether or not it ever really happened we will never know.

LM: In *Angels* you also described people who are part insect or vegetable at certain moment, but there your emphasis seemed less "mythic" or historical than symbolic — that is, you seemed to use this as a way of literalizing or exaggerating these people's insect-qualities or animal-qualities. You also weren't showing these people being "transformed" into these non-human forms so much as showing what they were already like....

WTV: Right: the people in *Angels* are much more allegorical than the characters in *The Ice Shirts*— so much so that "people" isn't always the right word for them. And whatever they are, there is very little transformation taking place in *Angels*. There is a little of that, but one of the big themes in the book is that basically the characters are *unable* to change their nature. Everyone is imprisoned with a nature, but it's the worst possible nature. So the "bugs" can't ever be anything but bugs. The revolutionaries who wanted to respond to the cruelties of the reactionaries by doing something positive become just as bad as the reactionaries. There's no hope for any real change there. Whereas the characters in *The Ice Shirt* see some way of escaping from whatever they are, either by changing their locations and going to Vinland, or becoming the sun, or whatever. That may or may not be an illusion on their part, but at least it's their hope not to be fixed.

LM: From the very beginning, American mythology has always had to do precisely with the notion of being able to change what you are (or *who* you are) simply by moving, changing your environment. Have we lost the belief that getting on the river or the road and getting the hell out of someplace will allow us to change our lives, change ourselves?

WTV: I think we have. Most of this continent's transformation is over with. What remains can be extrapolated from forces that are now already in place. I'm not trying to make an Hegelian argument that history is coming to end, or suggesting that I know what's going to happen in the future. Things will continue to change in this country, and perhaps very radically so. But my sense is that the other massive and violent transformations which are going to impinge on us (as they always will, because history is like that) are probably going to come from some outside source.

LM: What sort of thing are you thinking about?

WTV: Well, for instance, the possibility that the global balance of power will shift in such a way that we become a very backward country that gets broken up into smaller republics. Or let's suppose that environmental problems, which we brought about ourselves very directly, continue to operate and cause a lot of death and suffering and transform the country in that way.

LM: We see some of this happening already with the multinationals — they're already manipulating different aspects of our country (our economy, our relationship to our natural environment, etc.) in ways that aren't tied to our national identity.

WTV: That's right. A lot of the horrible ecological things that both we and the Japanese continue to do are outgrowths of very predictable technological decisions. That's another thing which the books in *Seven Dreams* are going to take up in different ways. Each time there's a new technological icon or fetish introduced, it's going to have a rather baleful effect.

LM: Like the ax in *The Ice Shirt*....

WTV: Right — the iron ax which the Norsemen bring with them and which the Native Americans reject. But for instance in dream number six (*The Rifles*), which involves the destruction of the Arctic, the icon is now the repeating rifle which the Native Americans *don't reject*. The result is mass starvation when the caribou are wiped out.

LM: The moment in *The Ice Shirt* when the Indian picks up the ax after killing one of the Norsemen with it, and then looks at it and decides to throw it back into the water, reminded me of the scene in *2001: A Space Odyssey*, where the cave man throws the bone up in the air and the bone is transformed into a space station. Both scenes seem to be describing one of those absolutely pivotal moments in history where technology is being introduced. Only in your scene, the Native Americans (at least temporarily) reject what's being presented to them.

WTV: I wasn't specifically thinking of the movie analogy, but the way you're describing it is reasonable. I see that moment in *The Ice Shirt* as being the beginning of American history. The Norse, with their characteristic combination of courage, ruthlessness, and arrogance, had decided they are going to take over this territory. To their mindset, these Indians are outlaws and can therefore be killed at will. The Indians, of course, don't see it that way at all, so there's a battle and the Indians with their stone axes lose to the iron axes. But they don't lose in the long run because they're so numerous and the Norse technological superiority is not so much greater that they can hope to be safe there. So eventually the Norse leave. But in one of the battles, one of the Norse axes has killed one of the Indians, and another Indian picks it up and kills somebody else with it. He understands how sharp and strong it is, but he throws it away anyway. This really happens in one of the Norse sagas, and when I came across it, I thought it was a really odd and extraordinary moment. Here was the first confrontation between a native, established way of life and this new power which the natives had never seen before. That ice was the beginning of this new power which was going to transform the landscape and pretty much ruin them — and pretty much ruin us, as well. Rejecting that power was an act which you can call the opening of American history. The scene with the acceptance of the rifles by the Eskimos many years later is the close of the whole process.

LM: The idea of creating this seven-volume saga strikes me as an astonishingly ambitious and confident undertaking for a writer of your age, and where you are in your career. How did the notion of this project evolve? Don't you have qualms about committing yourself to something this huge?

WTV: When I started I wanted to do something more or less along the lines of Ovid's *Metamorphoses* and I thought it would be really interesting to have the entire thousand-year period told, vividly and poetically, in one volume. But once I started working on the first part of it, I realized there was no way the thing could be done in one volume. Then, since I had already planned on calling the book *Seven Dreams*, I figured I might as well do the thing in seven volumes. So that's how I arrived at the overall conception.

As far as starting on this when I'm so young, if I want to do this thing at all, I *have* to do it now. It's going to take at least ten years to finish. Maybe longer. And [a] lot of the research involves traveling to places that require physical hardship. When I go to the Arctic I live in a tent and carry 110 or 120 pounds of food and other equipment on my back. Twenty years from now doing that may be impossible. My only real concern is whether I'll be able to continue making money from my writing in a way that allows me to travel to the places I need to. As long as that basic precondition is met, I don't have any qualms.

LM: There's a passage in *The Ice Shirt* where you remark of the history of the "Blue Shirt" that "Answers are nowhere and everywhere." That comment reflects the sense I get from your books: on the one hand, they're all filled with information and possible answers that arise and disappear — but in the end, there's no sense of closure or that you've provided a final explanation for anything. So when you are writing, are you looking for answers to specific questions that you feel you can answer for the readers? Or is writing more of a process of discovery for you?

WTV: When I begin a work I usually have a fairly specific issue that I'm interested in. In the case of *The Ice Shirt* I wanted to understand what this whole business with axes meant. But whenever I'm trying to understand a specific issue I always find that it becomes more and more complicated — which is why the books get longer and longer. With the Afghan book I really wanted to understand, first of all, whether the Soviets or the Afghans were right. Secondly, if the Afghans were right, then what I could do to help them. As I said, I ended up realizing that it's a very difficult process to help other people and that issues like these become very confusing and ultimately almost unknowable. So what winds up happening is much less a matter of me trying to provide answers or explanations about something I know in advance than the process of trying to deal with this ambiguous material. What you're left with is a movement of narrative more than anything else. Answers really *are* everywhere in the narrative. But also nowhere.

LM: A book like *You Bright and Risen Angels* is clearly a long, difficult, obsessive work. Were you at all aware when you were writing it that it was going to be difficult for this book to attract a large audience? Or do you just write the way the way you feel compelled to write and not concern yourself with the question of "audience" at all?

WTV: I just make the best book that I can. I like most individuals I meet, but I have a pretty low opinion of people in general. If I were to write for people in general, I would have to drastically lower my estimation of the intelligence of my reader, so I don't. I write the way it seems to me a book has to appear. I don't think that's egotistic. There are often things I would like to include in my books — things about me and other materials — that I feel I have to leave out because they aren't relevant to the book. I'm pretty ruthless along those lines, and I try to let nothing come in the way of what's best for the book. If that means that the book won't sell or that a publisher won't buy it, then that's my problem. *I'll* suffer for that, but I won't let the *book* suffer for it.

LM: Obviously there are a lot of differences between *The Rainbow Stories* and *You Bright and Risen Angels*, not so much thematic differences but in the manner of exposition, which seems somewhat more straightforward in *The Rainbow Stories*. Was that a conscious shift?

WTV: Somewhat so. In *Rainbow Stories* I was aware of not wanting to use the pyrotechnics when they weren't appropriate, whereas in *Angels*, particularly in the first half, pyrotechnics was the whole purpose of the book. I wrote *Angels* to enjoy myself by letting myself go to invent whatever I could come up with. That pyrotechnical or improvisational approach created the book's own structure, in effect — although, of course, once I let things loose, I would then go back and try and impose some kind of a story structure on it. But with *Rainbow* most of the time I was working at something which had a predefined structure, not just something that was creating its own. For instance, since I was working from a structure of fact with the documentary pieces (which for some reason the reviews have generally focused on), then I wanted to present the fact in certain way and I couldn't take such liberties as to obscure the fact. Even the non-documentary stories were also more focused and limited simply because they were stories. The reason I wanted to write *The Rainbow Stories* after *Angels* was partly a matter of my wanting to create these discrete artifacts as opposed to something like *Angels*, which used a sort of "writing-by-the-yard" approach and could easily have been ten thousand pages longer.

LM: What you've just said helps explain that comment you made somewhere about your view that the "diffuseness" of *Angels* was its main virtue of the book — while it was also the quality of the book most criticized by reviewers.

VW: The reactions to *You Bright and Risen Angels* were interesting. Some people seemed to be really bothered by the "diffused" quality of the book, while others have been increasingly disappointed with succeeding books precisely because they don't do that. My editor for *Angels*, Bob Harbison, was a big fan of that book, but he's pretty much hated everything I've written since. He has a right to feel that way because the other books are very different and in a sense (though not *every* sense) less ambitious.

LM: On the other hand, I see a lot of connecting threads through all of your books. And I certainly wouldn't say that *The Ice Shirt* is less "ambitious" than anything else you've done.

WTV: This has nothing to do with "ambition," but I've certainly tried to *improve* myself from book to book. For instance, I think that in each book my general ability to depict character has increased. I'm especially proud of this in the sequel to *The Ice Shirt—Fathers and Crows*. I'm also learning more about plot as I go — recognizing what's essential and what's extraneous. I'll never write a perfect book because no one ever has, but I feel that my books are constantly getting better. Which makes me happy.

LM: I was intrigued with the way you "appropriate" (or "collaborate with") the original materials you use as the basis of some of what appears in *The Ice Shirt*. What sort of research was involved in writing this book? I gather from your elaborate list of acknowledgments that you went around and looked up original materials. Were a lot of these translations of this original Norse material — the sagas, and so on?

WTV: Right. Unfortunately, I wasn't able to get any real professional help for *The Ice Shirt* on the Norse side, which was frustrating. There was one guy at the University of Greenland who would have helped me, but by the time a friend put me in touch with him the book was already in proof stage. The Icelanders and the people who specialize in Norse studies in the U.S. weren't really interested in what I was doing and couldn't be bothered. I'm sure there are some errors in my portrayal of the Norse. I've been interested in the sagas for a good twelve to fifteen years. I have a bunch of them in translations that I know fairly well, so it was easy for me to sit down and work with them. Visiting some of the places in Iceland and Greenland helped bring them alive for me in ways that just reading about them never could. But I've always felt that when an original text I'm using says something then I have no right to say the opposite. So, say, if there is a recorded speech somewhere, then I'll try and use that speech in my novel, although I may change it a bit. When novelists are working with original texts, we're always walking a tightrope between self-indulgence (if you don't try and do something "original" with this material) and plagiarism (if you go too far in the direction of "slavish accuracy"). My own feeling is that as someone who has an imagination I have a perfect right to work from these other sources, but my aim should be embellishing them, not distorting them.

LM: What sorts of "embellishments" are involved? For example, how much original information did you have about two main women characters in *The Ice Shirt,* Gudrid and Freydis, and how much did you supply?

WTV: They appear in "The Vinland Sagas," which have been translated by Penguin in a very slender paperback of fifty pages or less. The sagas are very taciturn and don't tell you much about the motivation of characters. Gudrid is the real heroine of the two sagas, although, in one of the sagas Freydis comes across as worse than the others (that is, in one of the sagas Freydis murders people and in the other one she doesn't). But in both versions Gudrid is this steadfast woman who is beautiful and fortunate and marries well. Everyone admires her and she seems to be a good person. And that was how I originally wanted to portray her. But the more I read over the sagas the more irritated I felt about her because she seemed too much like a goody-goody. I also started seeing that everything she was doing was really to her advantage, which to my mind made her actually worse than Freydis. I respect a villain who is an honest villain. In that way the character of Gudrid in the sagas was gradually transformed. If the anonymous authors of the two sagas could read what I have written, they'd probably feel I had very stubbornly and wrongheadedly distorted the character of this virtuous women they admired. But I feel that everything I've done with them is implicit in the tale.

LM: Why do you refer to yourself on the title page as "William the Blind?" Is that a reference to your worries about your eyesight, or is it something more metaphorical?

WTV: It's partly playing around and partly due to the fact that the sagas often have little monikers attached to the characters. "So-and-So the Lame," or "So-and-So the Priest," that sort of thing. "William the Blind" seemed like an appropriate one to give myself because I'm so nearsighted. It's maybe especially appropriate because I am always trying to understand or "see" things and I never really do.

LM: In your acknowledgments to *The Ice Shirt* you specifically mention Ms. Andrea Juneau, the coeditor of *Re/Search,* as serving as model for the form of Gudrid, and the transvestites Miss J and Miss Gidding for "a complete presentation of man to woman transformations" on which you based a scene in your novel. Most fiction writers don't present this sort of direct acknowledgement of specific autobiographical basis of a scene or episode, because they're worried this might either make their works sound "derivative" or destroy the illusion of the reality of the fiction. But all along you've never seemed much interested in erecting that illusion — or in maintaining that distinction between fiction and non-fiction, generally.

WTV: That's definitely true. I'm a very visually oriented writer. I have some painter friends who tell me that it's much easier for them to draw a picture of what my writing would look like than it is with most writers. That is because I'm always taking care whenever I can — particularly in something like *The Ice Shirt* or *The Rainbow Stories,* where it isn't just a work of the imagination — to try and see real things which then I can describe accurately. To do anything otherwise is an act of disrespect (again, that wasn't so much the case in *You Bright and Risen Angels* because there my purpose was to use my imagination solely). It's just as important and valuable to me to go to Greenland's Landsmuseum and handle a polar bear skull as to talk to my transvestite friends and see how they do what they're doing. I didn't feel any compunction about putting in the scene with the transvestites because that scene gave me the best access to what a transformation from a man into a woman would really involve. It's hard these days to find spirit women who'll go around touching men and making them turn into women. So this was the best I could do.

LM: In all of your books so far you transport readers fluidly from different worlds, times, and reality zones. It's almost as if you want readers to recognize that their own worlds are more open-ended and more fluid, temporally and spatially, than they realize — that they're not just sealed off.

WTV: People would be better off if they realized that their own particular world was not privileged. Everyone's world is no more and no less important than everyone else's. To have as many worlds as possible that are invested with interest or meaning is a way of making that point. I've gradually begun to see that I can use even my footnotes and glossaries and other sorts of materials to create some of this sense.

LM: This idea of forcing people to recognize that their worlds aren't the only ones — and of creating contexts that bring together different perspectives and world views — seems like one of the underlying impulse behind *The Rainbow Stories,* where nearly all the stories deal with people who have been radically marginalized in one way or another (prostitutes, homeless alcoholics, murderers, underground guerilla artists like Mark Pauline and the Survival Research Lab, and so on).

WTV: I definitely wanted to create a context so that people in these different worlds could see each other. I originally had more hope about that than I do today. Now the most I would hope is that people reading the stories would have a moment of thinking, "Oh, they're people too, and this is kind of nice." I'd hoped originally that somehow maybe if I described them well enough that then a few people would say, "Oh, they're people and maybe I should even *talk* to them." But I don't really have that belief or hope any more that any work of literature could do that no matter how well it was written.

LM: What changed your mind?

WTV: Getting a bit more experienced. Seeing the way people treat each other. Younger people like to hope that maybe somehow they can change the world — and not just change it in the sense of moving it from one random state to another (which is what is always going to happen), but somehow to make the world *better*. But at a certain point you see more clearly that the world is obviously no better now than it ever was. My current thinking is that literature isn't enough to bring people together to produce real understanding. Some sort of action is required, but right now I don't know what that action might be or how it would work. In fact, I'm pretty sure that it'll never be any better than it is now. Given that, all anyone can ever hope to do is either change a few specific things in a few specific ways (which will probably change again after you finish tinkering with them), or else help yourself and other people accept the fundamental viciousness and inertia of things. Religion does that, for example. Literature can too.

LM: It's a little like the way psychotherapy sometimes isn't able to help you change the way you are, but it helps you accept the way you are, so you don't feel so bad about it.

WTV: That's all you can ask really. And being able to change yourself isn't necessarily going to make you happy. You might be *less happy* if you could change, who knows? The people in *The Ice Shirt* aren't necessarily happier when they have the power to change from human to animal. King Ingjald wants to be manly so they give him the wolf's heart to eat, but even though that experience changes him, he ends up being this terrible, horrible person. He probably would have been better off if he'd just said, "Well, nothing I can do will ever make me be manly — but that's all right."

LM: Even if literature can't really change the situations you're describing, or even produce a deep understanding between people, isn't there some real value in simply opening a window on these other worlds?

WTV: If literature is valuable in and of itself (which is something I'm not sure of) then opening those windows or communication channels is one of the most valuable things that it can do.

LM: But of course, these are not just *any* worlds you've chosen to open windows onto — most of these realms are going to strike your readers as being particularly grotesque, repellant, violent, disturbing. Do you think there's something particular useful about confronting readers with things that aren't just unfamiliar to them but which will likely seem ugly or disturbing?

WTV: Absolutely. Because in doing that, you're raising the stakes. Just getting people to accept *anything* that's different without being disturbed is a step forward. But it's a far braver step to accept the presence of dignity and beauty and most of all *likeness or kinship* in something which is ugly. If more people could do that the world would be a better place.

LM: I'd like to have you talk a bit about the evolution of *You Bright and Risen Angels* and its relationship to the Afghanistan novel you had written earlier. You said somewhere something to the effect that after you had been involved in the Afghan struggle (which you couldn't really do anything to assist) that you wrote *Angels* with the objective of creating an optimistic view of revolutionary activity — you wanted "to make things better in my novel because I couldn't do this in reality."

WTV: I wanted to make things better in the book for angels because I couldn't make things better in the reality for Afghanistan. That's where the business about the triumphant revolutionary came from. Before I went to Afghanistan I'd just seen *Lawrence of Arabia* where (at least during the first half) you have this happy paradigm of the white man going out there and taking charge. On some level that's what I wanted to do when I crossed the Afghanistan border. Later, when I first started writing *Angels*, I still thought that if you could somehow put the right person in charge, he could do great, revolutionary things, could turn things around. Since I definitely had *not* been able to take charge with the Islamic commandos, I thought, 'Well, why not have *Bug* take charge, see what he could do?"

LM: Obviously, though, Bug and his revolutionary cohorts don't wind up changing anything in the end — they get sucked into the same shit.

WTV: That's because once I got more involved in describing what Bug was up against, I couldn't write the book from a positive standpoint. I couldn't honestly imagine any good things that he or any other revolutionary group could do to right the situation. The more deeply I described the situation and how it might have produced a person like Bug, the more I realized that after Bug had witnessed these bad things, he would end up badly. You see this sort of pattern everywhere. The little kids on the playground who are picked on by the bullies don't grow up being saints as a result of having been martyrs early. They end up taking it out on other people.

LM: Many readers are going to see what you're doing here in Marxist terms, with the Blue Globes and the Electricity people on the side of the capitalist system, and Bug and the other guys representing the communists.

WTV: Sure!

LM: Given the way that this revolutionary approach becomes corrupted and goes bottom up, are you implying that the whole Marxist notion of revolution is basically just a 19th-century utopian pipe dream?

WTV: Do you remember the guy who said, "If you're not a Marxist when you're under thirty you have no heart, and if you're still a Marxist when you're over thirty you have no brains?" There's some truth to that. Socialism, or something equivalent, seems to me to be a good system, something to strive for. All these puny little dogs who've been yapping about how the turn away from communism in Eastern Europe and elsewhere proved that socialism is bankrupt forever don't know what they are saying.

LM: There's a lot of specific historical contexts involved in those turns that don't have much to do with "socialism" at all.

WTV: It's like people saying the Inquisition proved that Christianity is no good — whereas it didn't prove anything. I'm personally hopeful that some day there can exist something like what the communists are talking about. The basic idea of "from each according to his ability, to each according to his needs" is very beautiful. And at some point it may be necessary to try for it.

LM: Is it possible, though, to imagine a situation in which political systems do not resort to violence? And assuming that repressive political systems do invoke violence, is it possible to have a revolutionary response that's not going to be infected with violence and bloodlust in the way it happens in *Angels*?

WTV: Probably not. Not even if your motivations are genuinely noble and pure. Violence is a part of the human character and always will be. It can't be avoided. For instance, I don't consider myself a conservative (I subscribe to a lot of notions that most conservatives would be horrified by, I'm sure), but I'm in favor of the death penalty. There are always going to be vicious, brutal, horrible people who have to be put to death for putting others to death. In that sense I think that revolutions will always have to be violent. To defend themselves against violence, they'll have to be violent too. Possibly the ugliness we've in seen Marxist governments (or so-called Marxist governments) in this century has not been the fault of the governments. I don't know. I'm no admirer of people like Stalin, but it might be that the violence used against them by the rest of the world, compelled them, at least in the beginning, to react violently.

I don't know whether Lenin was actually compelled to murder the Romanoff family and the little kids. I find that pretty vile. But I can imagine that maybe he did. When Hitler attacked the Soviet Union, obviously the Soviet Union had to respond. And we can understand the reasons, say, for the way that Albania and North Korea have become these horrible static fossils. Maybe it's not even their fault at all — although that still doesn't justify them to exist in the way that they exist.

LM: You describe J.G. Ballard's work somewhere as being "just mythological permutations of accidents and destructions with no message except there is nothing to say or feel any more." There's a way that description applies to Mark Pauline and his Research Lab, whom you devote a chapter to in *The Rainbow Stories*. But don't you feel that when people watch those things by Mark Pauline that they evoke fairly complicated responses from the audience?

WTV: No question about it. Part of what SRL does is very good and very much in keeping with what they say they're doing — which is to educate people about the extremely violent world we live in, and to help them get in touch with these vicious, empty, mechanical feelings and understand them. But another part of what they do is also very self-serving because people like to watch that stuff for the same reason they like to watch horror movies. Not because they're going to learn how to avoid it, but because they like to rub they're own noses in it. It may well be that seeing those things makes people *more violent* .

LM: There's something about this spectacle of machines crashing into one another that's very powerful to me, emotionally. It's like the response people get to car crashes, airplane crashes, or any machine malfunction. You get a kind of empathy or thrill watching machines being destroyed — the empathy of horror of watching this machine's "body" malfunction. And part of it may have to do with feeling that since we're imprisoned in this mechanical world, there's a private glee of liberation when we can watch the machines losing it.

WTV: Absolutely. For most of us the world we live in now is an immense trap or torture chamber. Everything outside this torture chamber has been destroyed by the torturers, so now there's just this vacuum. In this situation, we naturally take joy when we see that the torturers are malfunctioning. But at the same time we know that if we were to exert ourselves and actually destroy this thing we live in, then all the air would come rushing out and we'd suffocate. That would be the end. That's why violence is a very tricky issue, both for artists and ordinary people. We all share all these violent impulses, but we have ambivalent feelings about these feelings.

LM: These ambivalent feelings are certainly evident in your own work. On the one hand, there's a sense that your work is anti-violence, that you're satirizing or commenting upon the violent world we live in; but there's another sense that you empathize with this violence — almost like you're enjoying it.

WTV: I'm sure there's a sadistic undercurrent in my work, just as there is in almost anything which chooses violent subjects. At the same time, I feel it's also clear that I think that violence is wrong and that I'd be very happy if none of it was left. So, for instance, in "The Blue Yonder," it's my job to empathize with all my characters. That's what I'm after in all my work. And "The Blue Yonder" is partly about acts of violence. If I wanted to I could have tried not to empathize at all with this mass murderer, the Zombie. In that way I could have stayed righteous and pure, and the Zombie would have just been this two-dimensional character. Instead, I had to get inside the Zombie's head as well as the victim's head. The Zombie obviously enjoys killing other people in horrible ways and so if I'm doing my job, that enjoyment has to appear in the writing. In that sense the enjoyment of violence is definitely in the work. Whether or not that enjoyment is actually within *me* is something I don't know how to answer.

LM: Beginning with *You Bright and Risen Angels* and continuing right up through many of the pieces in *The Rainbow Stories* and then in *The Ice Shirt*, violence seems to be a twisted response to love, or lack of love , or love with the wrong kind of thing.

WTV: I think this kind of thing has happened in most violent people. They had feelings of yearning, or longing, or love, or whatever you want to call it, which couldn't be realized for some reason. So that love either becomes frustrated and they become violent in certain ways, or maybe the love is just completely burned out of them, so they don't care what they do to people. The other possibility (which is probably the most dangerous of all) is when these feeling of love become manipulated by someone who's suffered one of those other two things — someone who can then use that love for his own end. Someone who is a damaged soul, like Eichmann, would be an example. If Eichmann hadn't happen to have lived in Germany at a certain time, he would have died unknown. He was such a puppet of his setting that what he wound up doing wasn't completely his fault. He wanted somebody to love and then Hitler came along to fill that need; so Eichmann had to do what his puppet master made him do.

LM: That strange combination of brutality and insensitivity mixed together with passion and longing is something you really captured in *The Rainbow Stories*. For all their fascism and cruelty you depict in the skinheads, for example, there were also ways that they seem infinitely superior to people like middle-class businessmen or politicians.

WTV: Absolutely. That's one of the things I'm writing about in this new collection. There's this one guy in San Francisco who always calls Asians "gooks." Once he went into this Vietnamese restaurant and started screaming and yelling about "gook food" and how the gooks were an inferior race. Well, the door to this place didn't close properly, and later on, when he was finished screaming, he goes up to the woman and says, "Do you want me to fix your door for you?" She just looks at him and lets him. So he spends about three hours fixing the door, and then just kind of shrugs, goes outside and says, "You god-damn gook!" Then he goes off and leaves them. Now of course, you just know that it would never occur to most of these people sitting in the restaurant who thought this guy was such a horrible person for saying "gook" to fix her door. Life is strange.

LM: It's like what you just said about Eichmann. What people want to think about the skinheads or the Nazis or the people behind the Cultural Revolution in China is just that they were basically evil assholes.

WTV: That's the easy way because it allows you to feel this distance and sense of superiority. Whereas the truth is a lot more difficult to accept or deal with. Like that guy in the restaurant — what should you feel about that guy? I'm sure that's how most of the Nazis were, too. Perfectly fine people in their way.

LM: In one of your biographical statements you said that you lived inside of books as kid. Were you one of those kids who read all of the time and inhabited these realms in your imagination?

WTV: Pretty much so. I sat inside reading while the other kids were out playing. I really felt like I was *inside* those books, like I was trapped in them somehow. I was writing when I was six or seven, and I wrote a science fiction novel when I was in sixth grade. It was about these astronauts discovering another solar system, and various awful things happening to them at each planet until finally they were all killed off. I guess my work really hasn't changed too much [laughs].

LM: Were you writing pretty much steadily from the time of that science fiction novel onwards?

WTV: I've always been writing. I wrote stories and other stuff all through college, much of which I've since destroyed. I also wrote a novel just before I started the Afghanistan book.

LM: Were there any writers then who were influencing your sensibility, either through college or from your own reading? I was wondering in particular if you had discovered William Burroughs early on simply because he's about the only writer whose works I could think of which vaguely reminded me of *Angels*.

WTV: When I was working on *Angels* probably the writer I was most interested in was Lautréamont, not Burroughs. I've been impressed and influenced by different writers at different times. Right now, for instance, it seems like I've learned a lot from Mishima, Kawabata, and Tolstoy.

LM: When you were in college in the late 70s, were you reading the major postmodernists — Barthelme, Coover, Pynchon? I ask this partially because so many reviewers kept using Pynchon as a likely influence on *You Bright and Risen Angels*.

WTV: I had read some of those writers, but I hadn't read *Gravity's Rainbow* until after *Angels* came out, even though I'd read the other Pynchon books. But I don't think my stuff is a lot like Pynchon's.

LM: I don't either. Maybe there's some similarities in your use of scientific language and metaphors. But I felt Lautréamont's *Malador* was a more interesting possible source because of his emphasis on the grotesque and the dream-like, transformative qualities.

WTV: Yeah, that's a wonderful book. Lautréamont 's language is almost perfect. Poe was another writer who was influencing me. In re-reading Poe recently I was surprised at how limited the poor guy was. Basically his best few stories are almost duplications of each other. One of my recent stories, "The Grave of Lost Stories," is even about Poe.

LM: You said in an *Los Angeles Times* book review that you "admire writers who combine verbal and visual elements." And all your books, as physical objects, have a fairly complex design component that suggests that you're interested something more than just the book as medium for print. What is your background in painting and drawing?

WTV: I have no formal training. Painting or drawing for me is just an additional way of expressing that visual element that I think is so important. Just as a series of words is more than a random series of letters, a book should be more than a container for the words. So when I'm able to, I design my own books and build them with help from others because I like to collaborate. I've done this with some of my limited edition works and "book objects," like "The Happy Girls" and *The Convict Bird*. At the very least I like to have my books illustrated. I do the illustrations.

LM: What were the backgrounds of "The Happy Girls" and *The Convict Bird*?

WTV: *The Convict Bird* is about a friend of mine who is serving a life sentence in prison. I did it partly to raise a little bit of money for her, which I guess goes against this fallacy that somehow you can help people with books. I knew no one else would publish this poem in the way I wanted it to be published, so I decided I should do it myself. And since I was going to do it myself, I decided might as well go whole hog and make it exactly the way I wanted it. Matt Heckert of Survival Research Lab wound up doing the steel plate that binds the manuscript. The text of "The Happy Girls" is in my new collection, *Thirteen Stories and Thirteen Epitaphs*. In my Co-Tangent version it appears without the epitaph. As soon as I'd written the text I knew that Ken Miller's photographs would be appropriate because he and I knew some of the people in this massage parlor, and he'd taken pictures of them.

I also knew about his experience taking photographs of these prostitutes in Thailand, so the idea of a collaboration seemed like a nice idea. Our third collaborator is my friend James Lombino, who is a mechanical engineer who works for Steinway. I knew he could build an interesting box to house all this other material. But I was the person who mainly designed all these Co-Tangent book projects. So with "The Happy Girls," I wrote the story, made the metal plates, printed and painted it by hand. I'm binding it with Janice's help (she's better at threading a needle than I am). Ken Miller took the pictures and printed them and cut the mats, and James built the box.

LM: You say somewhere that "Writing or reading a book is always like being a voyeur." Has the experience of being a "voyeur" in order to write something been awkward for you at times? For example when you were doing *The Rainbow Stories*, people that were outcasts and victims in various ways were letting you into their lives and talking with you. Did knowing that you were going to be writing about these situations make you feel uncomfortable?

WTV: Reading about characters in any book is always voyeurism. And when you write, you have to develop this internal sense of yourself as a recording machine or video camera that you use to invade other people's privacy — hopefully with their consent. That part never bothered me, although I know it's bothered some of my reviewers, especially some of my British reviewers who seemed to feel I've shown very poor taste and was just using these people. I don't see it that way at all, though.

The Rainbow Stories got started because I wanted to understand more about love and how these feelings of love get misdirected. So I decided to write stories about prostitutes, and then that gradually began to encompass other lowlifes — street alcoholics, skinheads, and so on. It seemed like all these people really wanted was love, only they didn't have any idea how to get it, so their lives became more and more miserable. That misery wasn't something I had to seek out, though — it was right there, on the streets. My purpose in writing about this was to try and learn things about it — and, like I said, I started out thinking that maybe my writing could actually produce some kind of understanding between people who usually hate or ignore each other. I was hoping that maybe I could change the situation. That may have been naive, but certainly I still feel people should be given a chance to see these things and think about why they exist. In writing those pieces, one of the things that seemed very important to me was to be very faithful and accurate about what I had seen — to be as honest as I could be. I'd leave out something if it would obviously hurt someone (or hurt me), but since my goal is to be honest, I wound up having to include even a lot of things that are personally embarrassing. If you do things in that spirit of honesty, you're not using people.

On the other hand, if I were, say, Truman Capote writing *In Cold Blood* I think I would feel more ashamed of myself, because he must have known that people were going to read what he'd written more out of titillation than to learn something. Maybe I'm being unfair. I didn't finish the book because when I started reading it, it upset me in that way.

LM: Aren't you worried that people are going to read your books like that? Why wouldn't they?

WTV: It's OK if they do. I mean, I can't stop them from reading like that, and I wouldn't think of trying. It's just that I know that's not my intention, so I can feel comfortable with what I'm doing. People are free to think anything of me they want. What they think of me doesn't really matter to me.

LM: There must have been moments during the process of gathering materials for *The Rainbow Stories*. When you were frightened, or started thinking, "Uh oh, maybe I shouldn't have done this."

WTV: Sure, and I've mentioned a few of those moments in *The Rainbow Stories*. . When I started out doing the prostitute stories, I was pretty nervous about the pimps and drug dealers. One time a whore ran off with my money; when she saw me writing up my notes she must have thought I was a cop, so she had her pimp ambush me; I would have felt disgusted with myself if I had run away, but when I tried to just walk he took a shot at me (only one, though, luckily). For a while I was scared enough that I'd bring someone else with me, but that wound up being self-defeating. But these personal anecdotes aren't something really worth dwelling on. If I were to go on and on about them at great length, the whole point of what I was trying to do would be lost. It would sound as if the book is just about me.

Obviously, I didn't like it when those things happened to me. They were unpleasant and scary, and I did what I could when they happened. But that wasn't the meaning of the experience.

LM: A lot of readers would probably find it surprising that these people would talk to you at all. But my own experiences with, say, skinheads is that if you sort of talk with them on their own levels and don't treat them condescendingly, they're happy to talk with you. I mean, a lot of them were raised in the suburbs by parents who were lawyers and architects.

WTV: I know I never had any problem with the skinheads. A lot of them were warm, generous people. They all seemed to respect me when I'd show them what I'd written. I actually enjoyed the time I hung out with them. The street people were a lot harder to live with simply because their life is so awful — you had the fleas, this horrible booze you had to drink, the smells, shaking hands with people whose hands are covered with shit because they don't have any toilet paper. But the street people whose brains hadn't rotted were really interesting in a lot of ways, and they were willing to tell me their stories. Really, I think anybody will open up if you seem like you have a little bit of respect and show a little bit of your own vulnerability. A lot of times, they're afraid they're more vulnerable than you are, so if they have some way they can get back at you and hurt you too, then they feel more comfortable.

LM: *An Afghanistan Picture Book* is based on your experience entering

Afghanistan with Islam commandos in the early 1980s. What were the circumstances that led to that?

WTV: While I was in Pakistan in 1982 on a tourist visa, I made some contacts in the refugee camps with some of the resistance forces; eventually I crossed into Afghanistan illegally with Islamic commandos. I'd hoped to be there for about a month, but we had to wait on the border for about ten days for our ammunition. At the time the commandos would slip in at the beginning of the season and pretty much stay there until the end of the fighting season in the fall; they couldn't leave any of their ammunition behind, so they'd bring as much of it with them as they could, because they couldn't leave any out of the country.

Anyway, since we had to wait so long at the border I only wound up being actually inside Afghanistan for a couple of weeks.

LM: You said earlier that *Angels* was written in a sense as a response to what you'd done in the Afghanistan book — that notion of creating a fictional situation where the good guys (Bug and his group) could triumph over the bad guys.

WTV: It's hard to remember. With a long, involved book like *Angels* that wound up having so many twists and turns in it, it gets confusing as to what the initial idea really was after you're finished. The *main* impulse was probably just wanting to start a new book, since I'd just finished the previous one. But my conception of *Angels* also involved having seen all these bad things in Afghanistan and wanting to right the balance somehow. Writing the novel was the only way I could do this, since I couldn't do it anywhere else. Like I said, though, it wound up that in the process of doing writing the novel, I saw that actually there was no way of righting the balance. And that there never could be.

LM: Since your conception of the book changed so dramatically while you were writing it, you obviously weren't writing from an outline or something like that? Is that the case with all your books?

WTV: I never outline in detail. The very general scheme I've come up with [for] the *Seven Dreams* project is as far as I've ever gone with trying to formulate in advance what I'm going to be doing.

LM: Since you weren't working from an outline, or even from any kind of preset notion of what is going to be happening in the novel, how did you know the book was over? What was there about that very last scene with Frank and Brandi that made you realize the book should end there?

WTV: At that time, I didn't really analyze it. It just felt like this was right for the book to end. Later on, I realized that was the right place because in a way what the whole book is all about is disappearances. This happens with the characters, so that everyone dwindles away and vanishes. And even the richness of the language at the beginning becomes much more austere toward the end. Finally, the only thing that's left is just this debased war. It's not only that the Reactionaries have won. Their monolithic order is cracking and rotting and sprouting ivy; there are shorts and brownouts and everything is generally falling to hell. All we're left with is people like Frank — these overly adaptable, empty beings scuttling around in their shells, trying in their mediocre way to still love and manipulate people. Frank has basically been taken advantage of by everyone throughout the whole book. In fact, one of the passages I cut out from the book was about how the title of the book should have really been "Frank Fairless" — how the book was really *his* book, in a way; but he was so pathetic and ill-used that even in his own book he doesn't appear very much. Everyone has been using him: Dr. Dodger is pumping him and getting all this stuff out of him; Bug is trying to turn him into a revolutionary; Milly hates him. Everyone kicks him around. Eventually, the only chance he thinks he has for love is this prostitute, Brandi. But of course all she's doing is manipulating and getting money out of him, not really giving him love or anything else. At the very end of the novel, Frank realizes that all he needs to do to get her under his thumb is to start treating her the way that all these other people have been treating everyone else in the book — which means he should just start promising her all these things that he doesn't have and is never ever going to give her. So the book ends with old Frank sort of coming into his own. Now he's just as crummy and "mature" in his own way as the Blue Globes are.

LM: What was the origin of that image of the Blue Globes?

WTV: The first commercial transmission of alternating current took place in Telluride, Colorado around the turn of the century. They originally used wooden power poles, which weren't creosote or anything, the way they are now (they didn't have these PCB resistors or anything like that). As a result, often times the power poles would short and even catch on fire, and there would be these huge blue globes of ball lightning on top of the globes.

LM: There are several mysterious figures who are mentioned and kind of appear offstage-like that guy Phil Blaker, who is described as "owning Mars." I kept expecting you to clarify what the situation was with him, and the Martians (and the "Vegans") and so on, but you never did. Were you originally intending to do more with Blaker and the Mars business?

WTV: No. Blaker was never more in the book. I just enjoyed having him there. His presence in the book was absolutely pointless and inscrutable — just another one of the many sides of the Reactionaries squabbling among themselves. All the reader can know about him is that he was as vicious and awful as the other Reactionaries, and that's all you really need to know about him. Actually in terms of the Mars business, I'd thought at one point of having Wayne go to Mars. Wayne was doing these twelve Herculean labors for Parker and Mr. White — attacking the Beetle Guards, recovering the lenses of the miraculous Macropodia (which contains the entire universe in it), and in the end killing the Great Beetle and destroying the insect breeding grounds. I could have very easily whisked him off to Mars to do something for one of his other labors, but finally I felt like it wasn't needed.

LM: Do you recall what it was that gave you the initial idea to use the bugs in all these different ways?

WTV: Originally, I didn't know where the bugs were going to be in the lineup — whether they'd be with the Reactionaries or against them. But once I started working with them I realized that bugs are a good metaphor for [what] most of these characters are, deep down. Because bugs are amoral. You can't blame them for being that way. Bugs aren't courageous. They're always scuttling in and out of crevices, always trying to better themselves; they're always prepared to hide, and always ready to attack. With the possible exception of social insects, they don't have a concept of friendship or kindness, or mercy. In other words, bugs have developed the same kind of practical survival mechanisms that all the people in *Angels* have. Survival by this amoral expediency of hiding, scuttling, grabbing what's available, attacking when you have to. I also thought it would be interesting to imagine how bugs feel....

LM: A minute ago you said that sometimes the extreme case helps dramatize the general one. I'm reminded of your epigraph to *Angels*, "Only the expert will realize that your exaggerations are really true." I think there's an interesting aesthetic at work there that you find people like Kafka and the magic realists applying: by pushing something to the exaggerated or fantastic, the "reality" of the thing can come through more clearly.

WTV: There's a lot of truth to the idea that if there's any meaning or backbone to something, a lot of times the way to get at it is to keep forcing it into a more exaggerated caricature of itself. Eventually you'll reach some kind of limit where nothing is left but the exaggerated essence of the thing. Then you can see what the thing really is because everything is in sharper relief. That surface "realism" of ordinary life (and of most fiction) covers up a lot of important things that artists need to recover for people. You can also go at this from the opposite direction, where you take something real but extraordinary [and] make it sound ordinary, like what you find in Richard Hughes, *A High Wind in Jamaica*. It's about these kids who get kidnapped by pirates, who are very cruel; then later on when the kids get a chance they turn the tables and get the pirates horribly punished. The book works because it's so understated.

LM: Clearly thus far you've not been much into understatement....

VM: Well, certainly the reason that *Angels* works (if it works) is because it's an overstated book. There's no pretense of hiding the cruelty and anguish and everything else that the book is about. At the same time I wanted people to be entertained by the book and enjoy it, which they can also do when it's a cartoon.

LM: This method seemed very close to magical realism you find in Marquez and some of the other Latin American writers. Were they people you were interested in?

WTV: Sure. I loved *A Hundred Years of Solitude.* The problem right now, of course, is that this whole magic realism thing has become a gimmick; it seems very easy to do, so everyone is doing it. But at its finest it's really beautiful. I'd say that what I do with my own use of exaggeration isn't quite like this, though.

LM: Early on you, when you're referring to Ambrose Bierce being saved by Dr. Dodger's Special Elixir, and his inability to remember things, you say, "Such mental haziness is in order, given the delightful vagueness of the terrain — springy moss padding the continent, golden idols and lost gimcrack empires a dime a dozen, sentient insects and clean mountains without sharp peaks to puncture balloons and dreams; and a foggy sort of peace generally." That passage seemed to have to do with that idea of the "diffuseness" that you mentioned before — and why it's appropriate in this book. It's almost like a gloss on the narrative strategy you going to use here.

WTV: Yeah, I agree. It's the same kind of thing as when I refer to Wayne's "cartoon heart." You find phrases like that throughout the book, just by way of reminding people that, of course, the thing they're reading is far off and distorted from the literal truth — things never really happen this way, and there's no reason to pretend that they do. That's fine, because these distortions help us look at things more closely.

If, for instance, instead of bugs and electricity, I was talking about Capitalists and Communists, or white people and black people, most Capitalists, Communists, white people, and black people wouldn't be able to read it and get the point because everyone would be already emotionally or intellectually involved in their own particular side of things.

LM: So by taking it out of the realm of so-called "reality," you make it more available to everybody.

WTV: Right, because ultimately who cares whether the Blue Globes or the Bugs win? Turning everything into this cartoon helps us see the struggle for what it is. It's a bit like what happened with that Duetscher biography of Stalin. He wrote somewhere that certain people would sometimes say that his biography was too hard on Stalin (the Stalinists would all say so, for example), so they would then have the book banned in their countries. Then some other people would say that the book was too *soft* on Stalin and have it banned in their countries. He ended up feeling that these contradictory reactions indicated he had probably done a pretty good job. Which I think he did. But it's nice that *Angels* can avoid that problem because in terms of your response to the book, it won't matter whether you're pro or anti–Stalin.

LM: I'm not so sure — I mean, in the end, you're pretty pessimistic about the prospects for any revolutionary program.

WTV: Okay, maybe what I should have said was that if you were pro–Stalin and you were *smart,* you probably wouldn't like this book. You'd be irritated.

LM: The point of view in *Angels* is very unusual — there's nothing I can really compare it to. On the one hand, you have Big George, who implies he is able to shift in and out of various characters who were dead; and you also have "The Author," who is able to press the resurrection button and bring to life Bug, Catherine, and Parker. It almost seems there's a conflict going on there between Big George and the Author. What gave you the idea to use this very peculiar point of view?

WTV: It had to do with what I was talking about earlier about the book's initial purpose and failure to fulfill that purpose. You might say that "The Author" is the one who wants Bug to save the world (and the Afghans, and everybody else) while Big George is the one who actually controls events and makes sure that this can't happen. Another way to put it would be to say that "The Author" was the one who wanted his characters to be able to realize themselves and Big George was the force of life and fate, or God, or whatever you want to call it — or the computer. What George represents is that even if people realize themselves, eventually they're going to age and die. To start with, people are most likely not going to get what they want; and even if they *do* get what they want, they won't be able to make use of it. That's simply what life is. So "The Author" is optimistic and Big George is pessimistic — or realistic depending on your point of view.

LM: So these perspectives are really aspects of your own divided self.

WTV: Yeah. Except I like to think I'm a nicer person than Big George is.

LM: In terms of your use of yourself in your books, you said in one of your interviews that you felt *The Rainbow Stories* was an advance over *Angels* because your narrator "gives more away of himself." That's I suppose more obvious in *The Rainbow Stories* because there you directly reveal a lot about yourself, you take chances in making fun of yourself and playing with yourself in a sense, in all kinds of ways. I take it that was something you felt was important in that book — being honest about yourself, so you could be honest about what the actual experience was like.

WTV: Honesty about the beauty and brutality of other people is the big thing about *The Rainbow Stories.* Therefore I felt the least I owed them was to be honest about myself. So, for instance the scene in "Ladies and Red Lights" where I had a call girl up to my apartment was originally in *Angels*, except there I had that happen to Frank. Later on, it seemed like describing it that earlier way wasn't a particularly courageous or honest thing. If I was going to make use of that experience then I should do so in the way I did in *The Rainbow Stories*.

LM: On the other hand, *Angels* struck me as a very brave novel on your part precisely because even there you reveal a lot of your own vulnerability and foolishness in the book. You did this in various ways, not only as embodied through characters, but also through your presentation of "The Author" and his relationship with women, his blindness about love and the pain this causes him. You see this very strongly near the very end of the book, when you're talking Catherine, the Queen Bee. All this by way of saying: Didn't you feel that you were revealing a lot of yourself in that first book, too?

WTV: Sure I did. But in *Angels* these revelations are partly covered up simply because it's sometimes more difficult to know exactly where the fiction or the imagination stops and the reality begins. In *The Rainbow Stories*, it's usually a lot clearer which things actually happened. When I did things that a lot of people would disapprove of, I didn't try and hide or disguise them by presenting them through those layers of ambiguity that the narrative perspective creates in *Angels*. I don't want to knock down the way I was dealing with these things in *Angels*. It simply wasn't as direct.

LM: One of the commonplaces about writers is that it's usually their first novel that's the most autobiographical in some kind of direct sense. And even though it's obvious that *The Rainbow Stories* is the most "nakedly" autobiographical one of your books (and you interject yourself into *The Ice Shirt* in a lot of ways, too), I still had a sense that a lot of the materials in *Angels* had powerful autobiographical sources. Those scenes with Bug and the swimming team, and a lot of the other adolescent scenes, seemed very authentic in the way it *felt*, even though they often seemed very fantastic from a literal standpoint.

WTV: You might say that *Angels* reveals more of my emotions, *The Rainbow Stories* reveals more of actions, and *The Ice Shirt* reveals more of my thoughts.

LM: The color symbolism in *The Rainbow Stories* is one of the things that seems to unify the book in various ways. How did the use of color begin to work in with the evolution of the book?

WTV: The color symbolism occurred to me very early on, although it wasn't something I started out with. When I work, I tend to write several different things at once. In this case, the first things I started on were the "Skin Head Story," "Yellow Rose," "Blue Yonder," and "Ladies and Red

Lights." The first pieces I finished were the skinhead story ["The White Knights"] (which originally had a different name) and "Yellow Rose," followed by "The Wild Blue Yonder." About that time I suddenly realized that this color symbolism was starting to emerge. I didn't have much of the book completed at that point so it was easy to go back and adjust those pages to make them fit into the rainbow symbolism. "Violet Hair" was finished last and was the one easiest to write. It's also the one I think that is actually the best. The Poe epigraph I put in when I had about three-quarters of the stories finished.

LM: Once you recognized that this color symbolism was emerging, did you begin to consciously seek out certain types of experiences that would in some ways fit into this framework? Or was the framework always something you imposed later on?

WTV: I won't pretend that once I had the color scheme pretty well fixed in my mind that then I started cold-bloodedly trying to go out and make every experience I had try to fit this scheme. I knew more or less what I wanted this collection to be about, and the color scheme simply seemed to supply a kind of overlay or connection between the things I wanted to talk about. I thought of the book almost like a novel because it has a structure that allows specific patterns of themes and symbols to develop and clarify themselves . That's why I resisted when some of my editors wanted to cut and rearrange some of the stories. For instance, they thought that "Scintillant Orange" was anti–Semitic and so it shouldn't appear in the book at all. I wouldn't let them do that for various reasons. I feel very strongly that there is a real movement in the arrangement of the stories.

So, for instance, the stories are arranged so that "darkness" gradually emerges more and more from the stories, until at the end, you wind up with the X-rays, which aren't even in the visible spectrum. And this whole business about trying to know the Other, see into these Other worlds, should gradually become more and more obvious. I also more or less alternated the documentary stories with the imaginative stories to make the point that it doesn't matter in these worlds whether these things literally happened or not. They're both true in different ways.

LM: So these imaginative pieces were conceived concurrently with the more journalistic ones — they weren't works you had written earlier and then integrated later on?

WTV: They were all written at the same period I was writing the San Francisco pieces and more or less finished up at the same time too. That's why I feel the book falls somewhere in between a novel and a collection of short stories. There's definitely a certain movement and progression that's important in the book, that unifies what's being presented and justifies its arrangement. On the other hand, certain stories could have been replaced by other stories about different characters, so in that sense it's not quite a novel either. I'm not sure you can call something a novel if you can cut out one episode and replace it with a different episode involving different people without it really mattering.

LM: You've mentioned your desire for *The Rainbow Stories* to allow readers share to share different roles and worlds. How is this reconciled with your remarks in [the] *Melody Maker* interview that in order to stay sane, "Every individual has to think that their own world is more true than all others"? Does this ability for you to move into these other worlds, literally and empathetically, imply that the act of writing is for you a deliberate leap into a kind of insanity, or schizophrenia? Or is it the case that maybe you weren't ever able to really get into that other world?

WTV: My primary world is just this one basic "dream world" that I've been in from the time I was a kid. All these worlds that I see and write about are equally real and can coexist, so it's not like I have to leave my own world in order to inhabit them. That's my ability I guess. But this also means that these different worlds are also equally *unreal*, so I can't take anything too seriously. None of them take precedence over any others.

LM: Your works frequently have a powerful edge of extremity and violence to them. Were you involved or drawn somehow to the punk scene back in the 70s, while you were growing up?

WTV: No, I never was. I was aware that it existed, and of course being in San Francisco I saw it. But, no, I was never involved with it. I wouldn't say that I have ever been part of any movement.

LM: Were there any other figures who [you] feel might have influenced your sensibility while you were growing up? Painters or artists working in other art forms? What about other authors (I was wondering, for example, about Burroughs).

WTV: My influences are pretty spread out. I wouldn't say that there's anyone that has influenced me more than anyone else. I haven't read all of Burroughs's books, but some of them I like a lot. I think *The Ticket That Exploded* is terrific, and I liked *Junkie* a lot, too. In terms of visual artists, like I said earlier, I've never had any formal training in painting or drawing. I've been learning to express myself more with things like dock printing and so on and so forth. Certainly, there are a lot of visual artists I admire, like Paul Klee, who's given me a lot of intuitions in his work. I've gotten a lot of the obsessive love stuff from Klimt (and it's helped sometimes to look at his faces).

LM: Do you have any sympathy with the whole concept of postmodernism? Does it seem to make sense to you that certain things have been happening since the sixties — the various social, aesthetic, even technological things — that has created a situation so that artists growing out of the culture now are in some ways are operating differently than they were back in the 1950s, say?

WTV: I'd say that's true, but I don't think "postmodernism" is the greatest name for what this new context is. It's like in 1987 the auto dealers come out with the 1988 new car. By the time of 1988 they've now got to come out with a car they call the 2000 model. And what are they going to call the one the next year? Obviously postmodernism is bound to have its sequel, and that sequel's bound to have its sequel too. The truth is that every generation of artists is different and new from the one before it. That's certainly true today, but it's always been true.

LM: One of the things that's usually associated with postmodernism is something you seem to do very naturally or intuitively — that is, the way you problematize all sorts of distinctions that people used to make between fiction and autobiography, or between "realism" and fantasy or science fiction. You seem very comfortable with the notion that all these different worlds or perspectives co-exist and provide "windows" into each other. And in fact, it seems to me that your generation takes a lot of this for granted in ways that, say, the 60s generation of experimental writers couldn't.

WTV: At this point, what you're describing is probably true throughout the culture, not just in the arts. You see it in advertising, in television, in shop windows, anything. The gain from that is obvious: greater freedom in every way, more available options. The loss from it is a sense of disorientation, plus when it's done sloppily (the way it often is) there's no thought given to context. I honestly believe that most people nowadays, including writers, know less of the body of facts, and aesthetics — the basic core of information about the work and culture and so forth, that makes up our heritage — than people did earlier. That's very unfortunate because it make it impossible to place these new options or combinations within any context that means anything.

LM: Certainly one thing that strikes anybody reading your books is simply this wide, encyclopedic range of reading. Where does that come from?

WTV: About 95 percent of what I read is done for my work. But since my work is pleasure, I'm also reading for pleasure. The other readings I do are from random things I pick because they look interesting. For instance, the day before yesterday I went out to the bookstore and bought a catalogue on torture instruments of the Inquisition, Mishima's novel, *The Sound of Waves*, this Eliade book on Shamanism that I really want to read, a book on artistic methods (it's about various ways of painting and drawing and sculpture). That's pretty typical of what I might be looking at, excluding the stuff I read for my work, which I keep in this white box over here. It's mainly anthropological works about Indians, but also some religious materials.

LM: In *Angels* you created a lot of long paragraphs that seem to have a kind of musical structure to them (improvisation); it's almost like the reader can physically see your imagination grappling with an idea or image and just going with it, pushing it on down the page in the paragraph. That seems less obvious in *The Ice Shirt*.

WTV: I'd say that all the books in *Seven Dreams* are probably going to be more terse in that regard. In many ways when I'm working with these symbolic histories my own proclivities have to become more muted. I like what I'm doing here as much as anything else I've written, but the stylistic effects are more reined in by the overall structure I'm working with. Unfortunately, you can't do everything in a book anchored by fact that you can with something where your imagination is completely unbounded, like *Angels*. It can't be as spontaneous because it gets its legitimacy from something else. Hopefully, what it gains from that is greater than what it loses the other way.

The same thing is true with this stack of papers here called *Whores for Gloria*. It's a novel that was my first attempt to create a symbolic history. It's really a series of true stories which were taped. The basic devices are about this alcoholic who imagines this perfect woman, Gloria, whom he loves (we don't know if she actually existed or not). He pays all these prostitutes not just to have sex with him but to tell him happy stories he can use as memories of himself and Gloria. When I was interviewing prostitutes I found that these whores would start telling a happy story that would end up being just terribly sad. They could never tell a happy story. So this guy always keeps twisting these stories around in his mind to make them happy again, which they aren't. He's not either. He's a terribly pathetic, unhappy person.

LM: Don't you ever wonder or worry about suffering the fate of the moth who, as you say in "Scintillant Orange," "must die happily in the fire"?

WTV: Fire is neither a big attraction nor a phobia for me. But when my time comes to die, I hope I can die like the moth in the flame. That seems like the best way to go.

The Write Stuff ALT-X
Interview (1994)

AL

William T. Vollmann: I was born in Los Angeles. My dad was a graduate student there, and we didn't have a lot of money. We lived in this slum neighborhood. There were these reconditioned army barracks that got really, really hot in the summertime. There wasn't any air conditioning or anything. It was called veterans' housing. It was in Westwood. I think a freeway has been built over it since. There were lots of low-income families. I was kind of afraid of them. I used to get beaten up a little bit when I went outside, but I made some friends. My family was there until I was about five. Then we moved to New Hampshire where my dad had a teaching job. Then we moved around after that.

AL: When did you think that you would become a writer? Could you talk about your early days?

WTV: Real young. When I was about six. Started writing. I didn't think about it. I knew that I really liked to write. So that's what I did. I had a couple of jobs when I got out of college. My first job was being a secretary at this re-insurance company. I took guys' coats off for them when they came in. They would come in and stick out their arms like wings. That meant I had to pull off their coats and ask them what they wanted in their coffee. So this was in 1981. I was living in San Francisco. I did that for eight months. I was making about eight hundred dollars a month. I saved up enough money to go to Afghanistan. I went to Afghanistan with the rebels for a while. Came back. Went to Berkeley. I was going to be in the graduate program, but I dropped out after a year and never went back. I became a door-to-door canvasser. It wasn't too bad in the summer. Then, in the fall, it began to rain. Everyone dropped out except all these pimps and drug addicts. I had such a good time hanging out with them. I was a terrible canvasser though. I just really enjoyed how they talked. Some of these were really scary guys.

AL: So you wrote your first book about Afghanistan around that time, which was finally published a year ago. You came back to San Francisco. How did *You Bright and Risen Angels* come about?

WTV: *An Afghanistan Picture Show* wasn't published for a long time. I kept fiddling with it. I made revisions and rewrites. I added stuff about what I thought now, and what I did then. It has some depth to it. After I was a canvasser, I became a computer programmer. They sort of took me. I don't know why. I kind of fooled them because I didn't really know anything about computers. I lasted about a year or so before they fired me. When I was doing that I would go down there to the office. I don't drive. Sometimes I would stay all week. After everyone else had left, I would still be sitting at my desk, and I wrote *Angels* on their computer real late at night. I would eat candy bars from the vending machine for breakfast, lunch, and dinner. Then, when it was time to sleep, I would just get underneath my desk. I'd put a big waste basket in front of my head, so the janitors couldn't see me when they were vacuuming.

AL: That book was very strange and psychedelic. But soon after that, you turned to more documentary modes of writing with *Rainbow Stories*. What was the genesis of that much different book?

WTV: I guess it was because I was able to meet this guy, Ken Miller, the street photographer. At that time, he was in his heyday on Haight street. He knew everybody. Everybody knew him. He'd just go out, and all the alcoholics would call out "Hey Ken!" He'd just shaved his head, become a skinhead, and he lived with the skinheads. So they kind of liked him. He took all their pictures.

AL: With you, traveling and writing come hand in hand. From the beginning, you are going off to Afghanistan doing research. Since then, you've gone to the magnetic north pole. Could you describe some of these adventures?

WTV: With *Rainbow Stories*, I tried to go into all these different worlds, trying to understand what was going on. So it wasn't too much different going to different countries. Going from the Haight to the Tenderloin was like as different as going from Iceland to Greenland. It was very interesting for me, and I've never lost the desire to keep doing that. And now, I have a little more money. I travel to further places: that's all. It's all the same thing.

Going to the North Pole was pretty creepy. To prepare for such a trip I had to take a lot of food, a couple of stoves. You figure that in those temperatures, you can't count on one stove. In fact, when the gas runs out, you can't really replace the gas on one stove because if you take it apart, the O ring isn't going to stick any more. It's so cold. And if it leaks off the O ring, you don't want gas dripping near the open flame. The main thing is you've got to have lots and lots of clothes. You wear the clothes long enough, and they start freezing with your sweat.

AL: You talked about how *Rainbow Stories* had to do with Ken Miller. Is your new book, *Butterfly Stories*, also about your experiences with Ken Miller? The main story being about a journalist and a photographer going to Southeast Asia.

WTV: *Butterfly Stories* is strictly a novel. It's based on documentary research with prostitutes over there. It's about something that didn't happen, unlike the skinhead stories in *Rainbow Stories*. The journalist falls in love with one of the prostitutes in Cambodia. Gets AIDS from her. Can't find her. Goes back. Looks for her. Finally crosses the border into Cambodia just to let himself be captured by the Khmer Rouge, because he figures she's probably dead. He lets them kill him so that he can be sort of with her. Sure. I hung out. I met lots of prostitutes, but I don't have AIDS yet. I haven't been caught by the Khmer Rouge.

AL: When were you last tested?

WTV: A couple of months ago. How about you?

AL: Six months or so....

WTV: Maybe you're immune. I always tell these whores on Capp street, "Is it true what they say that if you get AIDS, all you have to do is give it to someone else and then you're cured?"

AL: You've launched this ambitious project called *The Seven Dreams: The IceShirt* and *Fathers and Crows* have been published so far. Can you talk about your experiences writing these books?

WTV: That came out of *Rainbow Stories* too, because *Rainbow Stories* was all these parking lots, where the whores were doing their business. I thought to myself, "What was the country like before all the parking lots were here?" I read a lot of Norse sagas when I was a kid, so that helped me for the first book. For *Fathers and Crows*, I didn't have any prior preparation. I didn't know anything about 17th-century Canada. It was fun to go to Canada and see what was there, read books about it, meet some Indians, work with some anthropologists. I'm real pleased with that book. I think it's a better book than *The Ice Shirt*. For that, I went to Iceland, Greenland, and Newfoundland.

AL: Do you feel that *The Ice Shirt* is your weakest book?

WTV: It's weaker than *Fathers and Crows*. It's got some good stuff in it. I'd say that my Afghanistan book is my weakest book. The first three-quarters of *The Ice Shirt* are OK. I think that the last quarter I'd do differently. I was still trying to figure out how to mix history and fiction as I went. That was the first attempt at the seven. It was harder with The Ice Shirt. I wish that I had more money too. For instance, I would've liked to have gone to Norway and Sweden for that one. If I had, that part would have been longer.

AL: Is writing an excuse to travel?

WTV: I love to travel and I love to write. I don't need excuses. I could stay in one place and write if I had to. Then it would be a different book. That's what I did for *Angels* when I was stuck in that computer place with freeways on three sides of me and sleeping under my desk. That was pretty awful. So I was just living in my head. If I had to do it again, I would. But I'd rather go to Pat Pong.

AL: So has traveling, having eaten all these candy bars, and smoking crack — has all that affected your health?

WTV: I feel like I'm in pretty good shape. When I'm at home working, I just sit on my ass, work on the computer, a Mac II. When I travel: the first couple of days are always hard. Then I get back into the swing of things. I just came back from an Arctic trip. I know every time that I go up there, for the first couple of days, I won't sleep very well because I'm not used to the cold and being on the hard ground. I get blisters. Pretty soon I get tough. The mosquitoes or the rain don't bother me so much. I take a notebook with me and write with that.

AL: How do you feel about technology? Are things getting out of hand with the growing indebtedness towards computers and technology? Are we heading towards a vortex of insanity?

WTV: I think it's really bad. I would like to abolish television and the automobile. Television because it has no reverence for time, and the automobile because they have no reverence for space.

AL: But if you abolish cars, where would whores go to do a quick hand job?

WTV: Well, I guess they would have to go under horses.

AL: Why do you write so much about prostitutes?

WTV: Why I'm interested in prostitutes is because they have everything interesting in life all together: there's love, sex, and money. What more do you want? I feel comfortable around women. Paying for sex is always an easy way to get into a woman's life, if she's a prostitute. It's always great for me when I travel someplace. If I really want to know what life is really like in one of those countries, just pick up a prostitute and live with her for a while. I see life as she sees it. I feel like I'm doing something and knowing something real fast. In a week, you learn as much as you would if you stayed in a hotel for a year. It's really great. *Whores For Gloria* is not autobiographical. I'm not an alcoholic or a veteran. I did go around in the Tenderloin asking prostitutes to tell me stories. I'd ask them to tell me happy stories, and they'd try. They'd always end up being sad stories. It's always sad when you see other people unhappy. It's not that prostitution is bad. I think that many prostitutes in Bangkok and Thailand have a pretty good life: they get boyfriends, husbands, they can go out of it when they want. Over here, there's all this shame we have about our bodies. So when someone becomes a prostitute, she becomes ashamed of herself. And then, it's a criminal thing. It's easier to get hooked on drugs. There's nothing wrong with taking drugs occasionally, but if that's all you do, it's easy to end up on your way out. So that stuff is sad for me to see. There's one story in *Thirteen Stories and Thirteen Epitaphs* that I wrote about a guy who goes to Bangkok and marries a prostitute. He would have done anything to stay with her. She felt bad that she wouldn't stay with him. There was a language barrier. She really couldn't explain to him why she wouldn't. Actually she married a couple of people, and kept doing her thing.

AL: Is observation as good as raw experience?

WTV: I think it depends on what's observation and what's participation. I started doing the crack stuff because these ladies that I was working with were smoking crack.

AL: We've talked about writing, research, observation, and so forth. Some people have accused the photographer Joel-Peter Witkin of exploitation. What is the difference between observation and exploitation? This is a culture that pays models 500 dollars an hour for their pictures, yet pays nothing to the poor or the destitute.

WTV: That's a good question. When I was writing *Rainbow Stories*, there was a piece on prostitutes in the Tenderloin called "Ladies and Red Lights." I was very concerned about exploiting them. I'd ask them questions. I'd always pay for the interviews. It was not actually that good a piece. It was a start of getting into that world. It was the best that I could do at the time. Since then, I've realized the best thing to do is that you try to become that person's friend. You do something for them. They do something for you. And everybody's happy. If you write a story about somebody, but in the meantime, she's puking in the sink because she needs her fix.... So you give her some money, and she can get fixed. She thinks you're the greatest. And you think she's the greatest too. You're both helping each other. I have some long-term relationships with some of those people. I feel like I've done good for them. I also feel grateful to them for letting me hang around and share their lives with them. So I don't think that I exploit anybody. But that's the kind of thing: it's always a matter of opinion. I was interviewed by somebody in Davis a few days ago. She kept telling me "What gives you the right to play God?" She thought I was kind of awful. All I could say was "You can believe it if you want." For instance, I'm going over to Burma to get this sex slave.

I guess they have really young girls there: eight- or nine-year-olds. They raise them like animals. Then they ship them out to whorehouses. Sometimes the Japanese want virgins and they don't want to use rubbers. So it's ideal for them to get one of these young girls. So I was interested to see how the process works, of buying a human being. Once I bought this person, I would have some kind of responsibility for her. I would try to set her up with a fruit stand, or a cigarette stand. I don't see anything wrong with voluntary prostitution, but I think that involuntary prostitution is pretty bad. So this woman said, "Well, you're giving her a taste of freedom, but probably she'll just end up the same way as she was before or worse. You're not doing her any favors." But I disagree. I figure you can't help anybody, but you can give them a chance to help themselves. If they take it, then that's great.

AL: Is the process of research crucial for writing a novel or a short story?

WTV: I think so. I think all kinds of things can qualify as research. Spending time on the street is research. The results are just as good as spending time in a library. But if you write, you have to do something like that. Or your life can be research. The important thing is you have to have something to draw on. Van Gogh and Gauguin used to frequent whorehouses. I'd call that research. They called it a "hygienic outing." I have a lot of respect for Gauguin. In fact, I was just in Madagascar for a month. I was trying to do some of the stuff he did. Not oils, but watercolors. Lots and lots of them. I made a lot of progress. Really exciting for me. Madagascar is a really wonderful place. Very friendly people. They would rip you off or kill you if they could, but they're very friendly.

AL: The other night, at Green Apple, you read a new story about crack. You said that "Crack is the only happiness." How does this figure into the new work?

WTV: I'm doing is series of real short pieces from all around the world. It's called *The Atlas*. It's set in Somalia, Sarajevo, San Francisco, and all these places I've been. So that crack story is one of them. Well, crack is certainly the only happiness in that story. Crack is a very American drug, but someone has told me that he's seen it in Belize. They're not smoking crack in Sarajevo but they would probably want it. That would keep them going.

AL: What do you think of the comparison to William S. Burroughs? I know that you have said previously that you think you are a better writer than him.

WTV: I'm not a big believer in the cut-up method. I think it was an interesting experiment. It's not how I work. I like looking at something, and writing down some notes about it, and correcting my notes, adding more notes, and so on and so forth. I like the feeling like it's totally voluntary and there's this control all the way through.

AL: What do you think technically about what you're writing?

WTV: When I write a sentence, oftentimes what I do is try to treat it like a kernel of popcorn. I'll keep packing more and more words in there. Sort of refine it, until it explodes. When it does, it has all this surface area. It's kind of complicated to trace the whole shape of the thing. But if you do, you get the whole round shape of it. And that's the way it has to be. Some of the earlier stuff is the most grammatically complex. I just try to come up with the right sentence for the right job.a

AL: Are there any contemporary writers that you think are good? You already said you liked Lautréamont?

WTV: Yeah, I like Lautréamont. I think Cormac McCarthy is really wonderful. He's terrific. Some of the older writers I like better than most contemporary writers. I like some of the real old stuff like the epics and sags. Ovid. Some of the Eastern European writers are neat.

AL: Do you write under the influence of anything besides crack?

WTV: Oh, that's no fun! Lautréamont helped me out a lot when I was starting off. I just loved those sentences. They were so beautiful, strange, and creepy, and very precise. Hawthorn I liked a lot. I liked his moral aesthetic. The stuff that I'm writing now: I try to listen to how people talk and how they live. Like that story about that crack prostitute. I think it's a good story, but I can't really take credit for it. It's not my story. It's her story. She let me into her life. I still see her. I was able to write some nice sentences. But they were her sentences and everything happened to her.

AL: You're a very visual writer and it makes sense that you would be drawn to art and painting. Could you talk about your attraction to art?

WTV: It's just another way of seeing, just like writing notes is a way of seeing. I have a whole bunch of watercolors that go along with the crack story. I think that the crack story stands alone, but it's just so much richer with the watercolors. You can see these portraits of women doing crack, spreading their legs on the bed, sitting on broken glass on the sidewalk. It just adds something. I'm doing more and more with the visual arts now. So I'm expecting in the next couple of years that there will be fewer books coming out. I'm doing these CoTangent books and I love illustrating my writing.

AL: Will you ever write some plays or do some theater?

WTV: I would enjoy doing theater. I started working on this story about The Queen of the Whores. I actually paid some prostitutes once to put on a skit on what they thought The Queen of the Whores would be like. I rented a space and let them go with it. I learned some stuff from them. I would really enjoy doing that some time.

AL: What would "the queen of the whores" be like?

WTV: I imagine her as someone who lives in the sewers underneath the

Tenderloin. She has all these pimps or enforcers. Everything is lit up by these trash cans that are full of trash and gas and diesel fuel. So there's these lurid orange flames shooting up all over the place. Some sort of concrete place. They bring people in, and she decides what's going to be done with them. When I was auditioning people for The Queen of the Whores, I realized there should be a good queen and a bad queen. A lot of them wanted to be the bad queen. They really got into the power. They wanted to torture people and kill them. What made me surprised and happy was that everyone got into it. I didn't even know what it meant. They knew. As soon as I said "queen of the whores." They would say "Oh yeah, I do this, I'll do that."

AL: Your novels are attempts to get to know the self, and simultaneously they are about knowing the other.

WTV: It's so hard. Everyone lives in his or her own world. You don't realize how small that world is. You exclude all these people in all these different worlds. They're just these featureless blurs that go on. It takes a lot of effort to get into these other worlds. There's an infinite number of them, so you can never know them all. But at least you can see a few of them. You realize that people operate according to these totally opposing value systems. I remember in Cambodia. It is really bad to touch someone on top of the head or the soles of their feet. There was this one beggar crawling around. He had his feet drawn up against his stomach to make sure he wasn't going to offend anybody. His knees were getting all cut up, crawling around in that broken glass. But he had to do it. He just couldn't point the soles of his feet at anybody. It was strange for me coming back.

AL: Are Americans self-indulgent and trapped inside the self? Is the self a prison? Do you feel that through your writing you've broken out of the self towards the other?

WTV: I think that I've tried, and to the extent I've succeeded I've become a misfit, because most people don't want to know the other. The more I succeed, the more people here really don't like me. They don't feel comfortable with me.

AL: Does that process subvert contentment and happiness?

WTV: I think it does. If you see someone that feels really miserable. And before, he was just someone that wasn't human. You go back home and can't be bothered. Then if you keep thinking about that person, it's kind of awful. When I was over in Sarajevo, I tried to get this Serbian girl out. I couldn't do it. I came back and I felt guilty. I'll probably not stop thinking about it. When I was in Kenya, there was one girl who wanted to stop being a prostitute. I got her into an eight-month course learning how to be a seamstress. It was 700 dollars. It was a lot for me. But there was no way she could have done it. I feel good about that. But at the same time, I think about all the people who would also want to take that course. It's harder to be happy when you think about that stuff. You just can't do enough.

AL: After all this time and travel, how American do you feel?

WTV: I was born here. I feel some identity and some loyalty to the place that I've eaten so many meals in. But I feel like I've become a little unglued. In a way, it's kind of liberating and other ways it's kind of scary.

AL: This is a time that we know all politicians are ineffective and mediocre. Can you think of one politician that actually helped anybody? If you really try to help anybody, they kill you, right?

WTV: Or if you try hard enough to help, there's a good chance you might get carried away, and kill them. Like when I was in Cambodia. I got to meet Pol Pot's brother. Very interesting guy. He said that when Pol Pot was a little kid, he would never take part in slaughtering any of the chickens. The old people loved him the best, because he was so kind to them. He went off to Paris just to get a better education. He started to learn some Marxist theory. He thought "The greatest good for the greatest number. This whole capitalist superstructure is really rotten. What we have to do is control the means of production." He went further than Marx and Mao. He said we have to get rid of all these specialists. Just get back to primary production. There's a lot of truth in it. Where I think he went wrong was he said I don't trust anyone but myself to do it. It's got to happen in my lifetime. So I have to eliminate all these large groups that will or might oppose my plans. I believe that the guy really, really meant well. That's what so depressing about it.

AL: What kind of influence do you want to have on your readers?

WTV: Sometimes girls send me naked pictures. Mishima's private army appeals to me. I think he used it for the wrong end. It was stupid and pointless. I would enjoy having a non-violent army to work against the automobile. Something like that. That would be satisfying. I've been working on a long essay called "Rising Up and Rising Down." It's about why I think violence is justified and when it isn't. Sometimes it is! What sorts of things it's right to try and do if you're going to cause some damage or possibly hurt somebody, or when you should get involved at all. I'm still trying to understand it.

AL: What is your theory on writing, communication, and meaning? You talk about "honesty" in some of your essays in *Conjunctions* and *The Review of Contemporary Fiction*. There is all this post modernism and experimentation going around. You seem to be opposed to all that?

WTV: I don't understand a lot of it. I studied Comparative Literature at Cornell. Structuralism was real big then. The idea of reading and writing as being this language game. There's a lot of appeal to that. It's nice to think of it as this playful kind of thing. But I think that another way to look at it is, "Look, I just want to be sincere. I want to write something and make you feel something and maybe you will go out and do something." And it seems that the world is in such bad shape now that we don't have time to do nothing but language games. That's how it seems to me.

AL: *The Seven Dreams* is an ambitious project. You've written about half of it. How long is it going to take to finish this? You still have four books to go, right?

WTV: Yeah, that's right! A few more to go. Let's see. The fourth one is half done and the last one is half done. So I'll finish it in five or ten years. I'm not in any hurry. I don't know if I'm going to be around because I do some risky things. So maybe it will all catch up with me.

AL: Don't you think that there are more important things to do rather than writing? Like enjoying your body or something?

WTV: Sometimes writing is fun. But if I didn't have something to say, maybe I would do watercolors or maybe I would improve my shooting skills, so I could be more useful in that way. I'm really interested in guns. When I went to Afghanistan, I didn't know anything about guns. I learned how important guns were in that situation. I spent a lot of time in the Arctic. I have Eskimo friends. They live by hunting. Guns have had some positive effects and done a lot of harm up there too. That's what the next of my "dreams" is about. I'm fascinated by guns. I've used a gun for self-defense a couple of times.

AL: When?

WTV: Once in the Tenderloin. I didn't have to shoot it. It was a Sig-Sauer P226 9mm pistol. I had it right here under my arm. Some black guys were going to stab me because I was a white guy in the wrong place. I just pulled out the gun and said "I'm really sorry to point the gun at you. I wish you'd leave me alone. I don't want to hurt you." They left me alone. It was really nice to have it.

Vollmann Shares Vision (2000)

MICHELLE GOLDBERG

William T. Vollmann gave me a bullet. It was hand-made, with a black pattern etched beautifully on it through some kind of oxidation process. That he'd have spare ammunition lying about didn't surprise me, but that he'd give a sweet little present to a visiting reporter did. One expects Vollmann, swashbuckling whoredog, war correspondent, quixotic freedom fighter, gun aficionado and fiction prodigy, to be gruff and imperious. After all, this is the man who, at 22, journeyed to Afghanistan in an attempt to join the fight against the Soviet occupation, who trekked into the Burmese jungle to meet one of the world's largest heroin producers and who, on a magazine assignment, kidnapped a child prostitute from Thailand and enrolled her in boarding school. His novels and short stories tend to dwell unflinchingly on the subterranean — he writes of whores, skinheads, junkies, terrorists, fetishists. Especially whores.

Yet in person, the man who makes Hunter S. Thompson look like Adam Gopnick comes off, at first, like any other suburban dad. Now 40, he lives with his wife, a radiation oncologist, in a big brick house light-filled house in Sacramento with hardwood floors covered in Middle Eastern carpets. Framed dust jackets from his dozen or so books line one wall, and there's a small jungle gym in the backyard for his young daughter. Bearded and dressed in a faded jeans, a milk chocolate brown shirt and white sneakers, he's welcoming and genial. Out of all the many writers I've interviewed, he's probably the only one who, after giving long, considered answers, looks at me and asks, "What do you think?"

None of this is to say that Vollmann's settled into middle-class complacency. He continues to report from the most brutal corners of the world, and his obsession with what the culture calls sin hasn't diminished at all. While he's also working on a series of books about the European conquest of the Americas and has recently finished a 4000-page manuscript about the ethics and justifications of violence, his art still gets much of its ballast from the intersection of sex and commerce. In his paintings — he's an enormously talented visual artist — lurid, hungry images of working girls recur incessantly. He has stacks of gorgeously done platinum printed photographs of the weathered women who work in Sacramento's Oak Park. He also makes block-printed, elaborately designed art books in editions of ten or twenty. One of them, a faux-children's story called *Convict Bird* has a steel, padlocked cover that needs to be opened with a key. Dedicated to Veronica Compton #276077, it begins, "Because so many children go about their play in ignorance of the true nature of the world, I have designed this little book for them, in sincere hopes that it will remedy this deficiency." An attached bookmark is made of a lock of black whore's hair affixed to a chain.

Finally, there's his new novel, a searing epic of almost 800 pages called *The Royal Family*. It's the kind of book that leaves reviewers grasping for adjectives, since words like stunning have been bled dry from overuse. *The Royal Family* follows down and out San Francisco private eye Henry Tyler on his search for the queen of the prostitutes, a search driven, in part, by his anguish following the suicide of his sister-in-law, whom he was in love with. Fevered, obscene and surreal, *The Royal Family* envelops you, sucking you into its strange moral universe. Partly, it's the tale of a failed utopia, as the whores briefly find succor in solidarity with their queen. But its also a parable about consumption — through John, Tyler's arrogant yuppie brother, Vollmann connects the voracious appetites of the underworld and those of the boardroom. The book resonates with questions about whether one loves people or what they symbolize. Most of all, its an engrossing story with a profundity that slyly creeps up on you while you're being blithely entertained.

MG: I read that when you were preparing to write *The Royal Family*, you hired whores to improvise some of the characters.

WTV: BBC radio was doing a little profile on me and how I work. When the reporter came to San Francisco, I was just starting to think about *The Royal Family*, and I thought it would be sort of interesting to see what people on the street felt about the idea of a queen of the prostitutes. As long as it was BBC's money, I thought why not audition them? So I got set up in a hotel with the reporter in the closet with his microphone and me on the bed with a bunch of beer and wine coolers, whatever the girls wanted, and then my friend Ken would just run out and grab them and bring them up. I asked them, "If you were the queen of the prostitutes, what would you do?" And it was really interesting and kind of fun. Everybody had a different fantasy. Some of them just thought it meant they were really sexy. This one girl said, "Oh, I'm the queen of the whores ' cause I can suck a baseball bat through thirty feet of garden hose."

MG: You gave the character Chocolate that line.

WTV: That's right. Then there were a lot of them who were very loving and generous, and the way they interpreted the role was they would be nurturing and take care of all the girls and give them whatever drugs they were addicted to. And I started imagining my queen of the prostitutes in that light. Then a couple of them, either because they were naturally mean or because they'd had a really hard time, just loved the idea of using power to be cruel. So then I started thinking about Domino, and decided there had to be a good queen and a bad queen. Then I thought about it a little more and thought well, Domino's not really bad. She does a lot of bad things, but in some ways she's my favorite character. I feel a lot of pity for her. She means well; she wants to trust people and love people but she can't.

That audition helped me. Then I got a couple of those prostitutes together and paid them to act some stuff out. I rented the 441 club for a night, and got six or seven of them just to see what they would do. They had a great time and I enjoyed it too. It was a little bit stilted — they had never done it before, and they were kind of overplaying to the audience, but I got a few good lines out of it.

MG: Who was the audience?

WTV: Just some of my friends, whoever wanted to come.

MG: Have you worked like that before?

WTV: No, that was the first time.

MG: I've read others interviews with you where people ask about your attraction to prostitutes and you seem kind of blasé, saying that having sex with whores is great and that you really enjoy it. At the same time, in this book and others your characters seem to be searching for an illusory kind of salvation in among these women — there's obviously much more to it than fun. Why do you keep coming back to prostitutes over and over again in your writing?

WTV: I guess there are lots of things that I'm searching for. I first got involved with prostitutes in my early twenties because the woman I was going to marry decided she didn't love me, and I was very, very lonely. I tried for a couple of years to find another girlfriend and I couldn't. I must have been very unattractive, probably because I was depressed, and depressed people can be a drag to be around. Finally I went to a call girl, and actually I felt so uncomfortable and embarrassed with her that I couldn't even have an orgasm, but after she had left I just felt so happy because finally somebody had let me put my arms around her and lie next to her in a bed. Even though she wasn't particularly nice and didn't like me and just wanted money, she really helped me so much, it was like a kind of therapy. And later when I got into a relationship and I didn't need that, I kept seeking prostitutes out as friends and as people that I could help and as people who could help me by teaching me things. They know so much, they've seen so much and they've felt so much, its like talking to a really old, grizzled war correspondent or police officer or maybe some monk whose been meditating all his life. Often they don't even know how much they know. And what they know sometimes destroys them. They learn some awful things because people can be very mean to them. People do bad things to them, and once I started thinking about that, I thought maybe they are even more elevated and exalted than I imagined. Some of them are almost like saints.

MG: Exalted through suffering?

WTV: Well, because it's their business to take these awful experiences and put up with these awful people and with things that no one else would put up with. If a psychiatrist is doing a good thing and all he or she has to do is listen to someone say, "I want to kill myself" or "I want to kill my husband' or whatever, than to have somebody who is maybe really mean and cruel and gives you diseases and stabs you and burns you, and you live that and accept it, it doesn't necessarily make you better, but it makes you worthy of a lot of respect in my opinion. I respect them so much. And so I started thinking about the queen as somebody who was really, really special.

MG: The idea of the holy whore goes way back.

WTV: It sure does.

MG: There seems to be a tension in a lot of what you write over the idea of victimization. You've said that you don't believe prostitutes are necessarily exploited. But at the same time, in your fiction there are a lot of rescue fantasies about these women.

WTV: Does that bother you?

MG: No. I just wonder what you're rescuing them from if they're not being exploited.

WTV: For one thing, there is a distinction between me and my characters. My characters sometimes do things that I wouldn't do or they do them in more extreme ways. But I guess if I see, for instance, a child prostitute who is trapped, I will feel terrible. One time I did kidnap a child prostitute. That was a very fulfilling experience to be able to go and help somebody. But a lot of people don't want to be rescued and maybe don't need to be rescued. I've been photographing and making platinum prints of some of the prostitutes in Oak Park, which is about a seven- or eight-minute drive from here. I'm trying to follow the same women over ten years. I'm now in the fourth year of photographing them, and I've got to know them pretty well and some of them have really, really terrible lives, but I don't feel that there's anything that I or anyone can do for most of them. For a person's life to change, he has to feel not only that his life is bad, but also that he wants to give up whatever makes it bad. In America, I believe that 99 percent of us are responsible for our actions and should be held responsible for our actions. So if somebody decides to be a prostitute for whatever reason and that person is an adult, I have to feel that that's a choice that that person has made.

MG: But you don't mean they deserve what they get.

WTV: No. What I mean is that just because someone is a prostitute, I don't want to say that she's exploited. And if bad things happen to that person and the person doesn't want to change, its not a question of the person deserving those things, but I would say we have to stand aside and hope that that person will either decide that she can live with them, or else that she wants to change her situation, in which case she can get some help. So much of the harm that has been done in this world has been done by missionary types who think that some aspect of a culture is really awful and that for peoples' own good we have to change it. I object to the people who call female circumcision female genital mutilation. That's what they want to call it, and they're convinced that it's a hundred percent bad and it should be eradicated no matter what anyone says. It might be true, it might not be true, but I think that sort of thinking is very, very dangerous. The people who see a prostitute and say, "Poor girl, I wonder who put her into this situation, and those awful men who take advantage of her should all go to jail," I don't think that that's true.

MG: But you've written that a lot of American prostitutes have incest or other horrible abuse in their pasts.

WTV: It's terrible, isn't it? But you know, I've had some sad things in my past, and that doesn't mean that I'm not responsible for the decisions that I make. I've been thinking about this a lot because I'm a gun owner, and I'm pretty sure that by the time my little girl is my age, handguns are going to be, in practice, banned in this country. When you look at the issue of guns, there are two visions you can have. One thing you can say is, and this is what I believe, that the second amendment is really wonderful. Unlike in other countries, our country trusts us to have guns. It's in our constitution — we have the right to defend ourselves against others, or even against our own government if it becomes a bad government, and I think that's amazing and wonderful. If that's the case, if I am allowed to have a gun and I ever misuse that gun, then I deserve some serious punishment. If I take my gun and shoot the next-door neighbors or rob a bank, I should be put in jail for the rest of my life or maybe killed. That's what I believe. The other way to look at guns is that we should cut people as much slack as we possibly can and try to be kind, and that if someone makes a mistake, then that person should not be held completely responsible and we should try and help that person and protect him from the consequences of his mistake.

MG: And you don't believe that?

WTV: I don't believe that. Because if that is the case, then the best thing to do to prevent these mistakes from being made is not to let people have guns.

MG: But in the chapter from *The Royal Family* about bail, you seem outraged over the callous coldness of justice.

WTV: It's terrible.

MG: So how do those two ideas reconcile themselves?

WTV: I don't think there's any way to really be very fair or very happy when you think about this stuff. If you look at it honestly, no matter what position you take, it's very, very painful and it's cruel and unfair to somebody. I feel tremendously sad for people who can't make bail. I think it's a very corrupt system, and I wish that we could set aside some kind of money to pay skip tracers so that we could let these poor people out and give them the same rights as the rich people. And obviously I don't think that women should be going to jail in the first place for street prostitution. But if somebody like my character Domino were going to jail because she had brutally slashed somebody's face with a razor, I would feel terrible for Domino and I would really pity her, but I would still think that she should go to jail and be punished. If I could refashion our justice system, what I would do is take all first-time offenders and maybe all second-time offenders and give them an immense amount of counseling and give them all kinds of options and be helpful and tender and give them every possible chance to understand that they had made a terrible mistake and that that mistake could still be rectified. And then give them another chance. And then, if they kept doing these things, I would be inclined to be punitive.

MG: When you were nine, your six-year-old sister drowned while you were supposed to be watching her. In his family, Henry Tyler is a black sheep — writing about him, you repeatedly use the symbol of the mark of Cain. How much of that is transposed from your experience in your family after what happened with your sister?

WTV: I tend to think that my parents are disappointed in me and angry at me, and maybe they're not, or maybe they're less so than I think, or maybe they've forgiven me after all these years, but it's very difficult for me to talk to them about it. I guess the difference between Henry and me is that Henry has just started out as kind of a small-time loser, and the sin that he commits is to fall in love with his brother's wife, but even before that, he was just not the favorite in his family. Maybe that's one of the reasons he can identify so well with these street prostitutes.

MG: Repeatedly in your writing there are characters who dive into underworlds initially as observers like journalists or detectives, and then get swept up in them far too deeply to ever return to their old lives. Is that something you fear for yourself or feel you've narrowly escaped?

WTV: Well, you never do really escape that stuff. I've been very lucky because I've been able to limit and control my exposure. I feel very lucky that I'm able to live right here. I never know what the future will bring, but I hope that I will be able to live here for a long time and die in a nice place like this, but you do get emotionally and intellectually damaged a little bit. I don't mind it, actually. I prefer the cost of that kind of knowledge to not having that knowledge and being smug and ignorant. Ignorant people can cause a lot of damage, and in a way they're not full human beings. They haven't experienced everything there is to experience.

MG: But what keeps drawing you back over and over again, now that you have so much experience of atrocity?

WTV: I want to understand people and I want to do good. There were a lot of reasons that were bringing me to the war zones. I was working on a long essay about violence.*

MG: What ever happened to that?

WTV: So far I haven't found a publisher, but I got an agent last year and she thinks she might have found somebody, so I'm hopeful.† It's about 4,000 pages, and it's devoted to the question of when is violence justified. Some of my *Spin* and *Gear* trips were to investigate it — I would write the long version and then they would abridge it and publish the short version. I've also thought that when people are in extreme situations, somehow their innate character, their essence is X-rayed by the blinding rays of horror. Under extreme circumstances people can be more selfish or more noble or more everything. Now I've learned a little bit and I'm interested in trying to get practical, and to see what I can learn that can make a difference, because I have not made a difference in my life for other people. I've done a couple isolated things that I'm proud of, but I would like to make a big difference for a lot of people. It's going to take me years and years to figure out what exactly I can and should do and how to do it.

MG: One thing that makes you really different as a journalist is the way you get involved with your subjects. Do you have a problem with the whole pose of journalistic objectivity?

WTV: Yeah, I think that's really wrong because, first of all, in the case of journalists there is always some agenda, especially if you go to any sort of

---

* *Rising Up* and *Rising Down.*

† The agent is Susan Golomb. This was before McSweeney's Books had agreed to publish the seven-volume essay. — M.H.

conflict. If you take a side you have an agenda, and if you don't take a side then you're implying that one side is no worse than the other, which is also often not true. When I was first starting to go to Bosnia, I believed what everyone else was saying at that time, that the Serbs were so terrible and so on and so forth, and it's obvious that they have done a lot of awful things. But what became clearer was that all these journalists I met just wrote off the Serbs as war criminals. I'd be in Belgrade and these Americans and Western Europeans were so rude and obnoxious, and everything the Serbs would say they would try and pick apart. Then some Croatian or Muslim would come along with an atrocity story and they'd write it all down and believe every word. And yet they probably believed they were being objective. But if someone were to come along and say well, I will be objective and so for every story that a Croat tells me about something bad that a Serb did, I will get a Serbian story about something a Croat did. And that's not fair either, because the Serbs have done more bad things than others. I would say the biggest problem now with journalism is that people are required to sum things up in such a tiny little space, so there's only room for black and white.

MG: In 1994, you were driving to Sarajevo with two friends and they were killed — you've said either by snipers or by a mine. Did that change your attitude towards going to war zones? Are you more afraid now?

WTV: No. It happened very quickly, and even if it hadn't the thing to remember is that we had the choice. We decided to go there, and so we have to take the consequences. Of course I will always grieve for my friends. It was really sad what happened, but they might as well have been killed in a traffic accident or something like that. In a way, their deaths are less sad than the deaths of the people who were stuck there. That's how I feel about it. My biggest fear is of being tortured. I don't want to be tortured. But if I were to be killed quickly — my friends died in a lot of pain but they died quickly — it's probably not so bad.

MG: So you're not afraid of death.

WTV: No. What's the point? We all have to die.

MG: Still, most people are.

WTV: Yeah, that's right. Everybody is probably afraid of certain aspects of death. I feel bad when I look in the mirror year by year and see a little bit more gray in my hair, and I notice that I can't work as hard or as long as I used to without getting tired. That gives me a sinking feeling. But everything that we have in life is only lent to us and we have to pay it all back at the end, so what can you do?

MG: You're pretty open about indulging in things that other people would consider vices. And yet even more than sex or drugs, the one thing that so many people lust after is fame, and you seem totally impervious to it.

WTV: Yeah, I'm pretty indifferent to it. The only thing I want, really, is for the books to sell well enough or for the journalism to do well enough financially so I can keep doing what I want. So far I've been able to do what I want, but it's an unstable career. The magazines could get tired of me, and then I'd be in trouble. But each year is a victory, that's all we can say. Otherwise, the only reason to be idolized I guess would be to get girls. I got lots of girls for a while and that was so wonderful for me and it made me really happy, and now I just like being left alone and being able to do what I want.

MG: I read where you said early in your writing career you started hiring prostitutes because it was an easy way to spend a lot of time with women and to get inside women's heads. How much do you think you've learned about them?

WTV: One thing I've learned is how difficult it is. I've learned a lot about prostitutes and there's a significant improvement from the prostitute characters in, say, *Whores for Gloria*, who were often based on specific women or were composites of specific women, to the prostitutes in *The Royal Family*, who I was pretty much able to make up completely.

MG: Has that knowledge translated to creating other female characters, like John's girlfriend Celia?

WTV: I have some experience with the Celias, but only a reader could tell me which of my characters are successful and which ones aren't. If I wanted to create someone like some of Henry Tyler's mother's friends, I can do it a little bit, but just because I've spent time with prostitutes doesn't mean I can create those characters. The more I meet different kinds of people the more I realize how many kinds of people there are, and it's sort of a lifelong thing to go after one world and the next world and the next world until you have a gigantic palette of things you can draw on.

MG: In certain ways Celia's longings are pretty parallel to the prostitute Strawberry's longings.

WTV: See, what I think, and I hope that it's not too didactic or irritating in the book, is that we live in such a horribly materialistic, consumer-driven world, that what Strawberry wants or what the johns want when they're looking for Strawberry is not that different from what Celia wants when she's shopping for plates. It's one of the things that really torments me, because I see so many people in America wasting their lives on very unimportant things, going to movies all the time, rushing to stores to buy something new that's not that different from the old thing, and meanwhile people are starving to death in other parts of the world. These people who just consume all the time don't seem to know that much about themselves or other people and I feel really sorry for them in the same way that I feel really sorry for some of these prostitutes. But at least these street prostitutes sometimes have a certain knowledge and self-knowledge as a result of all the things they've been through.

MG: There's an aphorism that to understand everything is to forgive everything. I thought of that reading about the pedophile Dan Smooth in *The Royal Family*, because he's a sympathetic character, certainly more sympathetic than John. This leads to a question that I think applies to your journalism, too — at what point does relativism and empathy run up against the need to form moral judgments?

WTV: First of all, journalists and novelists have different obligations than other people. Let's say that Hitler had escaped justice and he were hiding in Argentina somewhere, and I had a chance to interview Hitler with the understanding that I wouldn't reveal his hiding place. I would do it, and I would try to give him a certain amount of respect as a person because he would be letting me into his life, trusting me and trying to open himself up so that I could understand him. If I just said, "Hitler's a monster," period, we know that, that's not really advancing the cause of knowledge. And if I were writing about Hitler as a novelist, as I did about Dan Smooth, the biggest mistake I could make would be to just show him as a monster, because then he wouldn't come to life. Obviously most of the people who knew Hitler didn't think he was a monster, they thought he was the greatest. Otherwise he wouldn't have been able to do what he did. The most boring writing in the entire world is this socialist realist stuff where the good communist peasant always wins out over the bad landlord who is corrupt and disgusting in every single way. I've never met people like that. If you start thinking that that's how the bad people are, you're not going to recognize them.

MG: Does getting inside someone's head cause you to forgive what they do?

WTV: Well, the novelist should be at least as generous as God, because the novelist is God to his characters. So the novelist has to forgive them. I made Dan Smooth what he is, so for me to create his character and then not extend any sympathy or forgiveness to him would be very unjust on my part. If there were such a person as Dan Smooth and I found out he was one of my neighbors, if he invited me over for a beer I'd go and sit with him and I'd be curious about his life. I'd try and understand what he thought about the things he'd done and what his moral system was. It would just be so interesting for me. I'd probably watch my daughter around him a little bit, and if I ever caught him planning to do anything to any kid I'd turn him in. It seems like a pretty simple, common-sense thing. It's not like I'd say, "He's a convicted child molester so I have to judge him and I'm not ever going to talk to him." I think that's always a mistake. Because not only would I be isolating myself and not learning something from an interesting person, but also by isolating him, I would be strengthening his temptation to be evil, in my opinion.

MG: You've shot heroin and smoked crack without getting addicted to either. Do you think drug addiction is something that simply results from taking drugs, or do you think it's an expression of an instinct for self-annihilation?

WTV: I think that there might be a biochemical predisposition to addiction, and I also think that addicts can be seekers. Maybe my obsession with certain kinds of things in my writing and drawing is just my own peculiar expression of the same tendency that someone shows in obsessively hunting for crack, for instance. And maybe if you obsessively hunt for anything and you throw your body and soul into it, maybe that's what you were put on earth to do, and you might reach some amazing fulfilling place, even if you can't explain it to other people. If I were, say, a 50-year-old street prostitute selling ten minutes in my vagina and the one thing that I looked forward to every day was shooting myself up with speedball, the fact that I was willing to risk getting AIDS and to endure all this filth and danger and discomfort shows my devotion to the god of speedball.

MG: So you think there is enlightenment to be found in drug addiction?

WTV: Yes. And I don't want to romanticize addiction. I wouldn't recommend it to anybody. But I think that if it is the central part of your life and you're sacrificing everything for it, why not make it into something special?

MG: Have you found any enlightenment in your own drug taking?

WTV: I've had some powerful drug experiences. There's one story in my book *The Atlas* about one of those experiences, a mushroom trip that I went on after my friends were killed [in] Sarajevo where I felt that I was talking with God and asking God why my friends had been killed. I didn't get any kind of answer, but I felt that God was listening to me, and maybe someday I will get an answer.

MG: So you believe in God.

WTV: Yes I do. I didn't used to, but now I do. It doesn't matter whether there's a God or not, but it's a nice thing to believe. When I was in the backseat of that car in Bosnia and my friends were lying dead in the front and I was waiting for the next thing to happen, I was really frightened, but I thought if there is a God I could either beg for my life or I could say thank you for all my life so far, and I just felt like saying thank you. It gave me a lot of comfort. If I had begged for my life I would have felt dependent, but the fact that I was able to say, "It's been really interesting and wonderful in a lot of ways so far," it made me feel better about whatever was going to happen next.

Pattern Recognitions (2001)[*]

LARRY MCCAFFERY

Larry McCaffery: How has the *Seven Dreams* series evolved over the years? I'm specifically wondering how your conception might have evolved or changed during the actual process of creating these books.

William T. Vollmann: The main model I had in mind was Ovid's *Metamorphosis*. At that point I wasn't thinking in terms of doing a whole series of books but just a single, seven-part volume that would be this symbolic history of North America over the past thousand years. It would rely heavily on European and Native American myth, and I would retell these stories with my own slant as a way of providing some idea of the way that things changed. I stuck fairly closely to that conception when I started out writing the first book, *The Ice Shirt*. So at the very beginning of *The Ice Shirt*, I retold lots and lots of Norse myths and two or three Inuit myths as well, using those as a kind of a basic paradigm for other things that happened in that book. I guess the first important thing that began to change my conception of what I was doing was that I found that all the materials I wanted to deal with simply could not be compressed into a single volume. And since it was obvious that I was going to need a lot more room to do this, I worked up my original plans for doing seven different books, each with its own narrative and symbolic focus. The second thing that happened was I began to get more and more interested in being scrupulously accurate in what I was writing about. I decided that if I was going to use the Norse myths, for instance, I wanted to try to make sure to get all the gods and goddesses right, and that all my descriptions of the landscapes should be accurately based on my own expe-

* This interview was conducted in Borrego Springs, California. — M.H.

rience. That, in turn, made it seem only natural for me get interested in the ethnography and geography of that region so that everything could also be described as accurately as possible. So in addition to being a symbolic history of America, they also began to be sort of a classroom-type ethnography work that could be read for real information. I wasn't really thinking of this as something that would actually be used in a classroom, but I did want readers to feel confident that if they picked up, say, *Fathers and Crows*, they could be pretty sure that every detail about the Micmac Indians was correct and that what happened between the Micmacs and the Algonquin Indians had been rendered as correctly as I could make it. In order to do that, I started to get anthropologists and other specialists in these areas to look at what I was writing, to note any discrepancies between my version of things and theirs. And so fairly early on, I began to think of these books as being simultaneously fiction and nonfiction. A lot of the characters are made up and conjectured about, but I tried to be very careful that my treatment of everything was never purely invented, that it was being created within the limits of what I actually know about this stuff.

LM: Those were pretty rigid constraints. Didn't these make the actual writing process a lot more difficult for you in writing these books — as opposed to your other books, where you had a lot more imaginative freedom?

WTV: Very much so. Doing it this way so often felt exhausting and confining. It's pretty easy to give your imagination free play in the writing of something like *You Bright and Risen Angels*; that's even true of something like *The Royal Family,* which I also wanted to be meticulously accurate because I had lived in that particular world and it was easy enough to get all the details about everything I was imagining because it was right there. That's very different from writing about distant and bygone cultures, where everything that you come up with has to be researched and so forth. With the Dream Novels, I found that I was always getting ideas for a specific scene that seemed right from an artistic point of view, but then I'd find out that it never could have happened from an ethnographic or anthropological point of view. An important change that started happening in the Dream Novels was that all this research I began doing started making me recognize and identify real patterns of history as well as patterns of myth.

LM: At the very beginning of *Argall*, you refer to "the mark of Cain, dried up and the soles of my feet were the streams in Egypt, that's the story of Virginia and all the Seven Dreams." Is that the sort of patterns you began to recognize?

WTV: That's right, yes. At the most basic level, I began to see that each one of these dreams were reenacting the same depressing story and that all of them had the same sad ending. So in each one of these dreams you start off with a Native American culture that gets irreparably damaged by its contact with European white culture. Oh, sometimes there were some good change that comes through this contact, but usually just being damaged was the best case scenario for the Native Americans — usually their cultures were just obliterated by the combination of the superior European technology, the European disease vectors, plus its desire to remake the people and the land into their own image. But certainly there were times that the whole project just seemed so sickeningly depressing that I felt like I didn't want to do anything more with it. That's one of the reasons I've deliberately interrupted the work I've been doing with the Dream Novels, rather than trying to finish them up at all once, consecutively. But I'm sort of getting over that now.

LM: Have you been able to draw any sorts of conclusions from this pattern you've been able to identify?

WTV: The next step has been for me to say okay, can we extrapolate or interpolate or make any kind of induction from this pattern that we see? Is there anything about history or morality or anything else, the same thing happens over and over again; if it's universal, then maybe it's all the more important to think about it and not just say "oh how monotonously sad" —

LM: Depressing, yeah —

WTV: So, in the latest of the Seven Dreams, *Argall*, I take the approach of the Elizabethan morality play. And while there's still a lot of anthropological details that I had to research and make sure everything was correct and so on and so forth, that's not as much of a focus as in, say, *Fathers and Crows*, and even the landscape stuff is not as much of a focus as it was in *The Rifles* and some of the others. Part of that is because there isn't as much of the proto-historical landscape surviving in Virginia. I did go there several times and take a lot of notes, and the landscape appears in the book, but I would say that the Elizabethan language and ideology is probably the primary player.

LM: Given your stated intention to render everything in the Dream Novels as accurately as possible, I would assume that trying to deliver *Argall* in Elizabethan English must have been one of the most challenging aspects of writing the book. How did you go about doing that?

WTV: It took several years but I basically just got a hold of lots and lots of books that were written in that time and place. I read them, kept them on my desk to refresh my memory, and if I was having difficulties with anything in particular, I could consult them. But without a doubt the single book that I used the most in developing the Elizabethan voices was *The Complete Works of Shakespeare.*

LM: The period Shakespeare was writing his plays was almost contemporaneous with the events you're describing in *Argall*— one of those happy accidents, I suppose.

WTV: Absolutely. *The Tempest,* for instance, was even based on the ship-wreck of one of the sets of British colonists who went to Virginia shortly after John Smith left. So I kept Shakespeare on my desk and I referred to it almost constantly, especially during the last year I was working on the book. When-ever I was writing a passage where any of the words or phrasings sounded a little lame or flat, I would try and find a Shakespearean equivalent. Another tricky area for me was making sure that everything I described would have elements of hierarchy in it. Because Shakespeare and all the Elizabethans, as well as the Powhatan Indians, were very much top-down societies, it was very important not to make the mistake of thinking of these characters as acting in the kind of free and easy equal way people would be acting (at least the-oretically) in America right now.

LM: Back when you were first planning out the whole series, what was your selection process in choosing narrative materials that seemed resonant enough to be the basis of these book? For instance, in the case of the story of John Smith and Pocahontas that you deal with here in *Argall,* what was there about this specific historical episode that drew you to it? Maybe related to this is the question of whether you've ever felt at a certain point, okay, I really fucked up here, this material isn't working?

WTV: That's a difficult question. One of the general interests I had for all the *Seven Dreams* were any points of contact or communion or union between the two races. If you can have some incident where the people are close or even where they are lovers or have sex or are somehow intimate with each other, you're more likely to clearly see the effect the two cultures are going to have on each other. So in *The Rifles* you have Reepah and John Franklin, in *Fathers and Crows* you have Warren and Father Greg; so for *Argall* the John Smith and Pocahontas story seemed like a natural incident to pick. I was also curious about it since in many ways it was also, of course, emblematic of American history and the propaganda that's been used to propagate our own image of this history. But when I originally chose it, I honestly didn't know that much about the Pocahontas story. All I really knew was that it sounded promisingly romantic. I was assuming that would be important part of the novel. But the more I looked into it, the less romantic and the more depress-ing it became. That didn't make me feel I had fucked up by selecting it, but it certainly changed my conception of how I could use it in the novel. But once I got more deeply involved in what actually happened, the book cer-tainly wasn't what I thought it would turn out to be.

LM: Less romantic in what sense?

WTV: For one thing, Pocahontas was just a kid when she met John Smith, who was practically middle-aged by Elizabethan standards. So I think she probably did have sort of a childish crush on him but they were probably never lovers or anything like that. Now the familiar American version of the story makes us think of Pocahontas as having saved the colony, and then she had a nice marriage with another Englishman, and everything went on happily ever after. But things didn't happen that way. Pocahontas was actually kidnapped by Argall and probably brainwashed into converting to Christianity. There's no way to be sure about this — maybe she wasn't brainwashed and instead agreed to leave and convert out of some feeling of expediency — but it seems unlikely to think that she would have gladly embraced the Anglican faith after being kidnapped. And this guy who married her seems by his own words to have been a very, very pious patronizing sort of guy who looked on Pocahontas herself as being part of the Devil's generation, and so it's hard to imagine that he and she could have been very happy together. After all, he took her over to England to make a sort of a freak show for the Virginia Company, and she wound up dying when she was only 22 or 23 years old.

LM: The title of the novel doesn't refer to either Pocahontas or John Smith....

WTV: Argall is the guy who kidnapped her. He actually makes a cameo appearance in *Fathers and Crows*— one of his many activities was to destroy a Jesuit French-Canadian settlement or two in Canada. He possibly stopped on Manhattan on his way back, and since there was a dispute going on between the English and the Dutch about who controlled the island, he insisted on the submission of the Dutch to the English. But very little is actually known about Argall personally — he only pops in and out of the historical records occasionally, but when he does it's with a real menacing fury. In most of the recorded incidents, he just comes in, scourges something, and then departs. From the few letters of his that survived, he sounds like an extremely dry, methodical guy who was coolly calculating about whatever he wanted to do, and who then just went and did it. He had some real success — he ended up knighted and he died rich — but he didn't care much about how he did what he did. This all made him seem like a very eerie figure to me. An analogy: when you matte a print or drawing or painting, you pick a color in the image that's not a dominant color and then make the matte match that color; somehow that creates a certain sort of unity. Once I got going on the novel, I used the same principle —*Argall* is like one of those non-dominant colors I use in a matte, so let's frame the whole book around him and see what happens. Gradually *Argall* became more and more important to me. The more I found out about how little we really know about him, the stranger and more enigmatic he seemed to be, and the more important he became to the book. In the final version, he's become almost an inhuman force that comes in and out of the narrative like the wind of history. We see him arriving and then burning or blowing up a bunch of people's houses, and, like death — or progress or gunpowder — he irrevocably alters things. No one can predict him or stop him.

LM: For all your desire to be as meticulously accurate, historically, with this material, it must also be exciting to find these gaps or interstices in the historical records, and use them as a way for you to enter into this material from an original angle.

WTV: That's right. One of the things I do with *Argall* is to make him into this really, really weird, sarcastic, menacing character who is always saying things that sound very, very polite but then people start thinking about it, they realize he's just said something really terrifying and horrible. What we know about how Pocahontas was kidnapped is that she was in a place called Patawamuck, which is now on the Potomac river, not too far from Washington D.C., she was visiting a chieftain there who was allied with her father and probably traded for antimony. Argall had already established some kind of formal sworn brotherhood with one of these chieftains, so he went and visited the guy and told him he would have to trick Pocahontas onboard his ship, and if he didn't do that, Argall wouldn't be his brother anymore and the chieftain might just have to take the consequences. Well, I thought a lot about this and it just seemed like no matter what spin you put on it, Argall must have been a very menacing figure to this chieftain — he was basically threatening to burn down the guy's village and kill his wife and him and everybody else. This scenario seems likely because Argall had already burned some towns (there was a big war going on at the time between the English and the Powhatans; there were massacres on both sides), so I tried to figure out how Argall would put this to the chieftain. It seemed to me he would do it in a really, really creepy, nasty way. Once I had established that voice to the best of my ability, I tried to use it in a lot of his other encounters as well. So, for instance, at one point I have the governor, Lord Delaware, ask him if somebody has been loyal in his absence, and Argall says, "Oh certainly — he's been as loyal a knave as ever danced beneath the gallows tree." And Lord Delaware can't quite make out what Argall means by this. As it turns out, no one ever can quite make out what Argall means. But whatever it is, somehow it's not very nice.

LM: I recall thinking, as I read *The Rifles,* that you were using yourself (or some version of yourself) in a way that seemed different from the first two Dream Novels. You seemed to be a more active presence, let's say, than in the earlier books, where you were usually somewhat more of a neutral recorder.

WTV: I hardly appear in *Argall*. There were a couple of things involv[ed] with this. For one thing, downplaying my own role here was one way to make this book different from the earlier Dreams. As I've said, the story is basically the same in all the Dream books. One of my big concerns when I'm writing them is to make sure I can tell this same story as differently as I can, so I try to avoid writing anything that actually *is* the same. I certainly don't want them to be formula books, so each book has to be conceived in a completely different way, they're all retelling the same basic story but coming at it at different directions. I guess that what first happened with that voice was that in the first volume, *The Ice Shirt*, I realized that a lot of these myths were about the compression of time; that made me start thinking: Well, why not play around a little bit more with time? And since I'm always trying to imagine myself into these places, why not *really* do it and literally put myself in these stories, move in and out of them, because these books are acts of imagination. You know, sometimes when I'm writing, it really does feel like I'm actually in this landscape that probably felt the same for me as it had to my long-dead characters, with a shovel and pickax, digging a hole in some graveyard to look at the old skeletons (and all that digging is a lot of work!). For instance, those arctic landscapes I visited in *The Ice Shirt* and described had not changed much from the time when the Vikings were settling there — you can even still see the ruins of Eric the Red's house today, in Greenland. I never got to that particular place because it was too expensive for me to arrange, but in Greenland I did see the ruins of several other Norse houses, including one from the 1300 that had a Norse skeleton still inside. At any rate, the changeless quality of that area made it easy for me to sit on the shore of a bay as some Danish fishing vessels were going by and think: Okay, on this same bay 700 years ago something *else* could have happened; one of their historical myths was set here, so why not put the ship and myself and those long dead people right here? Doing that kind of imaginative extrapolation isn't difficult and in fact, it feels natural. There you are in their world, and it's still much the same world they explored and inhabited. I did a lot of similar things in *The Rifles* and to some extent in *Fathers and Crows*; when you go up to the forests and lakes and tundra of Canada today, they still have the same feeling to them as they must have had for the Eskimos and early European explorers, and it's not so very hard at all to imagine yourself into these places.

LM: In the case of *Argall*, it must have been a lot harder to project yourself in the original setting that is now Virginia....

WTV: No question about that. And not only have a lot of the landscapes been strip-malled over and developed but I also decided that introducing much in the way of my own voice and persona into the mix would be a needless complication. The Elizabeth voice is already so incredibly complex and introspective that it seemed superfluous to add another level to this by having my own character floating around. In the Norse world everything is very taciturn and straightforward, and so with the three earlier Dream books it seems helpful to have the author standing over Eric the Red's shoulder, embellishing and amplifying everything. But the Elizabethan rhetoric is so florid that it would have inflated the pattern into a scribble.

LM: Of course, you're not entirely absent here — your voice still occasionally works its way into the narrative, and in a different way you enter into the book through the elaborate series of notes and glossaries and so forth that you provide.

WTV: That's right. Not to appear at all would be disingenuous on my part.

LM: You've included a fairly large amount of glossaries, historical information, and footnotes that create a kind of running dialogue between yourself and the original you've relied on in all the Dream novels. What is the function of this material, in terms of the work as a novel — mainly to provide the reader with enough background so that then they can compare these sources with what you've made of them?

WTV: That's certainly part of it. They also remind the reader that the events in these books, however grim or awful or strange they might seem, are largely and literally true. I've always felt that the more we know about our own history the better off we are. But today a lot of people get their histories mainly from movies, television or other media sources where things don't have to be accurate. People will see movies like *JFK* or *The Patriot* and end up thinking: Okay, now I see how it really was. But the truth is that it's really, really dangerous for people to be thinking that way. It's so easy to be manipulated by the media, whose main goal isn't to provide historical accuracy but entertaining versions that will sell. I don't want to put people in that position in my books. I want the people who are reading this to respond by thinking, You know, maybe this is how it was, and these notes and information about the history, myths and other source materials lets me see where he's coming from, why he thinks this is actually the way it was; but in one of these footnotes here I can also see that this other guy disagrees with Vollmann about this, in fact this guy thinks just the opposite, so these things aren't black and white, nobody really knows for sure. In other words, I want to encourage readers to understand what my versions were based on, and if they disagree, they can go and look up this stuff and decide for themselves.

LM: I remember being surprised the first time I read *The Ice Shirt*, when I came across one of your notes about an exchange you had with one of the experts in the Icelandic sagas who disagreed with your own interpretation — most authors of historical fiction wouldn't want to air these sorts of disagreements because it would lessen their own version's sense of authority or believability.

WTV: Yeah, but including my sources and exchanges with people who don't share my take on this stuff is a really important part of what I'm doing in these books. If I were to pick up a book written about a period I hadn't studied, how else would I know how much was accurate and how much the author made up? I might just be interested in a good story and not even care about accuracy when I picked up the book, but ideally I'd have more interest in the period once I'd finished reading it. And once I'd found out more about it, I'd be in a position to say, "Oh, now that I have some sense of the period, I can see that this book is very accurate or completely wrong" — as opposed to just wondering if things really were that way or whether this is just romanticized or de-romanticized or whatever.

LM: In effect you create an instant dialogue with your own text, and the reader is invited into that dialogue.

WTV: It's also a kind of a useful trick on the reader — you'll be reading along in one of these books, and you think you're ¾ finished or ⅞ finished or whatever, but then you find out, no, actually you are finished, there's no more, the text itself has come to an end. A lot of the time when we read a book we kind of orient ourselves by where we are physically in the book —

LM: — so that you literally see the end coming.

WTV: That's right. You know if the hero and the heroine are about to get together and you're only three pages from the end, then they're probably going to get married and live happily ever after and that's that. Whereas I think its often useful or interesting to get to the end of the text but then discover there's still more stuff there in the book. When that happens you're kind of taken aback; you're stopped for a second and you think: Hmmm — maybe things kind of go on and on.

LM: That approach avoids the novelistic device of bringing closure to everything by the end of the book — which is mainly a dramatic convenience, a means of pandering to the reader's desire for conclusions, resolutions. Closure not only isn't "realistic" in the sense of not being very accurate about most of what happens in reality, it usually seems basically *inaccurate*, a sheer artifice.

WTV: That's right. And my Dream books work against that in two stages. There's the source notes and they way they open things up that have been introduced in the text, but in addition to those, there's the text proper, which is surrounded by a long introductory textual note and lastly by a series of what-happened-next commentaries — what is usually called "further history." Those two bookends for the text proper are in a lighter font and so they further position the status of the actual text. Hopefully doing this would make the reader think along the lines of something like, "OK, so this really happened and all these things, or something like them, happened to actual people these characters are based on, and it's really too bad now that the story's over because I'm not going to find out more from this book about these characters, but still, it *is* kind of interesting to start thinking about what happened after that during the next few hundred years, and then that makes me wonder what's going on now, and what's going to happen." Hopefully it serves some purpose of relevance in making the reader think that all these things haven't yet disappeared once the book is over — they still have their impact in the world today. It's like a slowly dying musical note — centuries later maybe you can still hear it, even if other notes have come in and drowned it out; so it might still be there and if so, what does that mean? What's it changing into?

LM: That seems to be one of the functions of the chronology of *Argall*. It brings people up to the present, in a sense.

WTV: Exactly.

LM: Those elaborate endnotes and glossaries that appear in your Dream Series must have been a lot easier to create on a word processor than they would have been on a typewriter. Of course, this could have been done previously by writers, but it was such a pain in the ass to create even a simple footnote on the typewriter that most writers avoided it. Partly what I'm driving at here is that one could almost describe these Dream novels as "assemblages," and I'm wondering if working on a word processor might have encouraged that way of thinking about what you're doing.

WTV: There's no question that a word process definitely does make creating these different textual layers easier. I'm sure that in the olden days, if you were organized you could have had shoeboxes full of index cards, so that every time you mentioned, say, a new Indian tribe in your text, you'd make an index card and put that in your shoebox and then at the end, you'd go through them all and make sure they were all properly defined and so on and so forth. That would probably have worked, but like you said, it would have been very tedious and time-consuming. So, yeah, the computer adds that option, or at least makes it a lot easier. But for everything the computer adds, something is lost. Before the typewriter existed and people had to write everything by hand, there had to be much more thought, and much more fluency, in everything you wrote because how many times could you write something by hand? So the stakes were higher with every sentence you wrote. Through a sad experience that happened to me once, I found how difficult it is to write out something by hand from memory one time when I lost a notebook coming back from Madagascar, while I writing "The Jealous Ones." While I was trying to reconstruct everything from memory, it was certainly obvious that what I was writing out was certainly less accurate and more difficult in some other ways, too — so much has been lost that your options are now fewer. But on the other hand, because you only remember whatever is most important to you about this experience, you can gracefully and eloquently create a story about it that's fairly seamless, whereas with the computer there's always a temptation to drop in another detail, another bit of text, another thing here and there, so that then you have to go back and smooth it over. If you can do that responsibly, the computer has given you a wonderful power, but it's awfully tempting to misuse that power.

LM: Yet another verification of the old maxim about absolute power corrupting absolutely? Certainly that power you've mentioned — specifically that power that comes from the computer's storage and retrieval capacities — would seem to put a premium in the composition process on the final selection process. Editing: what to leave, what to cut out? You can see an analogous situation in music — once the CD format, with its greater storage capacity, replaced the album, you had a lot of CDs released that obviously had too many songs, too many minutes of music; the ability to include more made it difficult to avoid the temptation to include it all, so the end result is lesser quality.

WTV: Sure: you can tell with a lot of stuff you see these days a lot of writers and other artists haven't learned yet to be responsible about this — at some point they've ended up with this huge number of little bits of data and they just don't want to waste them so they've inserted them. So it's hard to know whether or not computers are having a positive impact, overall, on writing right now.

LM: I suspect we're going through a transitional phase right now, sort of like what happened when other empowering technologies were introduced — electric amplification gave guitar players not only the power to play a lot louder (and that power was often misused) but a lot of other options that nobody could figure out what to do with. Then Jimi Hendrix came along....

WTV: Well, certainly in the case of writers, it would be a useful exercise for anyone who has a computer to try and write in lots of different ways, to try out different approaches until you can figure out what works best for you. One way to write is to keep putting things in as you go, which the way I often work, but another way is to say, "All right, I'm not going to insert anything until I've finished an entire draft, I won't backtrack as I go along, I'm going to write the whole thing in a nice linear fashion and then, once I've got that done, I'll see what I have and decide if any of this other stuff should be added somewhere." If you can try out both of those approaches, you're probably going to be a much better storyteller and a better writer generally.

Drinks with Tony (2005)

TONY DUSHANE

I hung out with Vollmann at his hotel room at The Rex on Post St. in San Francisco during the book tour of Europe Central.

TD: Let's talk about your writing process, your creative process. The material you pump out is a good quantity. You're writing every day I assume.

WTV: Oh yeah, absolutely.

TD: Mornings?

WTV: Whenever I can, morning, noon and night.

TD: You definitely have a unique voice. For a beginning writer, how would someone get to that type of unique voice or how did you acquire that yourself?

WTV: I guess you have to start by, as Hemingway says, write about what you know, which is usually yourself ... and trying to have as many experiences as you can and read as widely as you can so that you're capable of creating different voices and knowing more.

TD: Speaking of experience, you're the king of experience when it comes to what you've been through, your experience in war zones, etc. Do you feel the drive to really pursue the edge?

WTV: Well, I feel that I've learned enough to be able to write fiction and nonfiction about it. You know *Rising up and Rising Down* was sort of my life's work and I went through all those war zones so I could explain what I thought about violence and I've done that. When I wrote *Europe Central*, I was able to imagine myself into the heads of some of these characters in part because I've had a few experiences of war myself. I don't need to do that anymore for those reasons but I would gladly do it if I thought I could make a difference. If I thought that I could help people in the war zones or if I thought

I could help Americans understand what I thought our government was doing wrong, then of course I would consider it my obligation to do it.

TD: So your work is really a way of opening up to people who aren't able to have those experiences and showing them what's going on in the world.

WTV: In a way. You know in *Europe Central* it's too easy just to say, "Oh, the Nazis were terrible, the Stalinists were awful." And that's true, but where do you go from there? If you can realize the deeper truth, which is not only that were they terrible but if I were born in that time and place, I probably would've been one. And even if I resisted with all my being, I would still have characteristics of one, no matter what I did.

Just as in this society, everyone thinks that money is the most important value ... to such an extent that it's become invisible. Parents tell their children, you know you have to learn how to sell yourself. Of course they're outraged by prostitutes selling themselves, but that's what we are, we're a culture of prostitutes. It's a completely different value than is held by so many people in the world. And one of the reasons that we can't understand other people better is because we can't possibly imagine that they don't share that value. But they don't.

So if you were born in the third Reich, and all you ever heard was that Germany was the greatest and the Jews were very dangerous and poisonous and Slavs were inferior and this and that, maybe you could, if you were really compassionate and brave, throw some of that off. But deep down, you would probably still feel somewhat good about Germany. You know you would still think, oh Germany is a really progressive place and probably the rest of the world is a little primitive. That's probably the best you could do.

TD: Speaking of prostitution, you did live in the Tenderloin for a while or were you doing research for your....

WTV: I spent a lot of time in the Tenderloin, yes.

TD: Especially with *The Royal Family*, was that for research for that book, and for *Whores of Gloria*?

WTV: Yeah, that's right.

TD: Was that for research, in your mind, or were you just trying to experience it and then pulled creativity out of it?

WTV: Well, I wanted to come there and learn. I didn't know what the people were going to be like when I first started coming and I tried not to have preconceptions and just go and have the experience and take notes and repeat the process, until gradually over years, I began to be able to create prostitute characters. It's much harder to create a fictional character than to write about a living person. You have to see lots and lots of living people of these types in order to make up somebody who represents the type. But at the same time isn't just a concatenation of real people. So you know it's a real challenge.

TD: What got your writing bug started?

WTV: I was always that way even when I was a little kid.

TD: With the immersion and research, was that started young or was that developed over the years?

WTV: Well, I've really enjoyed reading, so I'm sure that's where it comes from. I'm very happy researching these books; it's really exciting for me.

TD: You deal with really serious topics, but there's a lot of humor in there, too.

WTV: I do my best.

TD: Do you feel your fictionalization of true historical events, is that a statement to how supposed history is absolute truth, when we read history?

WTV: I think literal histories are essential. At the same time I think that a literary portrayal of an historical event can bring out other sides, can make it somehow more immediate to the read. You know we can read any number of buried descriptions of what happened in General Vlasoff's (a character and historical person from *Europe Central*) life, but I feel that I make him real. The paradox of fiction of course is you make things real by making them up. The main thing is you remain relatively faithful to the facts and say okay, if I were this person, how would I get from point A to point B and why. Then if nothing else, you can instill a temporary empathy for General Vlasoff and people can kind of follow his career a little bit and meditate of all the paradoxes in it.

TD: I've been trying to figure out how a holocaust can happen, with a whole nation going along with it, but after reading *Europe Central*, you can see really being in the fever of what's going on and Germany trying to make its own name and the excitement of that.

WTV: Everyone's always looking for someone to blame. It's always easier blaming someone else for your problems than solving them yourself. Right now, for instance, if we had a terrorist attack that was, you know, was grander in scale than September 11, say a suitcase nuke goes off in Los Angeles or whatever, maybe it wouldn't be very problematic for many people in our society if we put all the Arab Americans in internment camps, like we did the Japanese Americans. That can quickly happen. If people can somehow be convinced that al–Qaeda cells are everywhere and these Arab Americans are extremely dangerous, you know, probably a lot of them could be murdered. You can see how easily those things can happen.

WTV: A lot of it has to do with lack of information. And most Americans are pretty ignorant, because the media just portrays Americans to America, so that's all we know. So a lot of people can't tell the difference between a Sikh wearing a turban and a Muslim wearing a hajib. So when you don't have information and somebody from this category has done something

wicked, it's very human to think that everyone from this category is dangerous.

TD: That just brought to mind your portrayal of prostitutes, because,
you know as a whole they're looked down upon, but you bring a lot of empathy towards those characters.

WTV: I have a lot of love and respect for prostitutes.

TD: And they're kind of keeping it real at the very core, like you said
earlier, we're all kind of prostitutes in certain ways.

WTV: Of course they're out to get what they can, and take advantage
of the johns occasionally. They rob them, they give them disease, well, that's
life, that's how people are. And at the same time, they make their customers
very happy, they keep marriages together, they console lonely people. I think
they're very, very spiritual in what they do.

TD: Speaking of spiritual, especially reading your latest book, some of
it felt like parables from the bible, do you feel that influence in your writing?

WTV: Definitely a lot of the stories are parables. I was reading "Operation Magic Fire" (a chapter from *Europe Central*) last night, at Booksmith,
and that's the parable of the guy who takes responsibility for everyone, so you
think, oh, he's sort of a Jesus figure in a way, except that he's absolutely vile.
I'm very interested in the Bible, not just in the Bible, but a lot of spiritual
text.

TD: The way you write is so conversational. Does it come easy for you?

WTV: Sometimes I can get a sentence right the first time. Other times
it takes 40 or 50 times to get it right. It all depends. It needs to feel easy and
look natural. If it's not, then you don't have the touch and you're not doing
it right.

TD: As far as editors at the publisher go, do they pull their hair out to
try to get you to cut even more than....

WTV: Oh, sure, I never cut anything that I don't want them to cut.
Sometimes they cut my royalties instead. That's OK.

TD: Were your royalties cut on *Europe Central*?

WTV: No, I was lucky.

TD: They were cut on *The Royal Family*.

WTV: Yeah, and on *Argall* too. With *Europe Central* I had a chronology at the end. A very detailed chronology, basically from about a little bit
before Hitler's birthday until about the late 1980s, and just everything having to do with all the characters, and what happened when in World War II,
in World War I and so on ... all the stuff I thought was important, it was
maybe 24 pages or something. Viking asked me to cut it. I thought about it,
and my first reaction was just to say no, as I always do, and I knew that they
only wanted me to cut it to save paper, and I bristled at that. Then I thought

about it and decided that since it wasn't one of the seven dreams, and there are all the source notes anyway, that probably it's not necessary, so it's probably okay to let it go.

WTV: I don't feel any regret about it and it does tighten up the book a little bit, but it's very very rare that I agree with suggestions to cut.

TD: Have you been working with the same publisher for most of your books?

WTV: I worked with Viking for many of my books.

TD: What are your influences, whether artists or other things?

WTV: I like Tolstoy, Lady Murasaki, Lautréamont, Hawthorne, Faulkner, Norse sagas, those are some of my influences.

TD: Any current journalism projects?

WTV: I just finished doing something for *Playboy*, with my button camera in fact, for my *Imperial Valley* book; we will see what comes next.

TD: What was the content from your button camera?

WTV: I went into a bunch of factories, in Mexico, these machiadoras, Ford-owned factories, to look for mistreatment of the workers.

TD: And....

WTV: There were some bad things, but not as bad as I would've expected, so that's good.

TD: Was that when you had the problem getting the button camera back over the border?

WTV: I used the button camera off and on several times, and I had a particular problem in January. I was detained at the border for five hours and they called the FBI and I was treated like a criminal.

TD: Did they recognize who you were, were there any fans among the heathens?

WTV: No, they went off and after a while they said, "Mr. Vollmann, we found out quite a lot about you." I said, "Oh good, whatever."

TD: Speaking more of the situations you've been in war zones countries or other similar situations, how do you handle the fear? I know you've been shot at, I'm sure there's a lot of other stories you can go on and on about. How do you handle that?

WTV: Well, you just have to make your best plan, like a good Boy Scout and figure out what might happen and make every effort you can to protect yourself in advance. Buy the best equipment, make the best friends, figure out the best route, know exactly what you're going to do, then once you have all that in place, you have to trust your plan and trust the people you've picked and be open and flexible and submit to the situation and just try to have a positive attitude, because once you're there, you can't control what's going to happen too much, and you have to be ready to be killed. And if that happens, hopefully you won't have too many regrets. And if it doesn't happen, you squeak through to do it again another time.

TD: It's not so bad. You know really, the people who choose to do that, the journalists, the people like me, if anything happens to us, we are less to be pitied than the people who are trapped and don't choose to go in that situation.

TD: Do you have to be really comfortable with your own mortality?

WTV: You bet, absolutely.

TD: Is death not that scary for you?

WTV: Well, it's always scary and it'll get you sooner or later, and since it's going to get you sooner or later and it's scary, then why not do what you want to do. You're not going to be immortal by refusing to take chances.... I think it's kind of liberating to be mortal and it really it can't be much worse than it already is; therefore, why worry?

TD: Have you had any interest from movie studios trying to get rights to your books?

WTV: Yeah, I wrote two screenplays on commission for two different studios, but they were never produced.

TD: Of course, was the money decent?

WTV: Yeah, it was like 20k for one and 30k for the other so it wasn't bad. It took me five or six hours in each case, so I can't complain.

TD: You busted out a screenplay in five or six hours?

WTV: Uh huh.

TD: How?

WTV: Well, I just cut out all the descriptions pretty much and wherever there was dialogue, I just added some capital letters and colons and it was all set to go.

TD: I have friends who will listen to this and just cringe. Do you write on computer or longhand?

WTV: If I go someplace like the Congo or a war zone or something, it's crazy to take a laptop, where it would just get stolen, and there's no reliable electricity. But I'll be going to Japan next month and I'll be bringing my laptop.

TD: What advice do you have for beginning writers?

WTV: I would say, don't fixate on getting published because that's really the least important concern. If you really care about writing, you should do it because it makes you happy and you should be just as happy if you can write something that you think is beautiful and you can keep it in a drawer and show it to a few people and they're thrilled. That's just as important. If you can have that attitude, then no one can take the pleasure of it away from you. So often there are beginning writers who put "copyright by" on every page of the manuscript, and they're so anxious to get an agent and do this and do that. That stuff is irrelevant. That's like asking a photographer, which is the best equipment, and all that matters is the image. With writing, all that matters is the word. You have to think of the sad lives and commercial failures, which so many great writers have experienced. Look at somebody like Melville. If you're an aspiring writer, do you want to write *Moby-Dick*? Sure. Well, if you're going to do that, that means you're willing to accept not just no success, but poverty and even a certain measure of disgrace for the rest of your life. Can you proudly accept that? If so, you may still not be a good writer, but you're on the right track. If your thing is getting recognition as quick as possible, then I would say why, why do you want that, and is writing going to help you do that? And are you going to be a happier person by having that recognition?

TD: I run a literary webzine, and when I get submissions that have the copyright on every page, those are always the worst writers.

WTV: Yeah, isn't that sad?

TD: How long did you live in the Tenderloin?

WTV: I just came in on and off. I would just stay at one of the hotels; sometimes I still occasionally stay there. You know, I like the kind of hotel, where you don't have to buy your own crack because the crack smoke kind of drifts through the walls from an adjacent room, and you can just enjoy the fragrance.

TD: You've smoked crack in the past?

WTV: I guess that I would say that I have.

TD: Is it a really great buzz?

WTV: It's like if you haven't had coffee for a long time, then you have really strong coffee. It's like that, only more so.

The Subversive Dialogues (2006)

KATE BRAVERMAN

When I moved to San Francisco, I gravitated to Berkeley's Black Oak sec-ondhand section. It's the cult library of books you meant to read, but didn't quite get to. The first year, the novels that most astounded me were Paul Bow-els's *The Sheltering Sky*, Don Delillo's *Underworld*, and the fictions of William T. Vollmann. In particular, *Royal Family* is a savage glittering novel of the San Francisco underbelly of prostitutes, pimps, private detectives and drugs writ-ten with the audacity, skill and authority of Cormac McCarthy's *Blood Merid-ian*. But the social and psychological issues are more complex and ambiguous. Vollmann's uncompromising anti-authoritarianism, his daring deviation from conventional narrative into literary criticism asides and essays, the sheer epic scale of the ambition unhinged me. I felt in the presence of Punk High Art, renegade genius and a contagious subversion I wanted to join.

As the new girl in town, I identified the most rumor-laden and incen-diary writer in the area and wrote him a fan letter informed by these impres-sions. We considered several interviews that our travel schedules, real and imagined on both of our parts I would guess, precluded. Phone negotiations sporadically continued. I wrote a prose poem in stylistic and emotional hom-age and dedicated to him:

"Autumn Women"

Autumn is a fiction, an acquired taste like opera and shellfish. Some women
need a pimp to open their eyes, show them the ropes, teach them the tricks,

153

turn them out. They were good girls once, didn't do drugs or smoke, could not conceive of the hills between Ravello and Amalfi. Big Sur to Mendocino seemed implausible. Athens and Shanghai felt contrived in their mouths. They were afraid of capitals. They were simple as bells. They smelled like glass on October afternoons, didn't wear make-up, want to speak French or see the Parthenon. Spandex and bronze did not occur to them. Lush are the ladies of the lamps, lit from within, heads dyed copper like coins. They didn't know they belonged in a shrine. Then came fall. They were terrified. That's why they needed a razor scar on the cheek, a fractured arm and black eye was all it took. You'd be surprised. Yes, they were autumn women, shy with their wine and yellow fires, their flagrant leaves. The forest turned. They heard the tinny tease of henna rinsed maples flaunting their stripped limbs and practiced tongues announcing the season of renegades. They didn't know they were looking in the mirror. They remember March. They were still cotton panty girls with aprons and Internet and collections of rocks and butterflies. A drawer just for bows. Then some ersatz celestial trajectory altered her range and hollowed out her vows. The auburn haired women of autumn are breathless as if calling from public phones on boulevards above subways. There's too much noise. Static on the line, but it's better than a beeper. Now they bring their accidents with them. Their coats contain a sadness that doesn't require translation. Even their wool looks contagious. And there's always a crisis. They don't know what to OD in, stand at closets, holding torn slips like they were precious ornaments, a crystal bud vase or a new syringe. Let's shoot up now while we're both in the mood. I have an apricot silk shawl for you. See how the air becomes charged? Lamplight is calibrated an elegant 14 carat and everything is tinged with pear. Such light can burn in deserted rooms for years with no fear of suffocation or fire. No, I don't want to know your name. Just lay down. Shut up. Now we can both die here.

This is how artists ring a classmate's doorbell, say, I've just moved in. I've seen you around. Want to play?

Finally the interview is scheduled. I call Bill from O'Hare, tell him I'm coming back to San Francisco and intend to drive to see him the next day. Bill asks, "Are you coming alone?" He doesn't mean in the Tibetan Monk-Sylvia Plath sense of the word. I say, "No. I'm bringing a male bodyguard who will be armed." Bill asks, "What will he be packing?" I say, "Probably a Berretta. Something he can just put in his jacket pocket. Now give me directions to your house."

The directions are unnecessarily complicated, as if Vollmann sees his current habitation as temporary camouflage. It's an unnaturally gray day. The land to the east looks veiled and sordid. Brush fires have turned the air thick and the sun is round, as if setting at noon. It's enormous, like a harvest moon after the dust of just cut barley, perhaps. I don't expect the suburban street, the brick house, the immaculate lawn with rose bushes and William T. Vollmann opening the door with the flourish of a Southern gentleman and giving the appearance of an academic prepared to discuss a student thesis. But then, what is he doing letting a complete stranger with avowed subversive intentions and an armed companion enter his house? Pleasantries are exchanged. Thus we begin.

KB: Black Oak has a wall of your books. I read your novels and short fiction and inquired about you to other writers. You have an enormous reputation as an outlaw, a recluse and a profoundly important literary force.

WTV: I'm sure they're all making a mistake.

KB: Why would serious writers who value your work be making a mistake?

WTV: They'd do better to write their own. But I'm flattered that people read my books. When they buy my books that allows me to write new ones. So I can't complain. But the world doesn't owe me a living. If they stopped liking my books, it wouldn't ruin my day.

KB: I've read *Whores for Gloria* and *Royal Family* and —

(Phone rings.)

WTV: That's all right. It's always like that around here. It must just be my blue eyes. That's why I don't pick up the phone much.

KB: Why do you have this barrage of phone calls? Writers find the phone intrusive and delete it from the environment. It's disturbing. You have a constant phone ringing.

WTV: I don't use email. And people use the post less and less. So they communicate with me by phone. Everyone is used to instant contact now. People are put out if I don't pick up the phone. But I figure they'll live.

KB: Why do you live in this particular city?

WTV: I'm here because this is where my wife got a job. She's a doctor, a radiation oncologist. I would have preferred to move back to San Francisco. We have a daughter. Lisa, six years old. We've been here 15 years. I'm from Los Angeles originally. I lived there until I was five. I went to high school in Indiana. I spent some time in New Hampshire, Indiana, was in New York for a while, now I'm back here. I'm really from the sidewalk. I'm from everywhere. I'm just a typical rootless American. My father was a business professor.

(It's a lovely but somehow unconvincing house. It looks like the residence of a senior professor, oriental rugs, wood floors, wedding photographs framed on the walls, and French doors. It has the trappings of substantial habitation, but the air seems somehow synthetic, as if it were a movie set. The props have just been unpacked and arranged. Vollmann might have just moved in. I have the unnerving sense that if I walked upstairs or beyond the formal dining room, nothing would be there. Nothing, no furniture, no walls or floors. It's a conceptual house, existing by the force of will. The illusion of a house, created by strings and mirrors and acts of misdirection. And the Southern gentleman construct doesn't quite

coalesce. Vollmann wavers into inappropriate invitations. I ignore them. We can discuss chasing the dragon another time. I am conducting a professional literary interview.)

KB: Your books deal with wildly marginalized people, prostitutes, drug dealers, and characters engaging in monumental substance abuse. Your literary fearlessness fascinates me. I think you're a genius and an original. I'm interested in your background. Where did you go to college?

WTV: Deep Springs. Its in the desert, in Death Valley. It was a two-year college. Then I transferred to Cornell University because Telluride House is affiliated with Deep Springs. I graduated from Cornell and started a Ph.D. program at Berkeley in comparative literature. I dropped out after a year and never went back.

KB: What comprises your literary framework?

WTV: The French surrealists. Blaise Cendrares, *Prose on the Transsiberian. Maldoror* by Lautréamont. *A Tune for Boris Davidovich* by Danilo Kiš. These two had the greatest influence on me in the beginning. *Whores For Gloria* is one of the few books that actually benefited from my college education. I studied the Russian formalists. They believed fairy tales are comprised of a finite number of motifs. For instance, the trickster appears. The wise old man or the fox gives the hero a present. The hero marries the princess. This kind of thing. There were 93 or 172 or whatever numbers of motifs. A fairy tale is like a necklace. Just take these motifs and put them on a string. It's the order and selection that determines the tale. In this way, it's not unlike a photograph. The only art in a photograph is order and selection. That gave me the concept for *Whores For Gloria*. It's a necklace, a narrative necklace; real stories of real women are the beads. And the string, I tried to figure out what would make the beads hold together. I came up with the idea of some guy who wanted to hear stories. Then, why would he want to hear stories? Eventually, I came up with the character of Jimmy. So it's real stories on a fictional structure. I've always been interested in writers like Lady Murasaki and Tolstoy, people who are patient and grand in their ambition and take over all the time and the space they need to say what they need to say. My work is still very dense; it doesn't flow as transparently as either of those two writers. In that sense I'm still more like Lautréamont. But narrative is very important to me. I've been accurately described as a character driven writer. Language came first. Then character. Now I'm trying to improve my command of narrative.

KB: That's an issue for me. Narrative. Consider the technological advances in the visual arts, photography and film, yet a book still looks and is meant to behave as if it came off the Guttenberg printing press. The consensual apparatus demands a recognizable story, rather than following up with Joyce or the revolutionary consciousness experimenters of the century. The marketplace doesn't permit writers the space to explore, with its stringent demands on little accessible stories. *The Royal Family* is impressive in managing to exist in this diminished climate.

WTV: I took a huge royalty cut for that. And that wasn't the first time, either.

KB: Let's address the subject matter issue. Why do you deal with whores and pimps, the denizens of the Tenderloin? What is the philosophical basis for this?

WTV: The fundamental intellectual level of humanity has and will always be low. These innovations might seem to be a development, but I'm not convinced. New technological possibilities mean more experimental things can be forgotten in new ways. There are amazing film makers, like the Soviet Dzija Zertov. Who knows who this guy is and who cares? Who knows or cares who Joyce was? That means people who want to write at that level, and I include myself, are only doing so because we love it. In the end, what else is there? There is no prize, including the Nobel Prize, which can compensate you for the work you put in. If it's not a joy, you shouldn't do it. If you don't get published, that's unfortunate in so far as whatever else you must do to stay alive consumes and prevents you from doing what you really must do. When I wrote *Rising Up and Rising Down*, it took me 23 years and my publishers all said if you want it to see the light of day, you have to cut it. And I said no. I fully expected that it would never appear. I was fortunate that McSweeney's agreed to publish it. Now it's out of print.

KB: Continuing to adhere to a Tolstoyan vision of the novel, it's immensity, grandeur, complexity and size, how have you been able to survive in the marketplace with an uncompromising vision completely outside of the mainstream?

WTV: When I write my books, I don't care about the marketplace. My father always used to say the reason academics fight so much is because the stakes are so small. When your book is published, the stakes are so low. Whatever they pay you is not enough. Therefore, why should you compromise? In the meantime, we're all prostitutes. Most of the prostitutes I know keep one little private thing. Some prostitutes won't kiss. Some of them save the anus for the person they love. Or they might refuse to say I love you except to the person they love. Whatever it is, they keep one tiny little broken shard of their integrity. I don't want to use the word integrity because it sounds as if they're doing something bad. They aren't. They're just living on the capital they have, which is themselves. My own way of being a prostitute is that I let magazines damage my work in any way they care to. My strategy is this. Except in cases of severe financial need, I only accept a story that really interests me. I am sure I can write it in a way that will please me and I can keep it in a book. Then I make money, get my expenses paid and do it my way. I put my heart into it, and then send it to a magazine. It gets butchered and l tell them it was excellent. They did a great job. Then they tell me how easy I am to work with. And I cash the check. Then when my book is finished, I'll cut my royalties in half or whatever is necessary, but you better not even change a comma without consulting me. In fact, the book I'm working on now has spurious commas and I made them remove them. So that's my own particular way of selling out. It's practical. I can't say it's noble. On the other hand, it probably doesn't do any harm.

(Phone rings.)

KB: Is the obsessional writing about prostitutes a metaphor?

WTV: Absolutely. We worship, or are attracted to, we are trapped by what Marx would call the cash nexus.

KB. The literary and experimental conviction of your work coupled with the boldness of your subject matter, the vivid and unflinching depictions, suggest a serious passionate political vision and literary agenda.

WTV: I'm pro-death. I believe in a woman's right to an abortion. I believe in euthanasia. I believe in anyone's right to suicide. I believe in capital punishment. I believe in gun ownership. I believe in violent self-defense. That's the common denominator. The left is disturbed by my belief in capital punishment and I own weapons. My buddies who go shooting with me are appalled that I'm not a Bush supporter. I believe in freedom of choice for everybody, which entails immense risks. Often people abuse the power that comes with freedom. Either way, society pays a tremendous cost. We pay for our gun violence and we are paying an ever more immense cost for the repressive policies of our government. I'm not just blaming Bush, either. This ridiculous war on drugs has incarcerated so many, ruined lives and made them violent. I don't see why it's anybody's business if somebody uses drugs or goes to a prostitute. If someone uses drugs and thereby injures or impairs his ability to perform a public function and as a result people are injured or killed, that person should be punished. But let's punish the person for what he's done, not what he might do. We are all prostitutes. We all do things we would not otherwise do just to survive. None of us should be too proud. It's good to remember that the people we see incapacitated, drunk and laying on the streets, are our brothers and sisters.

KB: That sounds like religious conviction, a conventional Judeo-Christian belief system operating.

WTV: Whether or not there is a God, it's good for me, personally, to be thankful for my life. Whether or not others give thanks or believe in God is irrelevant. I used to despise organized religion. But increasingly I respect its social functions and the basic minimum goodness it forces people to adhere to. I've been in Islamic countries where people are kind to me because Islam says they have to. I have to hand it to Islam. My neighbors next door are Catholic. They're involved in the affairs of the church, the schools. More power to them. I don't go to church. If there was a Jesus, he was probably not God. He was probably one of these drunk and irreverent homeless people who will say maddening, enigmatic things. You think about it later. Maybe it's bullshit. Maybe it's profound.

(Phone rings.)

KB: Your characters are compulsive womanizers. Is this autobiographical?

WTV: If I answered yes to that question, you might think I was a bad person. If I answered no, you might be disappointed.

KB: I'm asking this because the conventional reader might think you degrade woman in your writing. Your literary mastery and daring might be obscured behind the mesh of political correctness suffocating thought and criticism. It might deprive you of the legitimate credit you deserve as an experimental writer.

WTV: I have many female readers. They can see that I love women. In America, so many are ashamed of the body and sexuality. What passes for feminism and a defense of gender is Puritanism in a new disguise. I get annoyed when society tells me how I must behave. I feel the need to rebel. It's an immature and justified rage against authority. The hypocrisy, the idiocy and ignorance I hear offends me. But that element will always be there. I'm beyond being outraged or even engaged with such people. I'm involved with a certain kind of life. Be offended or not. But it's real; it's more real than any sort of life that denies the existence of promiscuity or drug use or poverty. I'm trying to say, this is how it is. These people are as good or as bad as everyone else. We should know one another. If you don't want to know the other, you don't want to know me.

KB: What are your current literary influences? Who do you read?

WTV: They just brought out the three-volume Isaac Bashevis Singer stories. I'm on the middle volume. They're great, beautiful and interesting. I'm fond of the work of Kawabata, maybe because he's so different from me. He won the Nobel Prize in the 60s and then gassed himself. He was very close to Mishima. He wrote a story called "House of the Sleeping Beauties" about a whorehouse just for old men who can't get it up anymore. They're allowed to sleep with beautiful girls who are drugged. The girls never even have to see the old men who are snuggling with them. Every now and then they give a girl a little too much by mistake and she dies and they just throw her in the river. It's very powerful. But most of his work is about non-bizarre, non-supernatural things, the ways Japanese relate to each other. And it's told in a simple way with a lot of material left out. You go back and read the same paragraph three or four times because you know you've missed something essential. I wrote a book, *The Atlas*, which is a series of, for me, very short stories inspired by his palm-of-the-hand stories. They're so small, one or two pages, they can fit in the palm of the hand. I'm going to get a glass of whiskey now. Would you care for a glass of absinthe?

KB: Yes. Thank you. Your depiction of the pedophile in *The Royal Family* is extremely poignant. He might be the most interesting character in the novel.

WTV: If freedom means anything, it's about being repulsive as well as being able to do flower paintings. I believe that we have to focus on the other. I'm not saying pedophilia is right. But I imagined someone who would be, by our culture's standards, the most vile and repulsive character, worse than Osama bin Laden. But let's make him wise and a guide or bridge to the Queen. And it's through somebody like that Tyler gains entrance to the Queen. He endures humiliation and insult from Dan Smooth. That's the price he pays. In so many ways, this novel is about degradation. One of the questions I've often had is when does self-actualization end and degradation begin? What does it really mean if we're going to try to be ourselves? We don't want to be conformists. We don't want to follow social conventions, but how far do we want to take that? The story of Henry Tyler in *The Royal Family* is a story of failure. In the end he's on the street saying I hate Irene, I hate Irene. Where did he go wrong? Definitely, he missed his opportunity to completely devote himself to the Queen. Everyone in the book connected to the Queen betrays her and that's inevitable. Because faithfulness and fidelity is impossible. Even if he had been able to utterly connect with the Queen, he would have still ended up in the same place at the end of the book. Dan Smooth is one of these ambiguous clues or markers. Smooth is not a good or happy person but he's not completely bad, either. What are you taking?

KB: Vicodin. I have Dexedrine, too.

WTV: Are those Vicodin 10s? I'll take some.

KB: No problem. *The Royal Family* is also the story of two brothers. What do they represent?

WTV: Cain and Abel. But I decided that Cain and Abel should both have the mark of Cain. When I read the Bible, I always think Cain does the best he can, Abel does the best he can, and God is not fair. We're never told why Cain's sacrifices aren't pleasing to God. Cain is jealous. Abel is smug and flawed. Yet after Cain kills Abel, God, who is so capable of killing for much less all through Deuteronomy and Leviticus, suddenly says I'm going to put the mark of Cain on you. And anybody who hurts you will be revenged 70 seven-fold. And that's so bizarre. Evidently, Cain fulfills a purpose, too. Who is God really for? It's not clear. But if we do have the mark of Cain, the mark of prostitution, the mark of imperfection, of humiliation and failure, dirtiness and sordidness, then we all have it, whether we're Cain or Able. The way I try to present them goes through a number of inversions. First you think John is dimensionless and a caricature. Later, you realize John is the one who consistently tries to help his brother, Henry.

KB: Tell me about your relationship with publishing. How are your books received, critically?

WTV: The *New York Times* tends to not like my work. Their reviews can be scathing. I get good reviews in Europe. I imagine it's because of the good reviews that I continue to be published. Because my books don't sell huge numbers of copies. And I anticipate that sooner or later I won't be able to publish any more because publishers are always upping the ante for what they say is the break-even point. They used to say 5,000. Those were the days. Now they say it's 10,000. And I think why is this? In every other industry, there are economies of scale. They produce more widgets for less. They should be able to tell you that the break-even point is now 10 copies.

KB: I want to pursue this from a comp lit perspective. You're an innovator and a postmodernist in a uniquely confrontational way. Postmodernism is minimal, it lacks scale.

WTV: When it comes to current critical categories, I feel intellectually inadequate. I don't read books by people who are alive. I think of myself as a child of the 60s. I was born in 1959 and when I listen to Jefferson Airplane or the Beatles, I'm always impressed by how subversive they are. I've shown my daughter Lisa *Yellow Submarine* on the video several times. It's really interesting to see people can still be shocked, offended and uncomfortable. There's nothing innocuous in there. At the same time, the values of the 60s, exclusivity, equality, free love and peace are wonderful. It makes me very sad people make fun of those values. Obviously, I was too young to be a hippy. I meet the children of hippies who grew up on communes, and they're bitter against their parents who didn't provide for them properly. But I see the 60s as a tremendous advance. I would rather be living in the 60s, in an era of love than living now, in an era of hatred and fear.

KB: What about this French magazine, *Topo*, saying you do punk as high art? *The Royal Family* is a singular punk document on every level. It's an act of vandalism, an indictment of society done with consummate craft. It's an incendiary compendium of punk violence against the American agenda.

WTV: I never know what to make of labels. People can call me whatever they want. I don't think I'd have the coldheartedness to put somebody up against the wall and shoot them. The representatives of the establishment in *The Royal Family*, John and Celia, are characters I feel sorry for. I feel sorry for almost everybody. I don't mind deconstructing or destroying some institutional sensibility. But when it comes to individuals, I would always try to have compassion. But I would make exceptions for obvious cliché cases. Take Hitler. Let's say Hitler granted me an interview, to ask and understand him. I would still vote for his execution and probably do it if I was asked to. But if he let me into his life and tried to help me understand why he was the way he was, I would execute him with a minimal amount of respect.

KB: OK. The Bay Area has embraced you. What do you think of the San Francisco art community?

WTV: I'm a loner. I love San Francisco. It's been very sad for me to leave San Francisco. For years I wanted to return there, though now I feel differently. I have a little girl and was able to buy this house and a studio for myself, which I couldn't have in the city. San Francisco is not only visually beautiful but is a stunning universe of separate and secret and easily discoverable worlds. *The Royal Family* is a love letter to San Francisco on some levels. I have an epiphany to Geary Street in *The Royal Family*. It's a love song, from the ocean to downtown. I wanted to write something like that for every district, Oceanside and so forth. In the end, I decided I had already tweaked the narrative as much as I could, with the essay on Bail. It belongs there. But I didn't want to overload the book anymore.

KB: If you had cut *The Royal Family* along commercial lines, it would have been a blowaway detective bestseller.

WTV: What good would that have done me? Why would I want that? I have enough money to have all the whiskey and prostitutes I want and buy things for my little girl and travel. So far I even pay the mortgage on my studio and get art supplies. When I consider my books, I'm proud. Not that they're perfect. I do a lot of rewriting. I wish I could go back and rewrite my first book, You *Bright and Risen Angels*; I could do a better job. But in the meantime, nobody knows as much about my books as I do. Nobody has the right but me to say which words go into my books or get deleted or edited. When I'm dying, I'll smile, knowing I stood up for my books. If I die with more money, that wouldn't bring a smile to my face. Unless I got better drugs or more delicious-looking nurses. You have to look on the bright side. Are my books autobiographical? Sex and drugs and love never hurt anybody. They might have killed a few people. But they didn't hurt anyone. So the more the better. I'm not a household name and that's fine with me. I just did a five-week reading tour in Europe. Then I have a five-week reading tour for Echo. I'll read at the New School. I could probably read at Columbia and Yale if I wanted to. Publicists set it up. If I can get some money, that's nice. I usually don't. Those trips are basically time deducted from your life. If someone is buying your books, it's a good gesture to be able to please that person. I am grateful to my readers. But I would never give readings otherwise. I don't go to other people's readings. If somebody wrote a good book, I'd rather sit here and read it with the music on and a glass of whiskey in my hand. Do I need any more friends? I have plenty of friends. You see how often the phone rings. The only reason to go on a reading tour is vanity or a sexual purpose. You can always get laid on those trips. But I don't have the vanity, so that takes away half of the reasons right there.

KB: You write the short story and the novel. Will you address the issue of how you see the two forms?

WTV: I write every form I can, including poetry. The most important thing I aspire to is being flexible. That means whatever I'm doing, I should also be doing the opposite. Short stories are wonderful because you can conceive of and see the whole thing, not just in general, but in its parts. With a novel you can't do that, it's too complex. A novel is like real life, it's infinite. There are more possibilities of random things, mysterious correspondences and synchronicities, which the writer can't even see. A short story is like a painting. A novel is like a photograph. You take a loop and look at a photograph and see things the photographer might not have. I deliberately alternate between the short story and the novel. I usually have three or four books going at once. The bulk of my energy will be in one book but I'll also be working here and there on other books, too. I wake up and work until the phone rings. Answer the phone, go back to work and the phone rings a few more times. Then I get irritated and stop answering. I work until I get hungry then I have lunch. Then I work until my little girl gets home and I play with her. Sometimes I keep playing with her or go back to work. Then it's bedtime.

KB: What is this project you were describing earlier? You have purchased a restaurant and you're trying to get hammocks and a TV for the crackheads?

WTV: It used to be a saloon in the 1890s. It's right by the homeless shelter. It's big, 3300 square feet. It's where I'll do my visual arts, my paintings, artists' books and block prints. It will be a good place to bring the models as well. Do you know the expressionist printmaker Kathe Kollwitz? She was in Germany in the 20s. She did pictures of mothers and children. Often the children were dead. The mother was starving. I want to do some stuff like that about homeless people. So it will be convenient for me. They're always asking for jobs and they're right in my parking lot. All I have to do is go outside, give them five bucks and they'll model for me. I don't think the artist has an obligation to anyone. I don't feel any artistic obligation. But I'm so worried about the way the world is, I have been for a long time. But I feel I'm good at loving people. Maybe if I can do drawings that reflect my love for people who others despise or fear, that would be my contribution as a world citizen.

KB: You have a mysterious reputation, a cult of mystique in the Bay Area. You're firewalled. You're a man of high secrecy and you inspire terror. Your name is whispered. You're keeping a very low profile.

WTV: I don't read. I have no vanity. If I were looking for pussy, I'd do it. But why bother? I'd rather be here getting work done. Honestly, if one of my books made a huge amount of money, I'd continue to publish because it makes people happy and I like to please people and give them things, but then I would completely disappear.

KB: *The Royal Family* is a surprisingly erotic novel. Was that a spontaneous effect when you engaged in acts of passion with the page? Or did you intend to write a scathingly vandalistic punk pornographic epic, using High Art as your tool?

WTV: I guess the former. But all my books are erotic. I never met a woman I didn't find beautiful and desirable. I don't care how old she is, how fat she is, whatever. All women are special and erotic. When I'm with a street prostitute covered with abscesses and soiled, my heart goes out to her. And when it does, I feel desire because I love her.

KB: Is this a problem for you in your marriage?

WTV: Marriage is just a state of mind. That means it's not a problem for me.

KB: In my mythological conception, I didn't expect you to be living in a totally suburban brick house with the trappings of a professional, in an atmosphere that projects normality in every polished floorboard. The oriental carpets and rolled leather sofas. The rose bushes in the front yard. In actuality, the biggest and most brick-encrusted house on the street. An immaculately tended and appointed house.

WTV: It's like I've already retired. The truth is, it makes no difference to me where I live. This place happens to please my wife. There might be a period of time when I'm in some 300-dollar-a-night hotel and the next night I'm in a six-dollar hotel. It's all maya and I get a kick out of it.

KB: Given your penchant for disappearance, who is part of the real Bill Vollmann circle?

WTV: My lesbian friend, Michelle. She lives here. She's a babysitter and works at the hospital. I have a friend who works as a commercial photographer. Sometimes we take each other out for lunch. My little girl. My best friend who lives in San Francisco. He used to be a house painter but he got cancer. I have a pal I go shooting with. He's Jewish. He's in Jews With Guns. That might interest you.

KB: It's conceptually interesting. But does it have meetings? I don't want to join anything.

WTV: No meetings. Anyway, those are some of my friends. I don't have friends in the neighborhood. I've survived without doing the soccer dad thing. I don't hang out with other writers. It's not that I'm a snob. It's just never really worked out that way. This society makes so many demands on our time. People are used to being interrupted. But I would rather not be interrupted. If you and I were going to be friends and I saw you every now and then, that would be great. Whatever I say I'm going to do, I do. But if somebody dropped in.... That's why my studio is great. No phone. Somebody bangs on the door and I don't answer. It's perfect. It doesn't have a bed or shower yet, but I put in a 30-foot workbench. It's got a men's room and a women's room. It's got a meat locker. I had the electrician put a light in the meat locker and he said, what's this for? I said, so when I dismember my victims, I can look at them. He frowned. There was a long silence. Then he put the light switch in and went away.

KB: I notice you have these recent literary awards prominently displayed. They're not stashed or thrown away.

WTV: My wife likes them. That's why she put them on the mantle. She used to have all my book jackets framed on the wall but then she had the living room painted. I don't know what she did with them. That was like a year ago. Maybe they're in the closet. Maybe she threw them away.

KB: What's your Dave Eggers connection? Is he your friend?

WTV: I don't think anybody is really Dave's friend. He's a very nice guy but he's so busy. You call Dave and get his answering machine. You're one of 50 messages. I like him. If I thought he were more available, I would enjoy seeing more of him. He's kind of a noble guy. I like Bruno Schulz. He's a prose writer. He was killed in 42 or 43. Cormac McCarthy, *Blood Meridian*, is a great book. Burroughs is a lot of fun. I love his stuff. *The Ticket That Exploded* is my favorite. *Naked Lunch* is great. *Junky* is a wonderful book.

KB: If anyone had picked up the Burroughs torch and continued to write with fearless abandon in content and style, it would be you.

WTV: That's nice of you.

I finish my second glass of Czech absinthe. He assures me he has a steady supply. This is how we part. The invitation to share narcotics replaces the standard let's have lunch sometime soon line. Vollmann, in his Southern gentleman at home quoting scripture while fielding phone publishing deals persona, is a generous host in all respects, and he looks tired. He's had a recent stroke and there's a residue. I shut off the tape.

Interview concluded. October 14. Vollmann on a day of grass fires burning in the hills outside San Francisco. Grass fires that have turned the sky gray and the sun is blood red. It hangs singular, in a perfect enormous ball, all the way to and from. California scrub oaks and sycamores are changing color for autumn, yellowing over alfalfa fields under this blood meridian sun. Not red, but neon Halloween orange. It's a singular and frightening sun, transformed by wild flames that burned 38,000 acres to the north. I snap photographs of the sun setting not over but into San Francisco Bay, like a bloated sea mammal returning to the fluid depths. Such photographs appear on the *San Francisco Chronicle* front page the next day.

I brought the camera to photograph Vollmann, but I don't. Vollmann elicits the desire to both injure and defend him. You want to beat him and have him arrested and yet, as a magical being, you intuit his vulnerability and do not violate him with a camera. I instinctively feel protective, as if encountering an endangered species at the edge of extinction. We all live our lives on multiple levels simultaneously. For some, the levels are profoundly mutually exclusive and the intensity of the juggling more obvious, in the conceits, sleight of hand and collateral damage ensuring from art lived on a cellular level. For some artists, the creative medium requires ingredients such as molecular scientists use for making mutants and clones, radioactive compounds like I-125 and P-32, lethal and necessary for the enterprise. A. Alvarez said of Sylvia Plath that art of a certain order is a murderous business. He didn't note that some know this from the beginning and deliberately choose and adhere to this path, writing as they bleed from the eyes and ears. Vollmann, who likes to please people, did not disappoint.

A Day at Vollmann's Studio (2007)

Terri Saul

William T. Vollmann appears at the door just as I turn in the drive. It's raining, so he helps me carry my camera bags in. I offer up a Christmas cactus and a box of clementines, also known as kid-glove mandarins, or simply, tangerines. Bill has a story, and after he first checks that I've locked my car, he tells it. He'd saved one segment of a Christmas cactus from when he was a child, and it lived, one of his many treasures, soon to germinate his rooftop garden, complete with parapet. His moral compass points towards the living. He nurtures voraciously, like "a white knight with a perpetual hard-on" (*Expelled From Eden*).

Walls covered, salon style in front, transition just past women's and men's restrooms painted in rough strokes of bold immoral color, to a dark bedroom/library complete with his oft-mentioned meat-locker closet, to a more academic critique-style corridor. Works had been lined up, propped on straight, blonde wall-runner rails. Ken Miller's prostitute photos lined the imitation café restrooms. Bill, being a prolific writer, has found the capacity for producing and collecting a vault of visual art. A collection of Soviet propaganda posters hangs over the entrance.

Everywhere art equipment announces itself— vintage, accordion-shaped view-camera bodies, vacuum-powered printing machines, ultraviolet cyanotype exposure unit, darkroom trays, an enlarger, baker's trays lined with drying prints, and a modular work bench as long as a strip mall parking lot.

Vollmann says everything should be displayed in the studio. "I figure, if you don't see things, all the things that you have, all your watercolors together, your engraving tools and everything else together, you're not going to use them all. And then you can get inspired and say, Oh, I'd like to do this right now."

It's an embattled sense of art one is tempted to link to his novels. If it's not used regularly, ink will dry up, watercolors will crack, woodcuts will gather dust. He's even made his workbench modular, so that if he ever was forced to downsize, he could take smaller pieces of it along.

His daughter has her own drawing space in the main room. Her notes to daddy and sketches are pinned up near low-lying tables. He's struggling with the creative parent's dilemma, how to have the freedom of a studio, a place where his individual work can germinate unhampered, in its raw state, without shame, and a place for his daughter to growup, where her friends and their parents will feel comfortable. How would it feel to be the daughter of Bill Vollmann? The conservative parents in his area aren't necessarily fond of his photos of prostitutes, even though in most of the photos the prostitutes are not acting particularly risqué, sometimes wearing everyday clothing, or simply posed facing the camera straight-on. It's pretty tame work. Only the subject matter is taboo, in a "family-friendly" setting. He's a good father. He says that having a child has been the most fulfilling part of his life. He enjoys having her around in the studio.

Vollmann is completely self-taught as an artist. He's never taken a print-making class, or a photography class. Everything he does with paper and images he's learned about in books. He makes the art for himself only, a purist who never considers his audience. He said he doesn't care about showing his work in galleries. His interactions with his daughter's classmates and their families may be the only time he's really had to weigh how he might be perceived. On the other hand he says we're all prostitutes.

We spend most of the day looking through his hand-colored illustrations for *The Butterfly Stories*, *The Best Way to Smoke Crack*, his Arctic journal, and his new oversized Candle Stories set, odes to friends and lovers.

I've been one of the first journalists (to borrow from the introduction sentence of heroic correspondence written by Vollmann to justify a deadline extension) to view an immense archive of art produced by one whom the Inuit call "Bill the Tourist," an ethnographer of everything that is unbelievable and startlingly true.

Bill shows me around. Pointing to a row of Oak Park photos (he was following Oak Park prostitutes in Sacramento, for quite a while, but had to quit after so many of them died violently, or became deathly ill. His bullet-proof armor couldn't protect him enough from the sadness):

* * *

William T. Vollmann: These are mostly platinum up here. This is kind of an experiment. This is platinum and this is gum over cyanotype.

Next to the figurative work is a group of abstract linear sketches appearing to morph from metal into light into photo paper.

Terri Saul: Are those photographs platinum drawings?

WTV: That's right. So, for this I just drew on a negative, and then printed the negative.

He points me towards more chemistry experiments and portraits.

WTV: This is a palladium toned printing-out-paper print, and it's been sitting out here for a couple of years without any change, so the palladium seems to really make it pretty stable. This is gum over platinum, and this is just straight gum. The gum is really, really hard. I don't know if you understand the process.

Gum Arabic, sometimes called "tears," is a substance used to increase the viscosity of ink and to make watercolors more transparent. It makes his fingers peel. He feels sick when he's working with it. But it probably won't do him harm in the end.

WTV: It's one of the first photographic processes. Basically you take gum arabic, with watercolor in it, and you make it photosensitive, and so it's as permanent as the watercolor itself. Artist's grade watercolors will last for hundreds of years, presumably. But, each time you print it, you get a very, very thin print. So you have to print over and over. So, this has about 12 or 13 printings in register on it. So you get this special kind of look to it. You can't get great detail with gum. It's just more of a moody thing.

TS: It looks like a ghost.

WTV: Yeah it does. And, she is a ghost. She's dead now.

We stand in the hallway silently staring at the photo of a ghost, together admiring her strong visage, before she was confronted with the brutal fact of her shortened life.

WTV: These are gum-printed negative drawings. So, each one of these is printed about four times. See, it has kind of a three-dimensional effect.

He shows me more platinum, more gum. We look at photographs of prostitutes posing any way they want.

Attending another set of photos, Bill is working hard on making lots of prints from his negative archive, from diverse sources, taken over many years.

WTV: These I'm just flattening. I just printed these yesterday. This one is 35mm. It's from Columbia from about 1999. This is a child prostitute. I think this is her mother, the procuress. I said, "Well, how about instead of paying for sex, how about if I pay for a picture?"

He shows me another photo from Columbia.

WTV: These two police had one machine pistol, between them, but they felt relatively safe in their police station, because they had a picture of Christ. I will say, they didn't really want to get in trouble with the criminals, so they tried to stay in their police stations. It was very bad for them.

I notice that Vollmann uses a medieval-looking WTV stamp as his signature, with the W on the right side, the V on the left side, and the T in the middle.

TS: Is that a hand-made rubber stamp?

WTV: It's soapstone. These are some of my block prints here.

TS: Are these documented anywhere? Do you have any books....

WTV: They're documented by you, Terri.

We continue the tour.

WTV: This is my darkroom here. These are mainly test prints and mistakes that I put on the wall so that I can work with them. This is the place where I do the processing.

TS: Renaissance man is an understatement.

WTV: I'm just getting started, Terri. Wait till you come five years from now. You'll see what I've done.

These exposure units are to print my gum prints, and platinum, and cyanotypes. Do you know what a contact print is? These are 35 millimeter. You have to put those in an enlarger, and you project it down here, and then you take it and develop it. These other prints here, the negative is the same size as the print. With the older style stuff, that's how you had to do it. So, what you do is you put the negative in what's called a contact printing frame, which is this thing here. You clean it obviously. You put the negative down first, and then your piece of sensitized paper on top of it, and then you lock it in place so it can't move, and you put it in here, and you turn on one of the ultraviolet lights, so you can probably see how there's blue light in there.

These older processes are called printing out processes, which means that you actually see the image form. You know with a photograph in an enlarger, the paper just looks blank, when you're done. You have to put it in the developer. But here it actually develops before your eyes, so you know when it's done. But it's very slow. You're looking at 20 minutes, 40 minutes. So, this cyanotype takes about 20 minutes to print.

TS: So, this is printed on sun print paper.

WTV: Yes, it is.

TS: You've placed a bunch of different objects on the paper itself to make an impression?

WTV: Yes. That's called a photogram. Some of them can be very dense. See these are some test gum prints, and as you can see they're still very weak and not right. Each one of these had to print for about two hours. So, there's a lot of time spent.

TS: What are these?

WTV: Oh, those are some photographic reproductions that someone did, some cheap things of some of my watercolors. I can show you those watercolors. Do you want some tea or some booze by the way?

Tchaikovsky plays and Bill makes me some kind of medicinal tea from a metal tin box he'd decorated with one of his etchings of a grasshopper. The incised metal has been rubbed over with printer's ink.

TS: Do you live here in the studio?

WTV: Sometimes, Terri, yeah. It all depends on my mood. But, I also have a home. I spend some time there. It's unclear which space I'll spend more time in, in the future.

TS: Where do you do most of your writing?

WTV: It depends on what I'm working on. I do a lot of poetry and stuff here, and if there's some current fiction or non-fiction, then I tend to work in the other house for that, because, it's my preference to have no phone here, and, you know, no one can reach me here at all, so I can get a lot done, and have a lot of peace. But, a lot of the time I need to be near the phone. So, if I'm at the other place, where there's a phone. That's a good place to be when I'm working on some of the books with deadlines. So, that's sort of how it works.

TS: Tell me about this.

I point to a door-sized table filled with hefty upright, over-sized books, balanced like a domino rally covered in plastic sheeting.

WTV: It's called "The Book of Candles" and it's a folio. There are 10 of them. Let's see, I started it in 95, and I've finished most of them this year. I finally sent one off to my dealer, and one off to the Lilly Library.

TS: Who's your dealer?

WTV: Her name's Priscilla Juvelis. She handles just my artist's books. She used to be in Cambridge, but she's now in Maine.

TS: Do they show in a gallery space before being sold?

WTV: Usually they go straight to collectors. The editions are really small, and I'm not sure that it really makes sense to have shows. I could change my mind on that, but, it seems like if you do that, you spend a lot of money, probably more than you're going to get.

TS: On airfare, hotels, and framing....

WTV: Yeah, that's right, Terri. And, I'm not really a vain person. I couldn't care less if people look at my stuff. I'm just happy to make it and if I can sell enough visual art and writing to get by and do more, that's all I care about.

TS: Do you think of yourself as an artist with a little writing problem?

WTV: I do my best. Yeah, I really like to do a lot of everything. I'm a curious person.

We arrive at the fully stocked wood engraving area. There's a block of wood covered with a sketch.

WTV: Back in February or March, I spent about an hour and a half in one place, standing in the snow on top of this truck, drawing this — the mountain. Here's a bunch of pine trees, and so on and so forth. And, so I've just started engraving it. This is the thing that I also used to engrave that metal box that you saw.

TS: Those illustrations in your novels, like in the *Seven Dreams* series, are they engravings?

WTV: Most of those are pen and ink drawings. But, sometimes I'll use them as masters for engravings. So, in *Butterfly Stories*, for instance, I did a bunch of drawings, which I then made into magnesium plates that I printed by hand. But, this is how this thing works. It's hooked up to an air compressor. So, it's a little loud.

He pulls me over to him and places some headphones over my ears. I turn off the recorder while he engraves. After the motor whirs to a stop, we take off for the island of tables in the center of the studio.

WTV: I was in Norway, and did some illustrations to some of the Norse Eddas. The ancient Norse myths are best preserved in the Eddas. So, they found me some professional models, and cut me some Norwegian pine wood, to get it just right.

TS: Norwegian wood.

WTV — That's right, Terri. This is one of them. This is the goddess, Freya. It says her name in runes, carved backwards obviously, so it'll be right reading, and then there were these petroglyphs that my editor showed me from the Sami people, the Laplanders. So, I did some drawings of some of those and put these ancient petroglyphs in too. This woman is actually an anthropologist who was excavating some Norse stuff at the time that she modeled for me. I just drew her. I'd already decided that all of the Norse things were going to have this border. I was staying in Lillehammer, where the Olympics were. So, I spent a lot of time outside, and found some birch trees, and kind of filled the area with the birch trees, and then it was ready for the first printing. I think it's going to be a suite of block prints. I'm not sure what I'll do with them yet.

This is Odin, and he gashed his side with a spear, and then after hanging for nine days the runes came to him. So that's the complete runic alphabet. That's the Well of Weird. He gave one of his eyes to get a drink from that water.

There's another one of Freya, a less successful one. So, I probably won't include that in the suite.

This is the seeress that Odin called to tell him about how the world was going to end. She was a woman in her grave that he called up, and she didn't want to come, but she had to thanks to his magic.

Vollmann refers to his model.

WTV: And this woman was like the perfect woman for it. She could actually recite some of this poem, the seeress's sayings to Odin, you know, in Old Norse. I did a bunch of drawings of her.

TS: Does printmaking remind you of the rubbings taken from old tombstones?

WTV: Yeah, sure, it does with these relief prints. That's Odin.

TS: It looks very natural, like it appeared there from behind, from behind the paper.

WTV: Well, that's nice of you to say. So, those are some of the Norse ones. Oh, and see, there's the one you were just looking at of my little girl.

TS: You hand-colored that?

WTV: Yeah. Usually I hand-color them, but I probably won't hand-color the Norse ones. There she is again [his daughter]. She was playing with some praying mantises.'

TS: Does she have pet praying mantis?

WTV: Right now she has a pet lizard. This is on a different kind of paper obviously. I did this in Cambodia. This one I did here. I found a piece of wood that had some knots in it. I kind of wanted this woman to be the wood spirit.

TS: You used the knotholes in the wood to represent her nipples and vagina?

I wonder if I should have said cunt, perineum, pussy, or vulva.

WTV: Yeah, she models for me quite often.

TS: You're kind of a Christ-like figure, considering the amount of time you spend with prostitutes.

WTV: Oh, sigh ... they are. They are like that. They take away so much suffering.

We look at the illustrations for "The Best Way to Smoke Crack."

WTV: This was a Vietnamese woman. This is a dry point. I used that engraver, and I carved into a copper plate, and then rubbed printer's ink, green printer's ink, and then printed it with a spoon, and then hand-colored it.

TS: Have you created a special edition of "The Best Way to Smoke Crack" with these illustrations?

WTV: Well, I've been thinking about it for a few years, and I'll show you a book that I have where I finally just bound all the possibilities for it.

He leads me to more prints.

WTV: This is a Hawaiian one that I did. There are a couple of versions of it, and I haven't yet decided whether I want to hand-color it or what color it should be printed in.

TS: Let's look at these foliage engravings.

The scene looks like a dense, complex mound of vegetation, very thick with leaves and spidery branches.

WTV: I really enjoy vegetation so much. It's just really beautiful. That's a gum print. That's another gum print.

We stop at an image of a budding vagina, the opening crowned by a string of small whitish flowers.

TS: Are those pikake flowers?

WTV: This was done in Thailand and they call them Phuang Malai, that garland.

TS: It's a vaginal garland?

WTV: Yeah, well, I mean, that's what I used it for. They just hang them from ferries or taxis or whatever for good luck. This took about seven or eight printings to build up.

TS: It looks like a shrine.

WTV: That's how it should look. I mean, that's a sacred place.

We open another set of matted photos.

WTV: I'm doing a lot of stuff with Japanese Noh theater. So, this is an ancient Noh mask the guy's holding. Here's another Noh picture. And again, these are gum prints. This is gum over cyanotype. This is a Noh actor acting out the part of Yoroboshi, the blind priest's song.

TS: Have you seen Mizogutchi's *Ugetsu*? In the film, there's a ghost character, who is a Noh figure, being played by a woman. Usually they're played by men.

WTV: No, I haven't. That's neat. I've interviewed one Noh actress. It's still pretty uncommon as you say.

Bill unwraps boxes and books wrapped in plastic sheeting,

WTV: I put this stuff out for the rainy season, because I don't entirely trust my roof. This is a folio edition of the *Book of Candles*. This is a wood block. It's actually two pieces of wood. I did this in Malaysia. I drew and engraved on the blocks of wood by hand.

He opens up a hinged door to a set of loose prints inside the first book.

Priscilla Juvelis's rare books site describes *The Book of Candles* as

"... a suite of eight religious and blasphemous love-poems to prostitutes ... housed in a sailcloth-covered basswood clamshell box which the artist / author has painted, collaged with hand-painted woodblock prints, and suitably adorned with gewgaws ...

WTV: There are the candles that I've engraved. See, even the screws I've engraved, and these little things. Each one of these is different. I decided not to bind them, but just to present them in a box. You can flip through if you want, Terri.

TS: Do you think the sentiments in your letter, "Crabbed Cautions of a Bleeding-hearted Un-deleter," would apply to your art too?

WTV: With the visual art, I'm probably a little more selective. Actually, you know, I do throw away, I mean I don't use a lot of the stuff that I write. I might keep it, but I don't use it, necessarily. And, with the visual art though, often, you know, I'll produce a print or an image, and I'll realize it's just not good enough. You know, like one of those prints of Freya.

He takes down an oversized handbound book of his various versions of "The Best Way to Smoke Crack," a life-sized book, the size of a small person, with a large cut-out of a cockroach on the cover. We photograph pages from the book.

TS: Who are your favorite artists?

WTV: I like Blake very much, William Blake.

Vollmann points to a painting of a prostitute.

WTV: She has abscesses on her thighs.

TS: Is she the one, Sunflower, from *The Royal Family*, who was asking Tyler to pop the pimple on her butt?

WTV: Hmmm. A lot of them say stuff like that.

TS: Back to William Blake. His work is really ecstatic.

WTV: Yeah, it is.

TS: The blue and yellow.

WTV: Yeah, it's beautiful. Absolutely. There are overlooked artists, like Andrew Wyeth, passed over because he wants to paint every pine needle, or every single blade of grass.

We look through more pages in "The Best Way to Smoke Crack." He tells me the story of a prostitute friend of his, a grandmother, who used his tube of Cadmium red paint as lipstick. Cadmium is the most brilliant red hue, but is a heavy metal, highly toxic, even in minute doses.

WTV: When she was posing for me here she was talking about one of her customers who was really, really nice to her and she said she didn't know what she would do if he died. And then, I was told later that she was strangled. I haven't seen her since. But, I knew her for probably about three years, and every time I would get a hotel room and I would see her, I would say, "You know, you can come in, and you can sleep here." Sometimes she would, if I wasn't around, she would steal my cadmium red watercolor and use it for lipstick. I said, you know, that's kind of bad for you. But, seeing as how she died from being strangled, well, I guess it didn't do her any harm. Poor thing.

We turn to another prostitute on another page.

WTV: A very, very nice intelligent woman.

TS: Her body is about four times the size of the car in front of her. She looks like an Amazon, or like Alice in Wonderland coming out of the gutter.

WTV: Yeah, she said that she couldn't decide what size she was, so I figured this would be a good way to draw her.

TS: Were you on anything when you did these drawings? Do you have any experience making art while using drugs?

WTV: I might have a beer or two every now and then. How about you, Terri?

TS: Beer. Wine.

WTV: That sounds good.

TS: Do you ever feel blocked, or have a hard time making new work?

WTV: No, because I do what I want. If I don't feel like doing this, then I do something else. How could I be blocked?

TS: You practice so many different art forms that you can always turn to something new.

WTV: Yeah, that's right. So, it's really fun for me.

TS: Are you a musician too?

WTV: No. How about you?

TS: Well, no, not really. But, I read the Shostakovich passages in the Palm Tree of Deborah in *Europe Central* over and over again.

WTV: Oh, you like Shostakovich?

TS: I like Shostakovich. But I liked more the metaphors about the chromatic scale, the "transgressive harmonies of the chromatic scale."

WTV: Oh, that was fun. Yeah. I really, really enjoy listening to Shostakovich now. It was a little hard for him to live the life he did. Actually, it took me a lot of work to get to the point where I could understand him a little bit. It wasn't natural for me to appreciate those harmonies. I'm sure it isn't for most people. It was a good stretch of self-improvement.

TS: Do you think that that's what people need to do when they see your work, or when they read your work, that they need to be open to the "transgressive harmonies of the chromatic scale?"

WTV: If they want to, Terri, but I think that if they don't like my work, or don't want to ever study it, or enjoy it, that's ok with me. That doesn't hurt my feelings.

He turns the pages of "The Best Way to Smoke Crack."

WTV: This is a small bar on Capp Street.

TS: Do you relate to Shostakovich, because he used so many notes in between the other notes, like you use so many complex images and words and marks?

WTV: Absolutely, Terri. Yeah. Yeah, I would say that I do. Yeah.

TS: Perhaps, you're a modern Shostakovich.

WTV: Well, thank you very much, Terri.

TS: Can you talk a little bit about the differences between printmaking and your more linear contour drawing with pen, where you're drawing the figure more loosely?

WTV: Well, I think, probably, if I had to choose, I would choose printmaking, because I love the crispness of the line, and then it's great to watercolor afterwards. But, what you gain with a print, you lose in spontaneity. And, with a drawing, it's really nice if someone is posing for you, and you can just go to town with a handful of watercolors, and that's very, very relaxing.

We turn another page.

WTV: This was a very, very nice woman. Usually, they say, "Oh, can you give me a little bit of money to "get well" before I pose for you?" And, you know, maybe 25 percent of the time they just run away when they have the money. But, I always think, that's ok. So, this woman went, and got her crack, and she really wanted to share it with me. You know, she wanted to be really nice. I thought that was so generous, it was giving me the thing that she most valued.

Bill switches out the Tchaikovsky. He asks me to choose a CD. I pick John Fahey, someone who strays off the map with non-standard tunings, and unheard of scales on the guitar.

WTV: I guess we'd better turn it down.

TS: Who are some of your favorite musicians?

WTV: You mean composers?

TS: Who are some of your favorite musicians you enjoy listening to here in the studio, lately?

WTV: Oh, Scarlatti, a lot. Shostakovich, of course.

Back to the art.

WTV: This one and this one (pointing to more colored prints of prostitutes) are of the heroine of "The Best Way to Smoke Crack."

We turn off the recorder to unpack one of his CoTangent Press books, "The Happy Girls," a heavy book, encased in metal, with a peephole that lights up when the batteries are functioning. Parts of the book are held in place by a black lace bra and its clasps.

After a break, we return to a discussion of literature.

TS: Have you read Laxness, Halldor Laxness?

WTV: I sure have, Terri.

TS: What do you like most about Laxness's works?

WTV: It's kind of funny, but at the same time it's just brutally true, and really, really sad.

TS: This drawing of a hanged person reminds me of Jon Hreggvidsson, in "Iceland's Bell." His life was ruined because he was caught stealing a piece of cord, fishing line. He's imprisoned over and over again, and never quite escapes.

WTV: Oh, "Iceland's Bell." That's a cheerful one.

TS: He's a survivor. He has these songs, the Icelandic Sagas, which soothe him, and help him think about ways to get out of his horrible situations.

WTV: That's true, Terri.

TS: How about "Independent People"?

WTV: That's a wonderful one.

TS: That one's my favorite.

WTV: Yeah, that's probably his best. I like "World Light" a lot, too. That one's about this guy who is a poet, and he can really appreciate the world and see the beauty incredibly well. But, he's a terrible poet. So, it just comes out as ... nothing. Nothing. He's got a very sad life.

We have a snack of potato chips and share a bottle of He'Brew, "The Chosen Beer." Vollmann lounges on the carpet, and asks me to sit down in his oversized pink chair. The chair's springs are busted. It's upholstered in some kind of embossed terrycloth.

TS: Kathe Kollwitz....

WTV: I have several monographs of her work.

TS: Compare someone like Kathe Kollwitz, someone who shows the true suffering of war to some of the modern war paintings being made now, like Steve Mumford, the Norman Rockwell in Iraq paintings, very heroic looking.

WTV: Yeah, the heroism, that's all they know. Well, now that the Democrats are getting a little bit of their own back, maybe there won't be as much fear on people's part. I've been called a lot of names for being against the war. I was against the war before it started. People booed me.

TS: Yes.

WTV: Well I'm glad you were against it too, Terri.

He rapidly changes the subject.

WTV: So, if I were going to draw you, how would you want to be drawn?

TS: I think I'd let you decide, since you're the artist.

WTV: Oh, that sounds good.

TS: How would you want to draw me?

WTV: It depends on whether you'd want to be drawn with or without clothes.

TS: I could think about being a model. Would you pay me anything?

WTV: Sure. What would you like me to pay you?

TS: What's the going rate these days for live figure drawing models?

WTV: Well, in a studio, there are lots of people there, so they might charge 80 dollars for three hours and it works out to about five dollars per person. But if I hire someone just to model for me, I'll usually pay 10 or 20 bucks for an hour. How much would you pay me, Terri?

TS: You'd model for me? I'd probably pay you a little more than that.

WTV: You would? You wouldn't have to.

TS: I would think that you would be charging a much higher rate, probably something closer to 100 dollars an hour.

WTV: Well, Terri, I think you are a lot more beautiful than I am. If I pay you 10, you should only pay me five.

TS: You know what? We could just trade. You model for me, and I'll model for you. It'll be equal.

WTV: Sure. That sounds good!

*   *   *

At the end of the day, I shuttle him from Sacramento back to Berkeley in a driving rain. In the car we, talk about parenting, the importance of patience, and on a broader level, the need to have a more lenient judicial system in place, that the overly harsh punishment of criminals, stretching of the three-strikes law, and lengthy prison stays for drug crimes are taking away the basic rights of people who require at most a slap on the wrist for petty crimes, like drug possession. He tells me about the research he's doing on a book about the court system's response to men accused of rape. Hydroplaning in my Cutter on Interstate 80 in a flood zone, I learn that the old standby of removing pressure from the gas and the brakes, while not attempting to steer, works wonders, and impresses a veteran of foreign wars.

We spend about an hour privately discussing the joys of marriage.

We also talk about his freight-train hopping research. He's been hopping freight trains on the weekends. He discovered an Atlas, originating in Portland, for freight train hoppers. I recommend the photojournalism of the Polaroid Kid, and he offers me the chance to be a box-car warmer, or to arrive via train on my next visit. Bill says I'm a good driver, because "We are still alive, Terri." He is, indeed, a genius.

Appendix: CoTangent
Press Book Arts

After writing the critical section of this book, I was given the opportunity to examine copies of most of Vollmann's handmade "book objects" that were either in the archives of the Lilly Library at Indiana University, or in the private collection of the Lilly's director, Dr. Breon Mitchell — Mitchell has the only complete collection in existence, which includes several one-of-a-kind volumes. Vollmann wears a few other hats beyond writer: photographer, painter, small press publisher, poet, and book designer. With his CoTangent Press, Vollmann has created what are commonly called "book objects" or "book arts" out of stories, poems and novels; they are printed in limited editions, lavishly designed, often with original art so no single copy in an edition is like the other. They also carry weighty price tags: anywhere from $5,000 to $30,000, sold to galleries, private collectors, museums, and friends.

Little has been written about Vollmann the book designer/publisher; since the editions are rare and expensive, few people own the works or have seen them outside the world of collectors and unique book aficionados. The summer 1993 issue of *The Review of Contemporary Fiction* includes Katherine Spielman's short article, "The Book as Apparatus: William Vollmann's Special Editions," which discusses the attributes of "The Happy Girls" as both a work of art and an object that *houses a text*, rather than the text itself, which is

> crafted to reflect the content.... "The Happy Girls," a story about prostitutes, is constructed so that one must ring a buzzer to enter the narrative. Once inside, the straps of a brassiere must be un-hooked to proceed. The result is the readers' sense that they are entering the world of prostitution. Once inside that world they are confronted with stark black and white photographs of prostitutes whose bleakness contrasts with the ornate color of the book's entrance.

Terri Saul, in her interview included in this book, visits Vollmann's art studio in downtown Sacramento to take a firsthand look at how Vollmann labors to put each copy of each edition together (in some cases, Vollmann works on each for several years, when he has the time). Her original online interview (truncated from the one herein) was accompanied by photos of various pages of art and text (especially paintings for "The Best Way to Smoke Crack") but have since been taken offline. In an appendix for *Expelled from Eden: A William T. Vollmann Reader*, my co-editor, Larry McCaffery, and I provide photographs from *The Happy Girls* and *The Convict Bird*, from copies McCaffery owns, along with the CoTangent catalogue descriptions. These are the only works in print that discuss Vollmann's art books; thus, I feel it necessary to add this appendix and believe it is important for readers to know and understand this particular side of Vollmann. (Vollmann as photographer is another important aspect; his photography is well-represented in a number of his books, such as *The Atlas, Rising Up and Rising Down, Poor People, Riding Toward Everywhere*, and *Imperial*. An extensive collection is housed in special collections at the Ohio University Library, along with his papers.)

In the following list of books, all except the first are published under the CoTangent Press colophon, owned by Vollmann and located in Sacramento, California. They are sold directly by Vollmann, through East Coast art dealer Priscilla Juvelis, and at specialty bookstores that handle these books on commission.

Descriptive Bibliography

A Tale of the Dying Lungs. Los Angeles, CA: Vagabond Press, 1988. The first handmade edition Vollmann put on the market. A 25½" × 12¾" printed and pictorial broadside, illustrated with a black and purple X-ray image of a human chest. Two hundred hand-numbered copies were printed on Rives Heavyweight by Patrick Reagh. Signed by Vollmann in blue ink and with an original pencil drawing of an octopus figure. Copies are still available from the publisher. I have seen it sold on eBay.

The Convict Bird: A Children's Poem. San Francisco, CA: CoTangent Press, 1987. Several editions were printed. There is an edition of 100 copies, of which ten were bound in steel by Matthew Heckert. From the limitation colophon: "For each of those ten, a street prostitute sold her hair to make the place-marker ribbon." A second edition of 12 copies was printed in 1993. The illustrations appear in black and white.

The book is dedicated to, and proceeds went to, "Veronica Compton #276077," an inmate in a women's prison. On page 15 is a letter to Vollmann from Compton about the ordeal she went through when taken to the hospital for a mammogram: "They put chains and cuff on both my ankles (which hurt) and a waist chain with cuffs on my upper body.... I could barely walk; I literally had a step value of about 4 inches! I had to ... walk about two blocks in front of children and parents. It was a most humiliating experience...."

Breon Mitchell owns a one-of-a-kind special edition with colored images and handwritten text, encased in a silver box. This copy was specially commissioned, as described: "This second edition of THE CONVICT BIRD is limited to one copy. Ben Pax bound the inner book and prepared the case. William T. Vollmann engraved the case before it was plated and wrote the illustrated the text [sic] in the inner book, whose cover he painted." Inside the case are two small painted bones, replicated femurs. On the outside cases, held in place by metal twine, are four objects: what appears to be an animal skull (or maybe a seashell?), a fish, three yellow and black beads together, and one yellow and black bead alone.

Epitaph for Mein. **1991.** From the CoTangent catalogue: "An unpleasant true story from *13 Stories.*" Lemon-gilded acrylic on iridescent pastels. Edition of one copy. Owner unknown.

The Grave of Lost Stories. **1993.** Edition of 15 deluxe copies only, 13 of which are for sale, all on Johannot paper, each signed and numbered by the artist/author and binder. Page size: 10⅞ × 7⅞ inches. Bound by Ben Pax: steel and grey marble box (a tomb) fitted to custom steel hinge by means of a copper sheet riveted to the steel and then crimped upward to form a pan. The hinge is powder-coated black as is the interior. The front cover is incised with the title, author's initials and [Edgar Allen] Poe's birth and death dates. The copy numbers appear in roman numeral on the back cover. Along the fore edge, 13 teeth have been set in handmade silver bezels. The inside covers each have four brass and copper rods, oxidized green. The book itself is bound in boards with linen spine which are "leafed, and variegated and painted in metallic fungoid patterns over which the author has painted a female figure to represent one of the stories" (Vollmann's description). The boards are copper colored and the female is in blue with on-lays of four small white bones outlining the skeleton. The book lays into the marble box-sarcophagus. The four illustrations are hand-colored by the author who has also made a number of small revisions in the text. The text is letterpress by Alastair Johnston in Electra and Cochin with display in Caslon, Marbleheart, Rimmed Lith and Astoria at Poltroon Press. The title page is printed in three colors, guards of black and gold gilt Japanese paper.

Another edition is owned by Breon Mitchell and described in Vollmann's catalogue: "A prior CoTangent edition of one handwritten folio copy (dated 1990) was illustrated on each recto side in the most poisonous pigments available (bound in galvanic battery and pickled squid)." This edition contains 11 loose folio sheets with handwritten text and water color illustrations. Text tends to be on the left side of sheet, illustrations on the right. Housed inside wood box with removable cover. The cover is painted black with a raised image of a woman, also in black, with a green face and red lips. The hair on the woman's head seems to be real human hair. Spielman discusses this edition in her article, and that it is in Vollmann's personal collection, which he later sold to Dr. Mitchell; Vollmann included three original paintings (two of Poe, one of a woman) with the sale. Price of the sale is unknown, as Mitchell paid Vollmann a single price for a number of these art books.

   The Happy Girls. CoTangent, 1992. One of the more intricate book objects. The text is housed inside either mirror glass or a birchwood box painted black by James M. Lombino, depending on which copy — I have seen both: Mitchell owns a copy of the metal box; Larry McCaffery owns a copy of the wooden box (see photos in *Expelled from Eden*). Each box is unique; all require a key to open the padlock. As Spielman explains, one opens the door and enters the world of prostitution, as seen by Vollmann, in Thailand: "The outside is severe, the inside colorful" (65). The peephole on the cover slides (in some copies, is hinged) and we see the face of a woman, a Thai prostitute. There is a doorbell; when pressed, the bell buzzes and a red light shines on the woman's face. Opening the door, we see the full photograph of this woman, taken by Ken Miller and produced in magnesium silver, who has self-inflicted scars on her body from a razor blade. The back cover shows her back and buttocks, with the words "HURT BY LOVE" etched in her flesh. The book contains four other photos of prostitutes by Miller. The book itself is 16" × 20", secured inside the box by a harness constructed from bra straps, sewn, the spine adorned with lingerie. The text, 12 pages, is hand-pressed by the author on smooth triple-ply acid-free 100 percent rag stock. Each page is a different color, using Daniel Smith etching inks. Four D-Cell batteries and a light bulb are included.

   Whores for Gloria. CoTangent, 1992. Two editions exist. The first removes the five signatures from the 1991 Pantheon American hardcover edition and rebinds them into new boards, each with an original water painting of a woman's face, with photographs by Ken Miller; some copies have ten photos, others five photos. This was an edition of 20. Each copy is different, from the hand panting by Vollmann on the cover to text handwritten in the cover's verso page. E.g., copy 11 of 20 (archived in the Lilly Library) contains a line drawing of what appears to be a poppy plant, and handwritten text: "Gloria. But later Gloria said I want you to be a boy not a girl" and in the back cover: "I guess you showed me all right." The five Ken Miller photos are: (1) a blonde woman in a white mini-skirt and black tank top with white socks and black loaders smiling and standing in a parking lot; (2) an African American woman in a mini-skirt and halter, grabbing her crotch like a man, standing in an empty alley at night; (3) a topless woman in a mini-skirt, black nylons, and high heels standing on top of a wood platform in a bedroom or motel room; (4) a naked African American woman leaning over a sink in a motel room, perhaps vomiting, with Vollmann sitting the right hand corner, watching her; (5) the same woman in 3, lying down on a couch and looking at the camera in a seductive pose. Copy 18 of 20 (also in the Lilly) contains on the cover verso page a line drawing, in black magic marker, of a woman holding a bottle of booze, and the handwritten text: "Wow, said Jimmy — you're BEAUTFUL. Well, I'm." On the back cover: "going to drink twice as much" and a drawing of a woman with her eyes closed. The ten Ken Miller photos are: (1) a faceless woman holding open her vagina; (2) a naked woman with an unclasped bra, eyes closed; (3) an African American man and woman on the bed, the woman holding the man's erect penis in her hand, the man handing her money; (4) a naked woman covering her face with her hands, standing in an artsy pose; (5) two African American women, one naked, the other topless, with the topless woman shooting heroin into her right arm as the other woman watches; (6) a transsexual prostitute sitting on the hood of a car by the street; (7) another transsexual in a long skirt and halter, sitting in a bar and holding a cigarette; (8) a woman with long braided black hair, in a white mini-skirt and white halter, leaning against a stool in a bar; (9) close-up of a woman's face; (10) close-up of a woman's spread anus and vagina.

The second exists in two copies only, as indicated by the inserted limitation page: "This copy is no. 1 of 2 deluxe copies of *Whores for Gloria*, bound in 8-ply museum board and nickel-plated rods. The boards were painted with acrylic and ink by the author. Ten photographs by Ken Miller grace this binding, and the text (taken from the Pantheon first American edition) has been illustrated by the author. This two-copy edition is the second (and more elaborate) CoTangent edition of *Whores for Gloria*, and was completed in 1993." Many of the Miller photos are the same in copy 18 of the first CoTangent edition. On the opposite side of the limitation page is a partial unfinished line drawing and would seem to indicate Vollmann cut this page out of a larger sheet he was drawing on. The boards are cut to resemble a woman's buttocks and legs and are painted to suggest this. The way this art object works is: one opens the legs up and the text is situated where a vagina would be. This copy is owned by Mitchell and has been sitting in his office at the Lilly Library. The sharp metal ends of the book make this object a somewhat dangerous work of hard to handle — one has to be careful. Maybe Vollmann intended this — just as it is hazardous to touch a prostitute in real life, so is this artist's symbolic rendition. Attached to the leg is a pair of black panties — it is unknown if they are new or used items Vollmann may have appropriated from a streetwalker. It is a heavy and unwieldy object.

It is interesting to note that Vollmann has re-created his book in both editions as issued by the publisher: removing the dust jacket and matte boards, adding in photos (some of the photos appear in the U.K. edition by Pan Books, but not the U.S. Pantheon edition), designing the novel into what's more in concert in his imagination than a commercial publishing product. This shows the artist taking a commodity sold on the open market and re-claiming the text — that is, this is what the publisher sees his work as, but for a select few who can afford it, Vollmann offers his work as he sees it. Without the Miller photos of the unattractive women scarred from cigarette burns and needle marks, the prostitutes in the text can look like anything the reader's imagination wishes, despite the surly descriptions Vollmann offers; *seeing* how these women actually look, and how they live, makes the reader approach the text in a different manner.

***Selected Prints from Butterfly Stories*. CoTangent, 1993–1996.** 20" by 18" cover housing 19" × 16" inches sheets, watercolored versions of the line drawings accompanying the trade edition of the novel. Limitation page: "These prints were hand-printed by the author from photo-etched magnesium plates, and then colored with archival watercolors and inks." There is no text from the novel. The prints are limited to 15 copies each and there are two sets of artist's proofs. The entire set of prints comprises 40 images. This book I have seen, owned by Mitchell [copy 3 of 14], contains 29 prints, plus two hand-painted endpaper images and a receipt from the Hotel 38 in Bangkok (numbered hotels are whorehouses). Vollmann bound this copy in boards incorporating Thai paper and shredded lingerie, hand-painted and varnished. Vollmann notes on the limitation page (unbound): "Copies 1 and 2 were given by the author to prostitutes in Southeast Asia. Due to the climate there and conditions in which those two women live, both copies are probably destroyed by now. Each copy of this edition varies in number of prints it contains, and is priced accordingly ... printed in Sacramento in 1993, and bound in 1996." Signed by author October [n.d.], 1996. This limitation page is loose, not bound into the book, and was created at the purchaser's request.

Incidentally, the U.K. publisher of *Butterfly Stories*, Andre Duetsch, issued a limited edition of 100 copies, slip-cased. This edition goes for $400–500 on the collector's market.

***Four Platinum Prints*. CoTangent, 1998.** Twelve bound pages, lavishly painted in thick, layered acrylics. Title page indicates "Portland, OR, 1996 — Sacramento, 1997 [Bound 1998]." This is copy 1 of 10, archived in the Lilly's vault. This is a large book, with a 40" × 46" black silk clamshell case, with printed black paper label mounted on spine. There is an abundance of line drawings of women in Vollmann's usual style. The 8" × 10" prints: Two women in the garden, holding apples; one nude woman sitting in a chair, eyes closed (appears twice on different pages); one nude woman standing before a water fountain; another naked woman standing before the water fountain. Each photo is glued to a sheet with a covering with a window cut out for the photo, then painted around it with acrylics and watercolors. Page two includes a faded cut-out photo pasted on of what seems to be a woman in a flannel shirt, not a platinum print. There is no text. From a note by Vollmann: "These are the first successful platinum prints I ever made, printed from the first view camera negatives I ever exposed. The ladies who posed for me lived in Portland, Oregon. At their request, I took off my clothes, too. I believe I took these pictures in summer 1995."

The Book of Candles. CoTangent Press, 2006. Unbound sheets housed in a 30" × 34" wooden box, hand-painted. Insert: "This first edition of *The Book of Candles* was relief-printed on Rives de Lin paper by the author in 1997. The text-blocks were photographically etched magnesium plates and the illustrations were woodcuts done in Thailand and Cambodia on Chinese ulo wood. The edition is limited to ten copies for sale and two artist's proofs." With Vollmann's signature: "Coloring completed 2005. Box completed 2006." Box includes brass hinges, brass inlay with author's name and book title, along with an illustration. This is a collection of love poems to prostitutes around the world, written in a rhyming scheme that calls to mind Blake's *The Marriage of Heaven and Hell*. This is a meticulously put-together art piece, nine years in the making. Page size: 19" × 16"; 75pp; (2 pp. per folio sheet, 32 sheets in all + 2 unnumbered double-page spreads). The text is a suite of eight religious and blasphemous love-poems to prostitutes and was composed in the Philippines in 1995 and relief-printed over a period of years (1997–2003). The text blocks and some illustrations are photo-etched magnesium plates. Other illustrations are woodcuts done in Thailand and Cambodia on Chinese *ulo* wood. Art dealer Priscilla Juvelis describes it in her catalogue: "Housed in a sailcloth-covered basswood clamshell box which the artist / author has painted, collaged with hand-painted woodblock prints, and suitably adorned with gewgaws.... The woodcut image on the underside of each box is different. Four Japanese 'doughnut hold' coins have been screwed in to the underside of the box to comprise protective feet [...]. Within this are set two wooden corner blocks mounted with selenium-splotched flower-engraved brass plates, a strip of painted walnut engraved with a print of a female nude, two engraved beeswax candles on engraved brass support wrapped round with brass wire.... The naive aspect of the art of this 'journal' brings to mind Gauguin's NOA NOA[...]. The beauty of the prints, which includes the vibrant colors, lead the reader / viewer to understand that a less sophisticated life has a beauty that cannot be extinguished." The two wax candles included on each end, held in by brass coil, suggests the reader is meant to view this book by candlelight. One poem, "Prayer to Angels," was published in *Expelled from Eden: A William T. Vollmann Reader* (2004).

The Best Way to Smoke Crack. Date? This story from *The Atlas* is a book Vollmann has been working on for some time. Terri Saul included photos with her online interview. The art and text have been created but, thus far, not bound. It is unknown if this edition is available yet, or when it will be.

Discussion

There may be specially commissioned or one-of-kind books that I'm not aware of, not in Vollmann's catalogues, or made for himself and not for the art market. (Saul mentions an "Arctic Journal" project.) The majority of these book objects concern prostitutes and the vocation of sex work, Vollmann's most obsessive subject matter. The prostitutes "are both victims and adventurers" (Spielman, 64) in these editions: from Gloria's story re-bound in creative ways to paintings of Thai sex workers Vollmann encountered to the religious awakening of the oldest profession in *Book of Candles*. There is death and redemption ("The Grave of Lost Stories"), crime and incarceration (*The Convict Bird*), which falls within Vollmann's concern with freedom (in a 2000 NPR interview, Vollmann states that he feels prostitutes are free because, "they work when they want to work," and do what they feel like doing, unlike most of the world stuck in jobs with time clocks and rules). Vollmann does not state the history of Veronica Compton, whom *The Convict Bird* is about, dedicated to, and for the welfare of. Compton is a nefarious figure in the annals of true crime, a serial killer groupie. Compton was infatuated with the Hillside Strangler case — two men were convicted of the murders associated with the case: Angelo Buono and Kenneth Bianchi, who left their victims' bodies scattered from New York to Los Angeles. Compton was a young playwright and actress and began a correspondence with Bianchi, asking for his insights on the serial killer's psychology; she had written a screenplay about a female serial killer and sent it to him. Their correspondence eventually turned to their mutual fantasies of rape, murder, and necrophilia. Compton began to visit Bianchi in prison. Bianchi convinced her to commit a murder similar in style to the Hillside Strangler and leave his semen at the crime scene, which would thus make the police believe they had arrested and convicted the wrong men. Compton smuggled some of Bianchi's semen out in a glove after a visit, and then set out to make her fantasies come true. Compton went to Bellingham, Washington. She checked in to the Shangri-la Motel and spotted a woman who worked in a bar. She thought the woman would be an easy victim, so she brought the woman to the motel and tried to strangle her. The intended victim was too strong and managed to escape, though, and Compton was arrested and convicted of attempted murder, with her first parole date in 1994. While incarcerated, Compton lost interest in Bianchi and began a romantic correspondence with another serial killer, Douglas Clark. She also wrote a sociological study, *Eating the Ashes: Seeking Rehabilitation Within the U.S. Penal System* (2002). Why didn't Vollmann indicate Compton's history in *The Convict Bird*? Or did he feel it unnecessary, that anyone drawn to the text would know who she is?

Compton, like the prostitutes, exist on the edges of society and against society's accepted norms. Vollmann is drawn to, and fascinated by, these women who sell their bodies on the street, in brothels, or fall in love with serial killers. Do they appreciate his efforts to create art for them? In the limitation age of *Selected Prints from Butterfly Stories*, he notes that he gave two copies to prostitutes in Thailand but doubts they still have them, or the editions still exist. What of the book for/about Veronica Compton? What was her reaction, and what did she think of Vollmann's interest in her, possibly the way she showed interest in prison inmates before she became a criminal herself? In *Rising Up and Rising Down,* Vollmann does not list Compton as one of his "moral actors," nor does he mention her in any of the seven volumes. There is no justification for murder for pleasure; her acts fall under Vollmann's list of "when is violence unjustified": "5. When it is in the service of no end" and "10. When its definitions are obscure or illogical" (Volume *MC*, 101).

Vollmann follows in the footsteps of William Blake, creating his artist books (mostly) by his own hand, where other writers tend to rely on specialty presses and artists to create the objects for them. The CoTangent Press offerings are an extra source of revenue for Vollmann, another hat for him to wear, another side of the complex, hard-to-pin-down creator.

Notes

Introduction

1. The full interview can be accessed at <http://www.pw.org/mag/dq_vollmann.htm>.

2. From Nunn's *The Grey Book*: "Deep Springs does not conduct a conventional school. It does not make a special point of preparing boys for college nor of providing a year or more of outing to build up their physique before they enter college. It does not reach agriculture or engineering, or specialize in any of the material sciences. Its purpose is not to finance education for those who cannot finance it for themselves. It is not endeavoring to prepare students for commercial pursuits ... but for a life of service, with the understanding that superior ability and generous purpose would be expected.... Deep Springs is endeavoring to add its mite to the creation of a class devoted to the country's needs and to be a pioneer in the method of education."

3. It should be noted that Vollmann frequently visited the former Yugoslavia in the 1990s. He worked as a war correspondent and had several traumatic experiences. It would appear that a book set in Yugoslavia which greatly influenced him was an impetus for his desire to go there, and there, his writing would still be affected by the influence of personal and political events. Others early influences of similar importance are Lautréamont, Melville, Hemingway, Faulkner, Steinbeck, and Mishma, but none had the same stimulus as Danilo Kiš.

4. Reported in Dinsmore's bibliography.

5. In the William T. Vollmann Manuscript Collection at Ohio State University Library, the box containing the TS for *WFG* includes rejection letters from Poseidon Press, Holt, SOHO Press; it goes without saying that no publisher readily recognizes a potential major new writer — Richard Brautigan's *Trout Fishing in America* and Jack Kerouac's *On the Road* both encountered years of rejection before finding a company willing to take a risk, and that's merely two examples. Many novels now considered important classics were initially declined by many editors and publishers.

6. Testing this new toy, Vollmann's first words into the microphone were, "Thanks Mom and Dad!" The computer translated it to: "This man is dead." See "Talking Prose" in *Washington Post*, 10 August 1997.

7. *The Los Angeles Times* assigned him to review his own book. He chose his alter-ego, "William the Blind," to write the review in the future, 2010. The review was titled "The Stench of Corpses," and it was not the best review a writer could hope for.

8. Eggers mentions Vollmann in his memoir, *A Heartbreaking Work of Staggering Genius*. Trying to get a contribution for his early magazine, *Might*, he sends a letter "to William T. Vollmann, soliciting for his predictions for the year. Vollmann writes back, in crayon, on the other side of the letter, indicating that he would like to contribute, but would like to be compensated. Because we have never paid

anyone for anything, and have less money now than ever before, we ask if there is anything nonmonetary that we can do. He says okay, this is what he wants: a) One box of .45 caliber Gold Saber bullets; b) Two hours, in a warm, well-lit room, with two naked women, to paint them, in watercolor" (283).

9. In a 15 November 2007 article in *The New York Times*, Motoko Rich comments on the fact that a National Book Award win has mixed impact on sales. He uses *Europe Central* as an example — while the typical winner will see an increase of up to 50,000 more copies sold, *Europe Central* sold (as of 2007) only 6,000 copies in cloth (priced at $40) and 26,000 in trade paper.

10. The Strauss Living Award has made a life-changing difference for some writers and altered the focus of their work. Raymond Carver was a recipient, and was able to quit teaching (a requirement of the award is that a writer cannot be employed full-time); after so many years of financial struggle, this, for Carver (and any other winner) was a grand acknowledgement from the literary community that the hard work has made an impact on contemporary literature. While Carver was given the award for his short fiction, he decided to spend the time (and last years of his life) writing poetry instead. It will be interesting to see if Vollmann's literary focus will change between 2008 and 2012.

11. From an unpublished interview with Larry McCaffery, dated 13 July 2001.

12. He sent *Picture Show* to the Russian consulate, offering them pages to voice opinion on the Afghanistan situation in the published version. In *Rifles*, he prints epistle exchanges with the Royal Canadian Mounted Police regarding allegations of human rights violations in the relocation of the Inuit.

Chapter 1

1. See Chapter Four for an in-depth discussion of freedom in Vollmann's work.

2. In the prefatory note to *Rising Up and Rising Down*, he states that his original intention was for *Angels, Picture Show*, and *Rising* to be companion volumes that bounced off each other, with "much reference ... to do-it-yourself politics of an extreme character" (ix).

Chapter 2

1. The novella is a curious form, popular in European literature but not American. "Novella" derives from the Italian for *a tale, a piece of news*. Novellas originally were news of town and country life worth repeating for pleasure and culture. The category for novella is usually 60–130 published pages. Vollmann has not explored this form outside his large collections, other than the 138-page *Whores for Gloria*.

2. When the skinheads finally read this account in manuscript, they do not like it. Dan-L says, in a postscript, "You need a lot of work with your grammar. You have a lot of run-on sentences" (64).

3. Solana Beach is an upper middle-class section of San Diego known as North County, south of Orange County.

4. Those in the Vollmann camp felt an accolade of this magnitude was long overdue, although there was previous recognition aside from the Whiting Award. The National Critics Book Choice Award nominated *Rising*; *Atlas* received the PEN/Hemingway; the Commonwealth Club of California acknowledged *Royal* and *Rising* with Silver Medals, for portrayals, fiction and real, of life in California.

Chapter 3

1. From McCaffery's previously unpublished 2001 interview, but published for the first time in this volume.

2. This information is found in "Seven Dreams: Description of Project" (*Expelled*, 447–450).

3. This is the only volume that has had an excerpt published, as "The Cloud Shirt" in *Grand Street*, 46.

4. Unpublished interview.

5. From Vollmann's essay, "Morrow's Conjunctions: A View from Below."

6. Citation from G.P. Lainsbury's *The Carver Chronotope* (2004).

7. Subzero's domestic life mirrors the Journalist's in *Butterfly Stories*: having a wife back home while carrying on an affair in the foreign countries he is doing research in.

Chapter 4

1. Regarding the size of this novel, his publisher, Viking, wanted Vollmann to cut the

book if not by a half, a t least by a third, to save printing expenses and allow for a moderate price tag on the cover. He wrote a lengthy letter to his editor, Paul Slovak, objecting to having the book cut, listing these defenses:

1. Most importantly, it will be a better book that way.

2. We did this for *Fathers and Crows* in spite of ... prophecies of doom. And it got a starred PW review, etc. Maybe it even sold thirty-seven copies....

3. This sounds crazed and immodest, but I actually believe I have a shot at winning the Nobel Prize or some other prestigious award someday. If Viking sticks with me that long, I think they may benefit from keeping me happy and by keeping the books intact. I am also getting more and more foreign sales these days. May the company please, please, just be patient.

4. It will be easier for me to help promote the book if I am proud of it [*Expelled,* 321].

True to his integrity, Vollmann agreed to have his royalties cut by a third to pay for the expense of paper. In the Beatrice.com interview, he comments about this: "Hopefully, any writer would do the same. I mean, the stakes are so low. In the course of three magazine articles, I can make as much as I made for this book. So I'm not doing it for the money, and, therefore, I can't see any reason to compromise."

2. Despite this negative criticism, Steven Moore has been one of Vollmann's most supportive reviewers, praising him in the *Washington Post Book World* and the *Chicago Tribune.*

3. Vollman jumped boxcars for his research. He tells Beatrice.com: "It's quite exhilarating, and I hope to do a lot more. But they're making it ever more difficult to do it. They really, really don't like the hobos riding the rails now, and I can't entirely blame them because there have been some gangs riding the rails, and they've done some vandalism and wrecked some tracks. And then, also, nowadays, somebody could lose a leg and sue the railroad." He was hopping train cars in the Imperial Valley in the late 1990s. The areas of Imperial that he describes in *Royal* are lush in detail — Coffee Camp, Salvation Mountain, Slab City; they are real places that he spent time in, resulting in the work-in-progress, *Imperial,* and his 2008 title, *Riding Towards Everywhere.*

Chapter 5

1. Vollmann's influence reaches beyond the literary community. In 2008, the hip-hop band The Roots released their political album, *Rising Down,* the title appropriated from *RURD.*

2. From a letter written to Joseph Priestly in *Essays, Articles, Bagatelles, and Letters, Poor Richard's Almanac, Autobiography.*

3. Zebu have humps, large dewlaps, and droopy ears. They have more sweat glands than European cattle (*Bos taurus*). They handle hot, humid climates well and have pest resistances not seen in European cattle. Because they were better adapted to hot environments, zebus were imported to Africa for hundreds of years and interbred with native cattle there. Genetic analysis of African cattle has found higher concentrations of zebu genes all along the east coast of Africa, and especially pure cattle on the island of Madagascar, implying that the method of dispersal was cattle transported by ship.

Chapter 6

1. *Some Other Frequency,* 316.

2. In 2000, Vollmann returned to Afghanistan. This is reported in Volume Six of *Rising Up and Rising Down,* the chapter called "With Their Hands on Their Hearts." Seventeen years older than The Young Man, Vollmann remembers the country well, and sees it with a more experienced gaze: "Afghanistan is a pomegranate, her sweet, shiny secrets hidden within the caves of dry bitterness" (103).

Chapter 7

1. He is also an accomplished photographer, engraver, watercolorist, printer, bookbinder, poet, song lyricist, and manufacturer of his own bullets for his pistols.

2. A forthcoming book, which may be published by the time this study is released, is a work of performance and cultural criticism on Japan and Noh Theater as artistic expression.

3. *The Royal Family* is dedicated to this woman, "Lizzy Kate Gray, the million-dollar vegan boxcar queen" (iii).

4. Hemingway is #6 on Vollmann's list of contemporary books most admired: "Hem-

ingway is usually a wonderful read, especially *Islands in the Stream* and *For Whom the Bell Tolls*— that is to say, the grandly suicidal narratives" (*Expelled*, 36).

5. The first chapter is titled "The Spirit of Place" and starts off: "The old American art-speech contains an alien quality, which belongs to the American continent and nowhere else" (1).

6. Ellison often utters this phrase at his lectures and appearances when interacting with his audience. The quote is cited in his biography at http://www.imdb.com/name/nm0255196/bio.

Bibliography

Books by William T. Vollmann

Listed by date of publication.

Fiction

You Bright and Risen Angels. London: Andre Deutsch, 1987; NY: Atheneum, 1987.
The Rainbow Stories. London: Deutsch, 1989; NY: Atheneum, 1989.
Seven Dreams [I: The Ice-Shirt]. London: Andre Deutsch Ltd., 1990; NY: Viking, 1990.
Whores for Gloria. London: Pan-Picador, 1991; NY: Pantheon, 1991.
Thirteen Stories and Thirteen Epitaphs. London: Deutsch, 1991; NY: Pantheon, 1991.
Seven Dreams [II: Fathers and Crows]. London: Deutsch, 1992; NY: Viking, 1992.
Butterfly Stories: A Novel. London: Deutsch, 1992; NY: Grove.1992.
Seven Dreams [VI: The Rifles]. London: Deutsch, 1994; NY: Viking, 1994.
The Royal Family. NY: Viking, 2000.
Seven Dreams [III: Argall]. NY: Viking, 2001.
Europe Central. NY: Viking, 2005.

Non-Fiction

An Afghanistan Picture Show. NY: Farrar, Straus & Giroux, 1992.
The Atlas. NY: Viking, 1996.
Rising Up and Rising Down: Some Thoughts on Violence, Freedom and Urgent Means. Seven volumes. San Francisco: McSweeney's Books, 2003.
Rising Up and Rising Down: Some Thoughts on Violence, Freedom and Urgent Means. Abridged edition. NY: Ecco, 2005.
Uncentering the Earth: Copernicus and the Revolutions of the Heavenly Spheres. NY: Atlas Books/W.W. Norton, 2006.
Poor People. NY: Ecco, 2007.
Riding Towards Everywhere. NY: Ecco, 2008.

Book Objects

The Convict Bird: A Children's Poem. [10 steel copies, 90 paperback copies.] CoTangent Press, 1988. A poem about a woman in prison, encased in steel, with a lock and a window.

The Happy Girls. [Edition of 13.] CoTangent, 1991. A story from *Thirteen* about massage parlor prostitutes, encased in mirror-glass, with a red light and buzzer.

Epitaph for Mien. [Edition of 1.] CoTangent, 1991. Lemon-gilded acrylic on iridescent pastels.

Whores for Gloria. [Edition of 15]. CoTangent, 1991. Bound in archival eight-ply matboard, with nickel-plated hinges, cover shaped like a woman's legs drawn up against buttocks, photographs by Ken Miller, illustrations by the author.

The Grave of Lost Stories. [Edition of 13 +2 h.c. copies, and "Mass edition" of twenty copies (which do not include the marble covers)]. CoTangent, 1993. Slightly revised from the *Thirteen* version, bound in sarcophagus of toothy white marble covers by Ben Pax, with custom hinge, Spring-loaded skeleton hands, sterling silver bezels, custom screws, and screwdriver with cast silver skull-headed hangs (for special screws).

Butterfly Stories. [Edition of 14]. CoTangent, 1993. Bound in lingerie, with butterfly wings, illustrations, facial studies, hang-printed figures, and watercolors.

The Book of Candles. [Edition of 10] CoTangent, 2006. The text is a suite of eight religious and blasphemous love-poems to prostitutes and was composed in the Philippines in 1995 and relief-printed on Rives de Lin paper by the author over a period of years (1997–2003).

Periodical and Anthology Publications

Short Fiction

"The Grave of Lost Stories." *Conjunctions* 14 (Spring 1992).

"DeSade's Last Stand." *Esquire*, November 1992.

"San Diego, California, U.S.A. (1988)." Larry McCaffery, ed., *Avant Pop: Fiction for a Daydream Nation.* Normal, IL: Black Ice Books/FC2, 1992.

"The Answer." *ZYZZYVA* (Summer 1992).

"Alaska." *Granta* 40 (Summer 1992).

"The Ghost of Magnetism." *Paris Review* (Fall 1992).

"The Cloud Shirt." *Grand Street* 46 (Summer 2003).

"Incarnations of the Murderer." Larry McCaffery, ed., *After Yesterday's Crash: The Avant-Pop Anthology.* NY: Penguin, 1995.

"Breakout, Pt. 1." *Grand Street* 71 (Spring 2005).

"Breakout, Pt. 2." *Grand Street* 72 (Fall 2005).

"De Sade's Last Stand." Maxim Jakubowski and Michael Hemmingson, eds. *The Mammoth Book of Short Erotic Novels.* NY: Carroll & Graf, 2000.

"The Best Way to Smoke Crack." Michael Hemmingson, ed. *What the Fuck: The Avant-Porn Anthology.* NY: Soft Skull Press, 2001.

"Widow's Weeds." *AGNI* 66 (Fall 2007).

Journalism and Non-fiction

"Scintillant Orange." *Conjunctions* 11 (Spring 1988).

"The White Knights." *Conjunctions* 12 (Fall 1988).

"The Quest for Polar Treasures." *Conjunctions* 13 (Fall 1989).

"American Writing Today: A Diagnosis of the Disease." *Conjunctions* 15 (Spring 1990).

"Pornography's Top Components." *Fiction International: Pornography and Censorship Special Issue*, No. 22 (1991).

"Letter from Somalia: KillingTime with the Windowmakers." *Esquire*, May 1993.

"Something to Die For." *The Review of Contemporary Fiction* 13, no. 2 (Summer 1993).

"The Best Things in Life Aren't Free." *Esquire*, October 1993.

"Pages from *The Atlas*: New York." *Grand Street* 51 (Winter 1995).

"Preface." Ken Miller. *Open All Night*. Woodstock, NY: The Overlook Press, 1995.

"Doctor's Orders: An Unnatural History of the Dead." *San Francisco Examiner*, 20 July 1997.

"Writing." Will Blythe, ed., *Why I Write: Thoughts on the Practice of Fiction*. Boston: Little, Brown, 1998.

"Melville's Magic Mountain." *Civilization*, 5.1 (1998).

"The Very Short History of Nunavut." Bill Bryson, ed., *The Best American Travel Writing 2000*. Boston: Houghton Mifflin, 2000.

"Television ate My Town." *Gear*, January 2001: 118–19.

"Morrow's Conjunctions: A View from Below." *Review of Contemporary Fiction*, 20 (Spring 2000): 142–146.

"Afterword." Danilo Kis, *A Tomb for Boris Davidovich*. Normal, IL: Dalkey Archive Press, 2001.

"The Old Man : A Case Study." *McSweeney's Quarterly Concern* 7 (2001).

"From *The Atlas*." David L. Ulin, ed., *Writing Los Angeles: A Literary Anthology*. NY: Library of America, 2002.

"Across the Divide." *The New Yorker*, 5 May 2002.

"Muslim Dreams." John Miller and Aaron Kenedi, eds., *Inside Islam : The Faith, the People, and the Conflicts of the World's Fastest-growing Religion*. NY: Marlowe & Company, 2002.

"Three Meditations on Death." *McSweeney's Quarterly Concern* 9 (Fall 2002).

Selections from "Delineations" (*Imperial*). *Pacific Review: A West Coast Arts Review Annual 2002*.

"Two Dead and One Maybe About to Die." *San Francosco Chronicle*, 9 December 2003.

"More Benadryl, Whined the Journalist." Dan O'Connor, ed., *Wanderlust*. NY: Thunder's Mouth Press, 2004.

"They Came Out Like Ants! Searching for the Chinese Tunnels of Mexicali." *Harper's*, October 2004.

"Blood, Sweat and Trade Secrets." *Playboy*, December 2004.

"The Mask is Most Important Always." *Tin House*, Fall 2005.

"Catching Out: Travels in an Open Boxcar." *Harper's*, January 2007.

Excerpt from *Riding Toward Everywhere*. *Sactown Magazine*, January 2008.

Book Reviews

Rev. of *Biography of Conrad Aiken*, by Edward Butscher. *San Francisco Chronicle*, 18 September 1988.

Rev. of *Hot Jazz Trio* by William Kotzwinkle. *Los Angeles Times Book Review*, 18 November 1989.

Rev. of *The Drummer of the Eleventh North, Devonshire Fusiliers* by Guy Davenport. *Philadelphia Inquirer*, 2 December 1990.

Rev. of *Pinocchio in Venice* by Robert Coover. *Philadelphia Inquirer*, 27 January 1991.

Rev. of *The Mysterious History of Columbus* by John Noble Wilford. *Philadelphia Inquirer*, 13 October 1991.

Rev. of *Wrong: Stories* by Dennis Cooper. *NY Times Book Review*, 26 April 1992.

Rev. of *Arise and Walk* by Barry Gifford. *NY Times Book Review*, 3 July 1994.

Rev. of *On The History of Destruction* by W.G. Sebald. *The Believer*, May 2003.
Rev. of *Dreamland: America at the Dawn of the Twentieth Century*, by Michael Lesy. *LA Weekly*, July 2003.
Rev. of *You Alone Are Real to Me: Remembering Rainer Maria Rilke* by Lou Andreas-Salomé. *American Book Review* 24, no. 6, September/October 2003.
Rev. of *Exit A,* by Anthony Swifford. *New York Times Book Review*, 14 January 2007.

Archived Papers

Hogue, Sarah. "The William T. Vollmann Collection: Guide and Inventory.
Spec. CMS.98." A detailed catalogue of 49 boxes containing Vollmann's papers archived at the Ohio State University Library. Retrieved at http://library.osu.edu/sites/rarebooks/finding/vollmann.php

Selected Works About William T. Vollmann

Listed alphabetically

Critical Essays

Bell, Madison Smartt. "Where an Author Might be Standing." *Review of Contemporary Fiction* 13, 2 (Summer 1993): 39–45.
Christiansen, Peter. "William T. Vollmann's *The Ice-Shirt*: Updating Icelandic Traditions." *Critique: Studies in Contemporary Fiction* 38 (1996): 52–57.
Kelly, Robert. "Notes Towards Four Meditations on William T. Vollmann." *Review of Contemporary Fiction* (Summer 1993): 62–3.
Laidlaw, Mark. "Suicide Notes on WTV's *You Bright & Risen Angels*." *Review of Contemporary Fiction* (Summer 1993): 46–52.
LeClair, Tom. "The Prodigious Fictions of Richard Powers, William T. Vollmann, and David Foster Wallace." *Critique: Studies in Contemporary Fiction* 38, 1 (1994): 12–37.
Lewis-Kraus, Gideon. "An Oral History of *Rising Up and Rising Down*." *McSweeney's Internet Tendency*. Retrieved at
http://www.mcsweeneys.net/authorpages/vollmann/vollmann18.html.
McCaffery, Larry. "Everything Is Permitted: The Post-Pynchon, Post-Modern Fiction of America." *Positive* (Tokyo), 1 (Spring 1991): 248–267. English trans., in *The Novel of the Americas*, ed. Raymond Weslie Williams. Boulder: University of Colorado Press, 1992.
Smith, Carlton. "Arctic Revelations: Vollmann's *The Rifles* and the Frozen Landscape of the Self." *Review of Contemporary Fiction* 13, 2 (Summer 1993): 53–61.
Spielmann, Katherine. "The Book as Apparatus: William T. Vollmann's Special Editions." *Review Contemporary Fiction* 13, 2 (Summer 1993): 64–7.

Profiles

Beckett, Andy. "A Nerd in Action." *The Independent*, 26 June 1994.
Bell, Madison Smartt. "William T. Vollmann's Risky Business: The Writer as Empiricist, Obsessive and (Nearly) Corpse." *New York Times Magazine*, 6 February 1994: 18–22.
Ehrenreich, Ben. "Double Agent for Cain: William T. Vollmann and the Case Against God." *LA Weekly Reader,* 17–23 November 2000.
Goldberg, Michelle. "Author William T. Vollmann Shares Vision." AlterNet.org.

Hemmingson, Michael. "Free Radical: William T. Vollmann in San Diego." *San Diego Weekly Reader*, 18 Feburary 2004.

Huic, Davor. "Journalists Killed by Mines Not Wearing Protective Gear." Reuters News Service, 3 May 1994.

Hooper, Joseph. "The Strange Case of William Vollmann." *Esquire*, February 1992.

"Mine Kills Two Photographers." The Associated Press, 2 May 1994.

Reed, Dixie. "Sacramento Writer Wins Prestigious Award." *Sacramento Bee*, 28 November 2007.

Saul, Terri. "A Day at Vollmann's Studio." Retrieved 29 November 2007 at http://esposito.typepad.com/TQC_6/Vollmanns_Studio.html.

"William T. Vollmann." *Contemporary Authors*. Vol. 134. Ed. Susan M. Trotsky. Detroit: Gale, 1992.

"William T. Vollmann, Author of *The Royal Family*, Silver Medal Winner for Non-Fiction, 2001 California Book Awards." Profile of Vollmann on receiving an award at 70th Annuel California Book Awards, posted at www.commonwealthclub.org.

Interviews

"An Interview with William T. Vollmann." Alt-X.com.

Bell, Madison Smart. "William T. Vollmann: The Art of Fiction CLXIII." *Paris Review* 156 (Fall 2000): 256–290.

Braverman, Kate. "The Subversive Dialogues." *San Francisco Bay Guardian Online*. http://www.sfbg.com/40/21/lit_conversation.html.

Brush, Ben. "William T. Vollmann on Writing with Integrity, Bending Genres, and Humanizing the Villains." *Poets and Writers Magazine*, March 2005.

Coffey, Michael. "PW Interviews: William T. Vollmann." *Publishers Weekly*, 13 July 1992: 36–37.

Dushane, Tony. "An Interview with William T. Vollmann." Bookslut.com, November 2005.

Hogan, Ron. "Interview." Beatrice.com, 2000.

McCaffery, Larry. "An Interview with William T. Vollmann." *Review of Contemporary Fiction* (Summer 1993): 9–24.

_____. "Moth in the Flame: An Interview with William T. Vollmann." *Some other Frequency: Interviews with Innovative American Fiction Writers*. Philadelphia: University of Pennsylvania Press, 1996: 301–334.

_____. "Running on the Blade's Edge: An Interview with William T. Vollmann," *Mondo 2000*, August 1992: 91–95.

Steinberg, Sybil. "Interview with William T. Vollmann." *Writing for Your Life #2*. NY: Pushcart, 1995.

Thorne, Matt. "What's in the Meat Locker, Bill?" *The Independent*, 6 August 2006.

Bibliographies

Andersen, Allen S. *William T. Vollman : An Annotated Bibliography*. Masters Thesis, 1996. San Diego State University, Malcolm Love Library.

Dinsmore, John. "William T. Vollmann: Bibliographical Checklists." Self published 12-page photocopy.

McCaffery, Larry. Selected Bibliography of Primary and Secondary Sources included in "Moth in the Flame: An Interview with William T. Vollmann." *Some Other Frequency: Interviews with Innovative American Fiction Writers*. Philadelphia: University of Pennsylvania Press, 1996: 312–16.

Other Works Cited

Primary

Adams, Richard. *Watership Down*. London: Rex Collings, 1972.

Agee, James, and Walker Evans. *Let Us Now Praise Famous Men*. Boston: Houghton Mifflin, 1941.

Bailey, Stephen A. *L. L. Nunn: A Memoir*. Ithaca, NY: Telluride Association, 1933.

Ballard, J.G. *The Atrocity Exhibition*. London: Jonathan Cape, 1970.

Baudrillard, Jean. *Simulations*. NY: Semiotext(e), 1983.

Bell, Madison Smartt. *Lavoisier in the Year One: The Birth of a New Science in an Age of Revolution*. NY: Atlas Books/W.W. Norton, 2005.

Capote, Truman. *Answered Prayers*. NY: Random House, 1987.

Chiaromonte, Nicola. *The Paradox of History*. Philadelphia: University of Pennsylvania Press, 1985.

Cooper, Dennis. *Frisk*. NY: Grove Press, 1991.

Debord, Guy. *Society of the Spectacle*. Detroit: Black and Red, 1983.

Delany, Samuel R. *The Mad Man*. NY: Masquerade/A Richard Kasak Book, 1994.

Denzin, Norman K. *Interpretive Biography*. Thousand Oaks, CA: SAGE Publications, 1989.

Doctorow, E.L. *Ragtime*. NY: Random House, 1975.

Dos Passos, John. *U.S.A.* NY: Houghton-Mifflin, 1960.

Dostoevsky, Feodor. *Notes from the Underground*. NY: Vintage International, 1993.

Dunant, Henry. *A Memory of Solferino*. Geneva: International Committee of the Red Cross, 1986.

Ellis, Bret Easton. *American Psycho*. NY: Vintage, 1991.

Franklin, John. *Thirty Years in the Arctic Regions*. Lincoln: University of Nebraska Press, 1988.

Gibson, William. *Neuromancer*. NY: Ace Books, 1984.

Hemingway, Ernest. *The Snows of Kilimanjaro*. NY: Charles Scribner's Sons, 1933.

_____. *For Whom the Bell Tolls*. NY: Charles Scribner's Sons, 1940.

_____. *Islands in the Stream*. NY: Charles Scribner's Sons, 1970.

Kawabata, Yasunari. *Palm-of-the-Hand Stories*. Trans. Lane Dunlop and Martin Holman. San Francisco: North Point Press, 1988.

Kerouac, Jack. *On the Road*. NY: Viking Press, 1957.

_____. *The Subterraneans*. NY: Grove Press, 1958.

_____. *The Dharma Bums*. NY: Viking Press, 1958.

_____. *Vanity Duluoz*. NY: Coward-McCann, 1968.

Kiš, Danilo. *A Tomb for Boris Davidovich*. NY: Peguin Books, 1980.

Lacouture, Jean. *Jesuits: A Multibiography*. Trans. Jeremy Leggett. Washington, D.C.: Counterpoint Press, 1995.

Lainsbury, G.P. *The Carver Chronotope*. NY: Routledge, 2004.

Lautréamont, Comte de. *Maldoror & The Complete Works*. Trans. Alexis Lykiard. Cambridge: Exact Change, 1994.

Lawrence, D.H. *Studies in Classic American Literature*. NY: The Viking Press, 1964.

Leavitt, David. *The Man Who Knew Too Much: Alan Turing and the Invention of the Computer*. NY: Atlas Books/W.W. Norton, 2005.

Mailer, Norman. *The Naked and the Dead*. NY: Little, Brown, 1943.

McCaffery, Larry, and Michael Hemmingson, eds. *Expelled from Eden: A William T. Vollmann Reader*. NY: Thunder's Mouth Press, 2004.

Melville, Herman. *Moby-Dick*. NY: Harper, 1851.

Miller, Ken. *Open All Night*. Woodstock, NY: The Overlook Press, 1995.

Monod, Jacques. *Chance and Necessity: An Essay on the Natural Philosophy of Modern Biology*. Trans. Austryn Wainhouse. NY: Knopf, 1971.

Nunn, L. L. *The Grey Book*. Privately distributed, Deep Springs College Library.

Orwell, George. *Animal Farm*. London: Secker and Warburg, 1945.

Pynchon, Thomas. *Gravity's Rainbow*. NY: Viking Press, 1973.

Rich, Motoko. "Vietnam Novel Wins National Book Award." *The New York Times*, 15 November 2007.

Rolfe, John. Letter to Edwin Sandys. 8 June 1617. *The Records of the Virginia Company of London*, ed. Susan Myra Kingsbuy. Washington, D.C.: U.S. Government Printing Office, 1906–1935. Vol. 3, p. 71.

Ronell, Avital. *The Telephone Book*. Lincoln: University of Nebraska Press, 1989.

Russell, Paul. *Boys of Life*. NY: Dutton, 1991.

Shirer, William L. *The Rise and Fall of the Third Reich: A History of Nazi German*. NY: Simon and Schuster, 1960.

Smith, Michael A. *The Students of Deep Springs College*. Revere, PA: Lodima Press, 2000.

Spiegelman, Art. *Maus*. NY: Pantheon, 1988.

Steinbeck, John. *The Grapes of Wrath*. NY: Vintage, 1992.

Sterling, Bruce. *Schismatrix*. NY: Arbor House Publishing, 1985.

Swift, Jonathan. *The Writings of Jonathan Swift*. NY: W.W. Norton, 1973.

Wallace, David Foster. *Infinite Jest*. NY: Little, Brown, 1993.

_____. *Everything and More: A Compact History of Infinity*. NY: Atlas Books/W.W. Norton, 2003.

Wittgenstein, Ludwig. *Tractatus Logico Philosophicus*. NY: Hudson Humanities Press, 1951.

Secondary

Aird, Robert. *Deep Springs College: Its Founder, History, and Philosophy with Personal Reflections*. Deep Springs College, 1997.

Aldiss, Brian. *Billion-Year Spree: The True History of Science Fiction*. Schocken Books, 1974.

Bailey, Stephen A. *L L. Nunn: A Memoir*. Ithaca, NY: Telluride Association, 1933.

Barron, Neil. *Anatomy of Wonder: Science Fiction*. 2nd ed. NY: R. R. Bowker, 1976.

Blake, William. "The Garden of Love" [illuminated ms. plate]. *Songs of Innocence and of Experience: The Illuminated Books*. Ed. and with an Introduction by Andrew Lincoln. n.p.

Blish, James. *Cities in Flight*. NY: Avon, 1970.

Buddha. *The Teaching of Buddha*. Tokyo: Bukkyo Dendo Kyokai [Buddhist Promoting Foundation], 127th rev. ed., 1980.

Dostoevsky, Feodor. *Crime and Punishment*. Trans. Jessie Coulson. NY: Norton Critical Edition, 1964.

Ignatius of Loyola. "All Things to All Men." *Epistolae et Instructiones*, vol. I, pp. 179–80; trans. appears in Jean Lacouture, *Jesuits: A Multibiography*.

Kawabata, Yasunari. "Gleanings from Snow Country." *Palm-of-the-Hand Stories*. Trans. Lane Dunlop and Martin Holman. San Francisco: North Point Press, 1988.

_____. *Snow Country*. Trans. Edward Seidensticker. NY: Perigree Books, 1981.

Kellogg, Robert. Introduction. *The Sagas of Icelanders*. NY: Penguin, 2001.

Konrad, George. *The Case Worker*. NY: Harcourt Brace Jovanovich, 1978.

Lacouture, Jean. *Jesuits: A Multibiography*. Trans. Jeremy Leggett. Washington, D.C.: Counterpoint Press, 1995.

Machiavelli, Niccolo. *The Prince*. Trans. Luiigi Ricci; revised by E. R. P. Vincent. NY: New American Library, 1952.

McCaffery, Larry. "The Fictions of the Present." *The Columbia Literary History of the United States*. Emory Elliot, ed. NY: Columbia University Press, 1988, pp. 1161–1177.

Minsky, Richard. "Book Arts in the USA: An Exhibition." Center for Book Arts, Manhattan, April 7–May 12, 1990.

Russell, Bertrand. *The History of Western Philosophy*. NY: Clarion Books, 1945.

Seymour-Smith, Martin. *Who's Who in Twentieth Century Literature*. 1976; NY: McGraw Hill, 1976.

Smith, John. *The General History of Virginia: The Third Book, Chapter 2* (1624). Text taken from *Travels and Works of Captain John Smith*. Ed. Edward Arber and A.C. Bradley. Edinburgh: John Grant, 1910.

Smith, Michael A. *The Students of Deep Springs College*. Revere, Pennsylvania: Lodima Press, 2000.

Index